THE ULTIMATES 2

GODS & MONSTERS

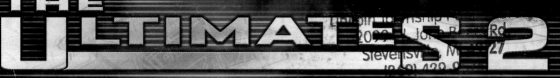

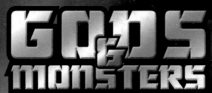

WRITER: MARK MILLAR

PENCILS: BRYAN HITCH

INKS: PAUL NEARY

COLORS: LAURA MARTIN WITH LARRY MOLINAR

LETTERS: CHRIS ELIOPOULOS

ASSISTANT EDITORS: JOHN BARBER & NICOLE WILEY
ASSOCIATE EDITOR: NICK LOWE
EDITOR: RALPH MACCHIO

CAPTAIN AMERICA CREATED BY JOE SIMON & JACK KIRBY

COLLECTION EDITOR: JENNIFER GRÜNWALD
ASSISTANT EDITOR: MICHAEL SHORT
SENIOR EDITOR, SPECIAL PROJECTS: JEFF YOUNGQUIST
DIRECTOR OF SALES: DAVID GABRIEL
PRODUCTION: LORETTA KROL
BOOK DESIGNER: JEOF VITA
CREATIVE DIRECTOR: TOM MARVELLI

EDITOR IN CHIEF: JOE QUESADA
PUBLISHER: DAN BUCKLEY

PREVIOUSLY IN THE ULTIMATES:

THE ULTIMATES HAVE HAD TWO DECISIVE BATTLES SINCE NICK FURY BROUGHT THEM TOGETHER. THE FIRST WAS WHEN THEY SAVED NEW YORK CITY FROM THE RAMPAGING MONSTER KNOWN AS THE HULK. WHAT THE WORLD AT LARGE DOESN'T KNOW IS THAT THE HULK IS REALLY BRUCE BANNER, A SCIENTIST WHO WAS WORKING ON THE SUPERHUMAN DEFENSE INTIATIVE.

THE SECOND BATTLE THE ULTIMATES WON WAS AGAINST AN ARMY OF SHAPE-SHIFTING ALIENS BENT ON DESTROYING THE WORLD AND KILLING ALL HUMANKIND. THESE TWO VICTORIES MADE THE ULTIMATES THE BIGGEST CELEBRITIES THE WORLD HAS EVER KNOWN

When faced with Nazi Germany's military advances, the U.S. government decided that the best weapon against them was a person, not a bomb. With this in mind, Steve Rogers volunteered for a covert military experiment that turned him into Captain America. After a few years of exemplary service, Captain America fell in battle-- his body wasn't recovered.

Years passed and Captain America was found frozen in suspended animation. When he awoke, he was convinced to join Iron Man, The Wasp, Giant Man, Black Widow, Hawkeye, and Thor in forming the superhuman defense initiative run by Nick Fury, called The Ultimates.

PREVIOUSLY IN THE ULTIMATES:

The Ultimates have had two decisive battles since Nick Fury brought them together. The first was when they saved New York City from the rampaging monster known as The Hulk. What the world at large doesn't know is that The Hulk is really Bruce Banner, a scientist who was working on the superhuman defense initiative.

The second battle The Ultimates won was against an army of shape-shifting aliens bent on destroying the world and killing all humankind. These two victories made The Ultimates the biggest celebrities the world has ever known.

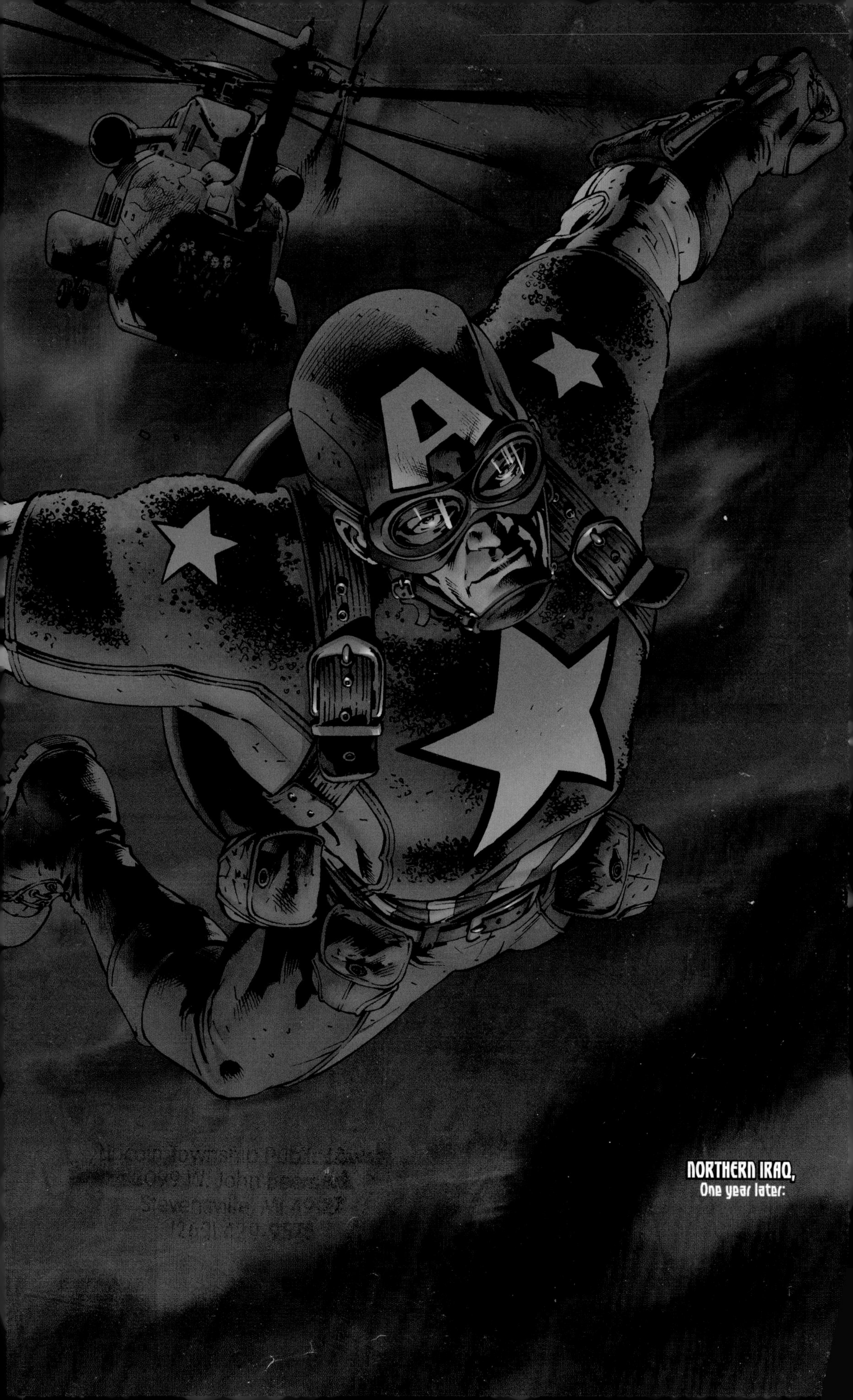
NORTHERN IRAQ,
One year later:

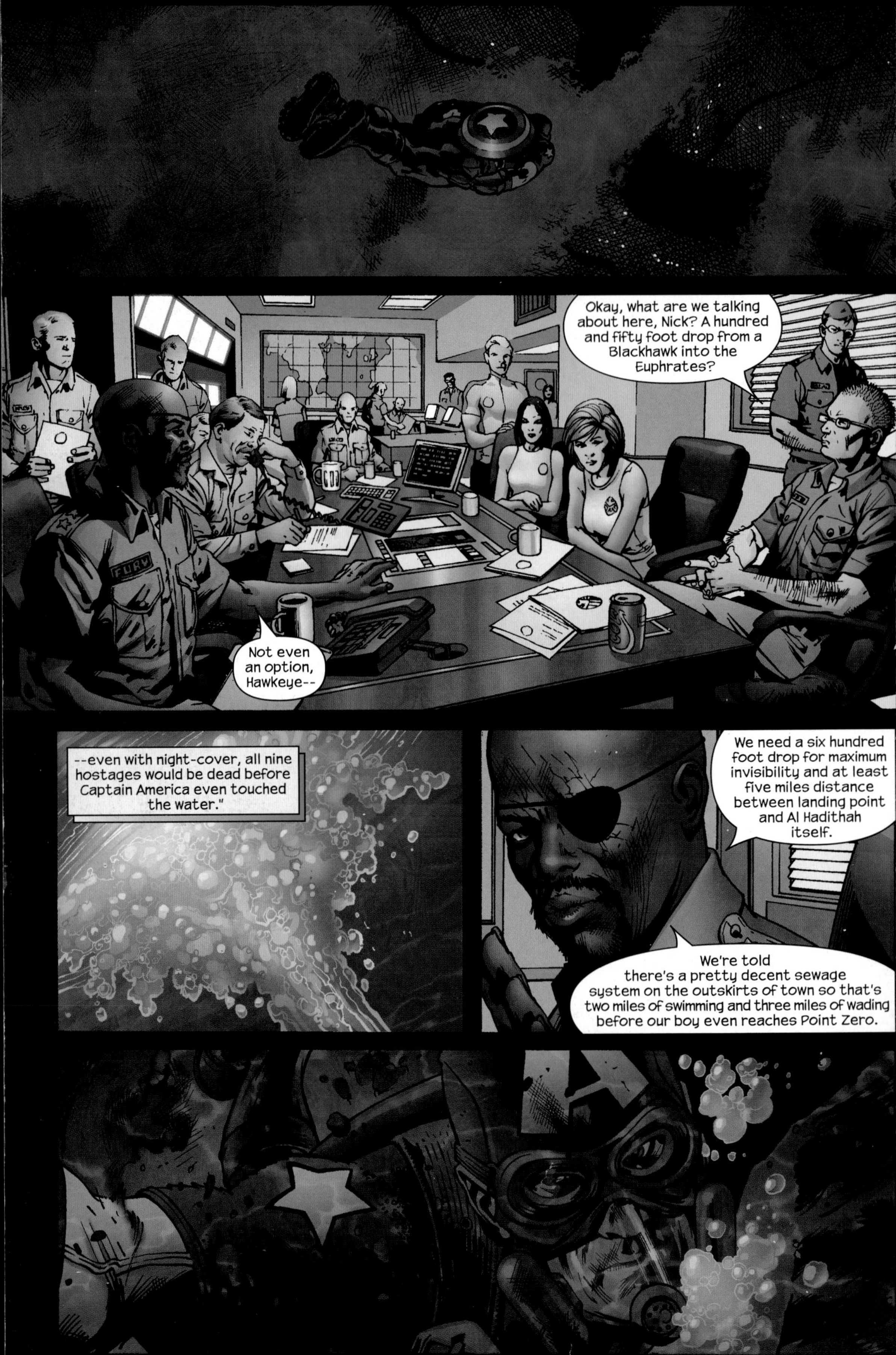

Okay, what are we talking about here, Nick? A hundred and fifty foot drop from a Blackhawk into the Euphrates?
Not even an option, Hawkeye--
--even with night-cover, all nine hostages would be dead before Captain America even touched the water."
We need a six hundred foot drop for maximum invisibility and at least five miles distance between landing point and Al Hadithah itself.
We're told there's a pretty decent sewage system on the outskirts of town so that's two miles of swimming and three miles of wading before our boy even reaches Point Zero.

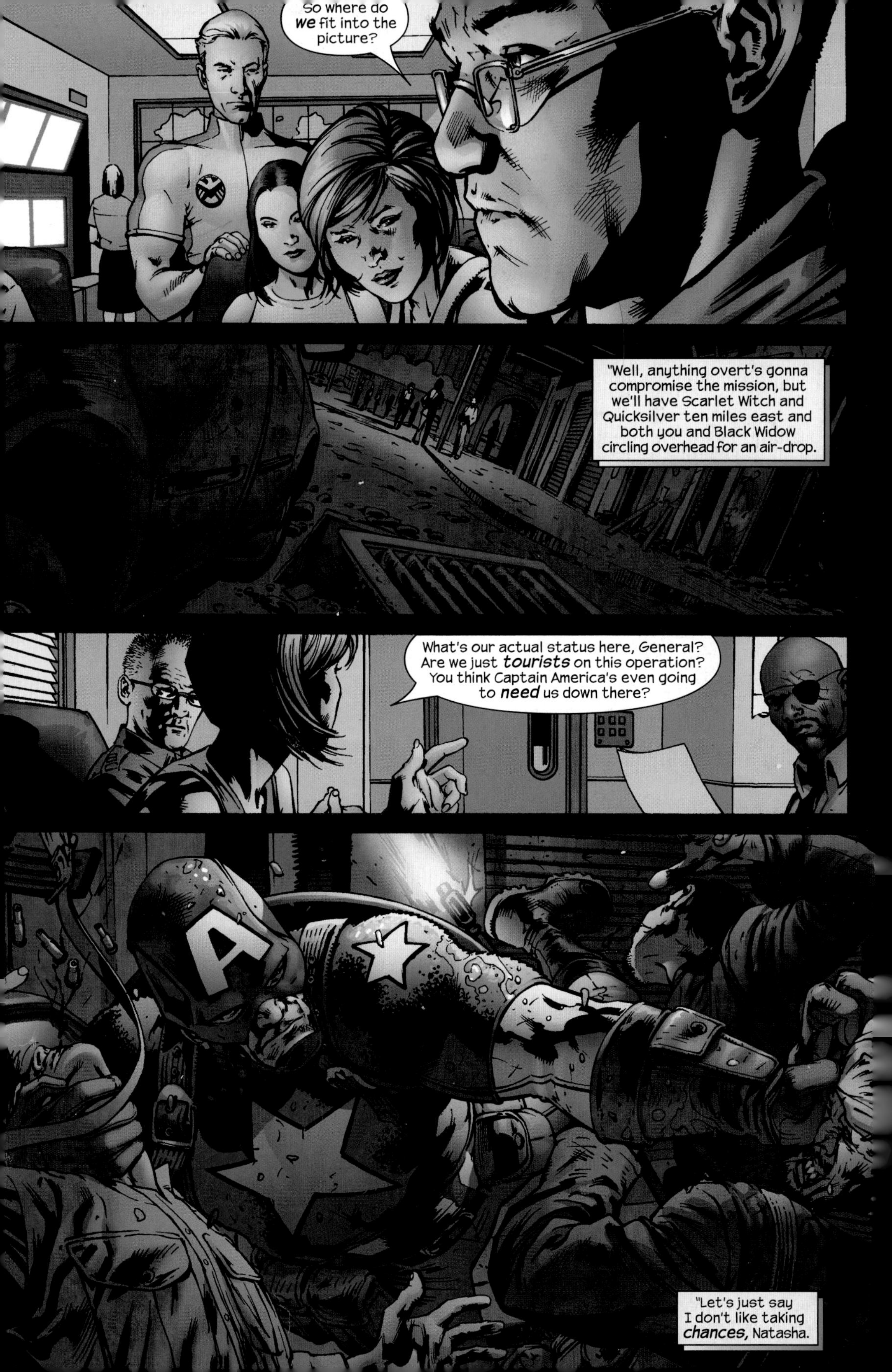
So where do *we* fit into the picture?
"Well, anything overt's gonna compromise the mission, but we'll have Scarlet Witch and Quicksilver ten miles east and both you and Black Widow circling overhead for an air-drop.
What's our actual status here, General? Are we just *tourists* on this operation? You think Captain America's even going to *need* us down there?
"Let's just say I don't like taking *chances,* Natasha.

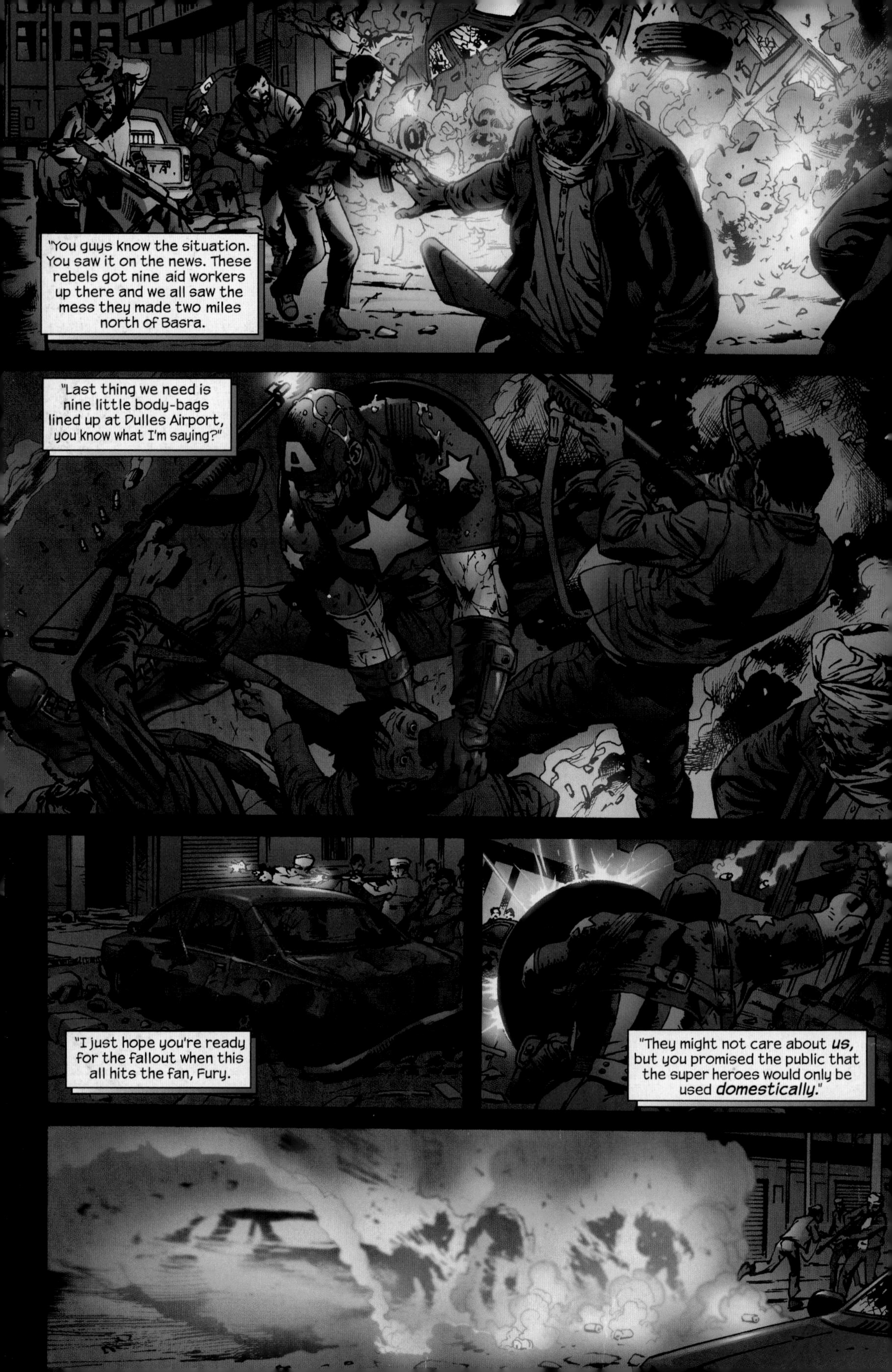
"You guys know the situation. You saw it on the news. These rebels got nine aid workers up there and we all saw the mess they made two miles north of Basra.
"Last thing we need is nine little body-bags lined up at Dulles Airport, you know what I'm saying?"
"I just hope you're ready for the fallout when this all hits the fan, Fury.
"They might not care about *us,* but you promised the public that the super heroes would only be used ***domestically.***"

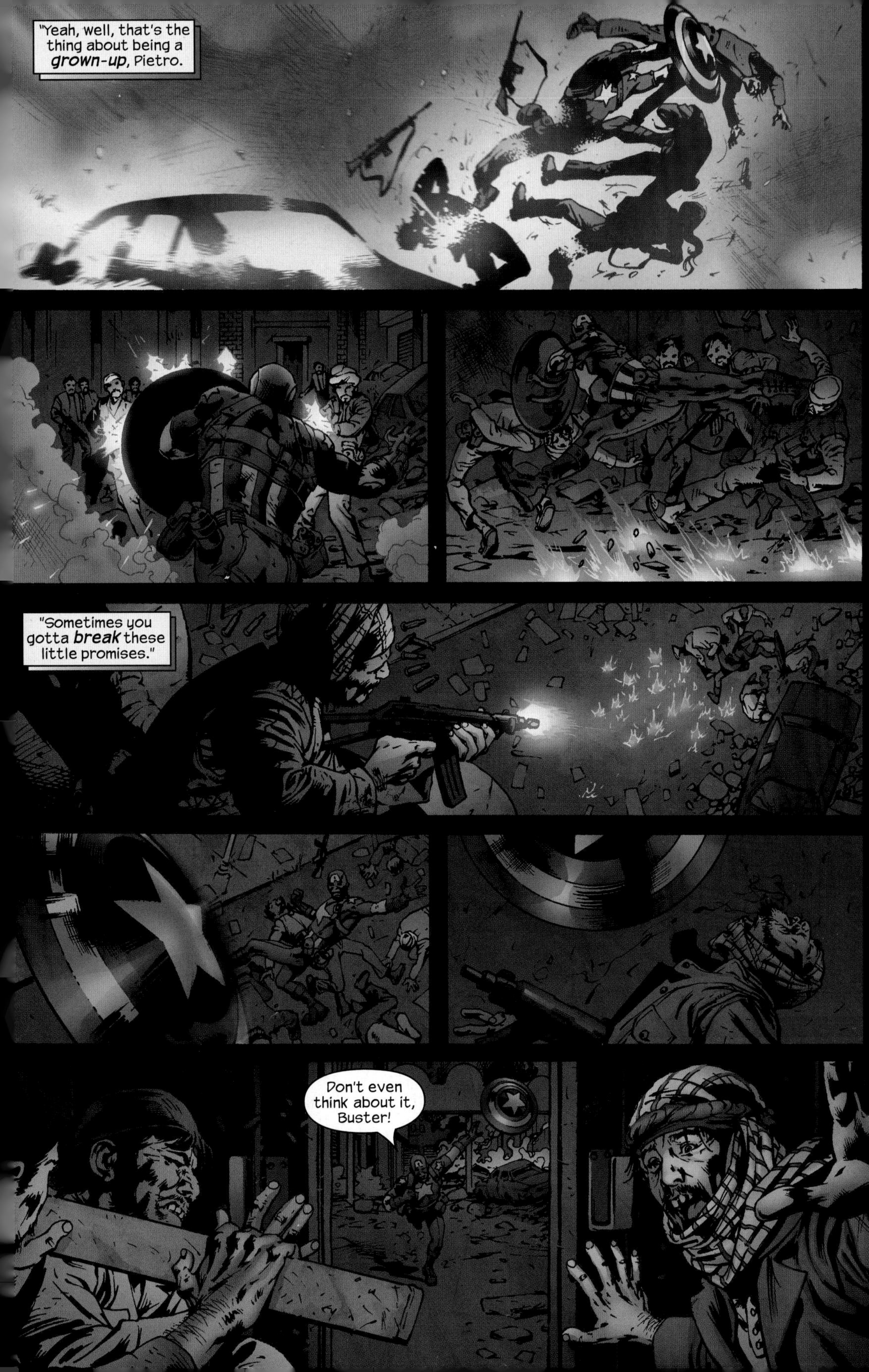
"Yeah, well, that's the thing about being a *grown-up*, Pietro.
"Sometimes you gotta *break* these little promises."
Don't even think about it, Buster!

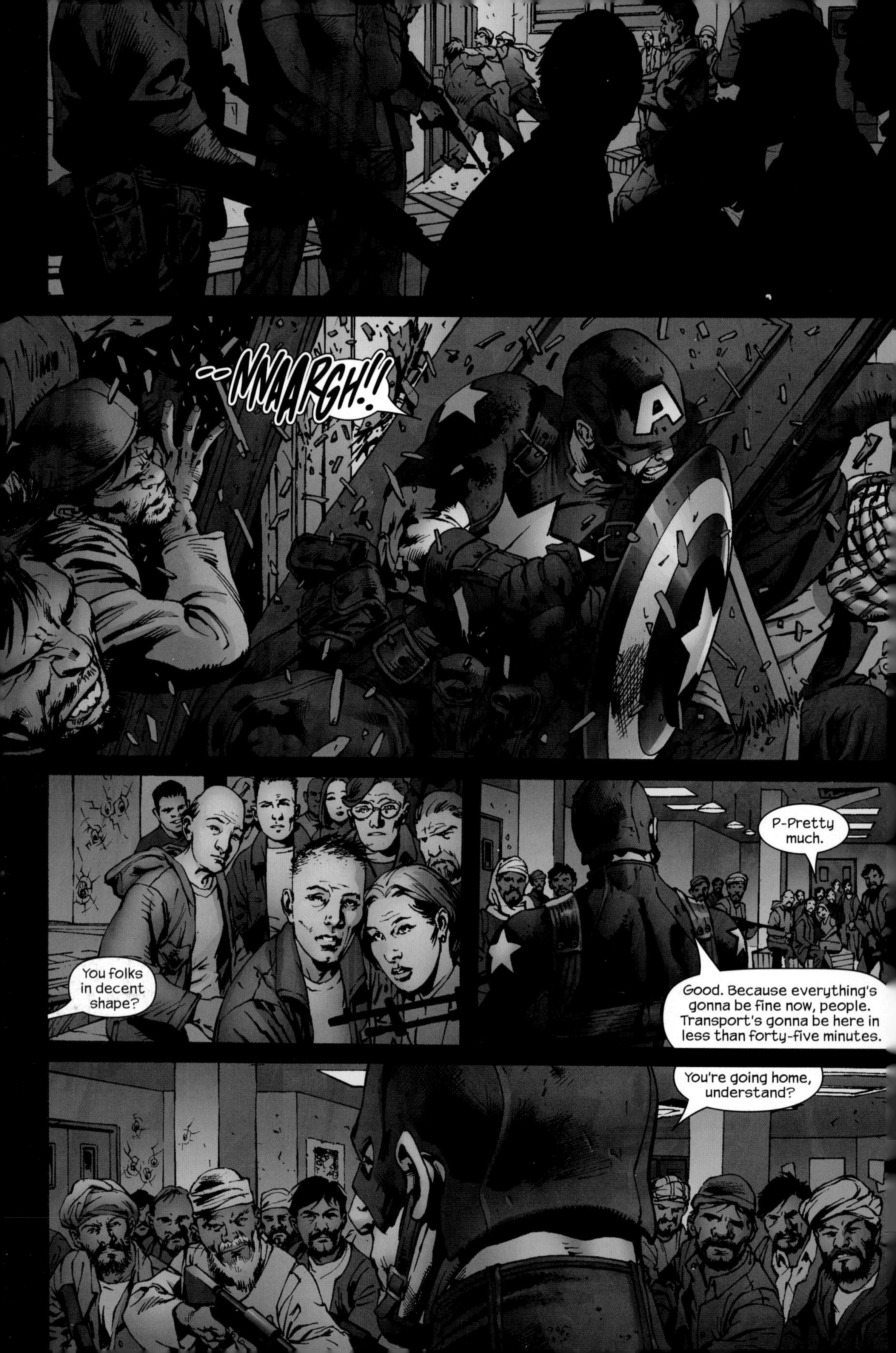
--NNAARGH!!
You folks in decent shape?
P-Pretty much.
Good. Because everything's gonna be fine now, people. Transport's gonna be here in less than forty-five minutes.
You're going home, understand?

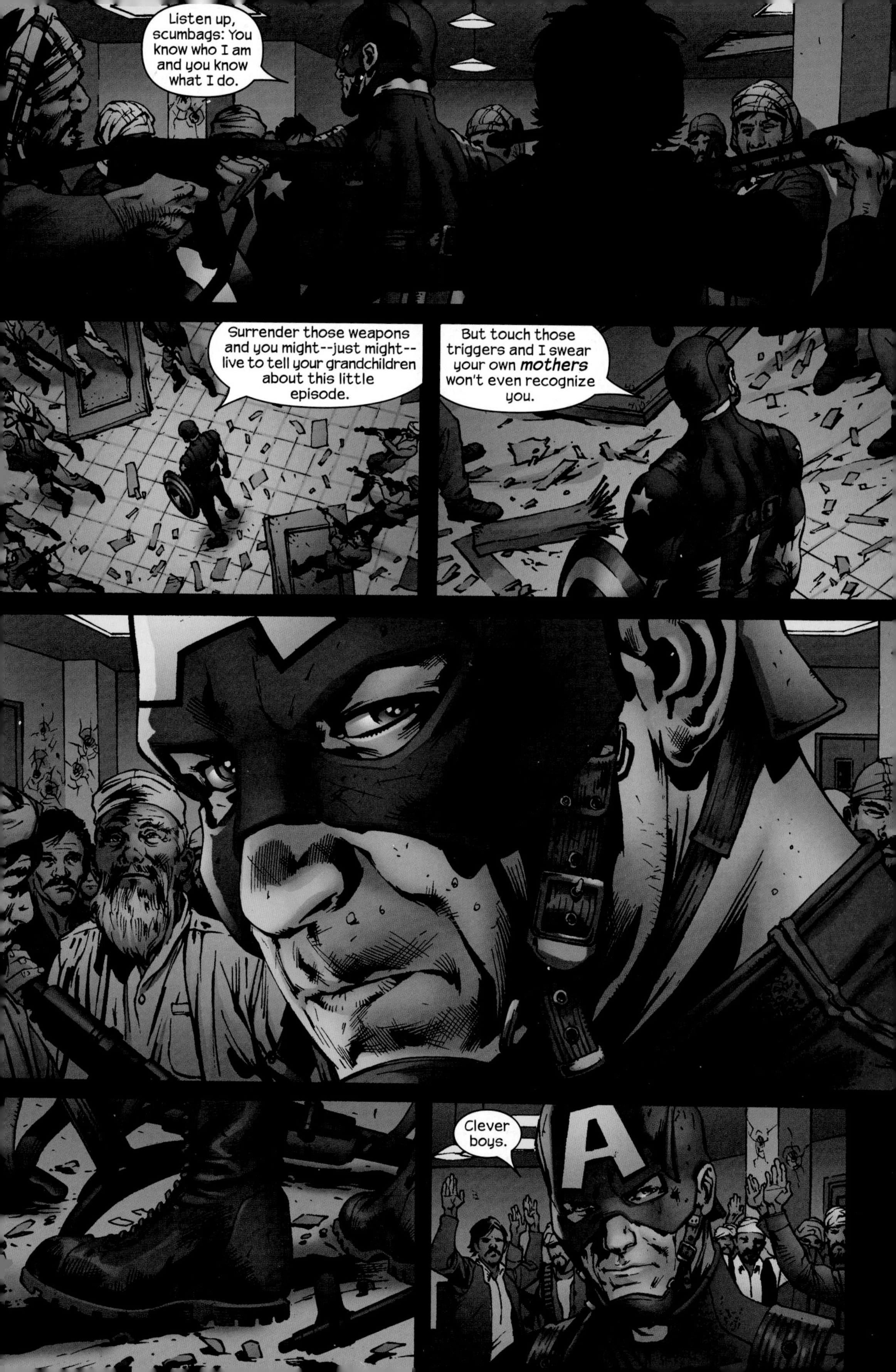
Listen up, scumbags: You know who I am and you know what I do.
Surrender those weapons and you might--just might--live to tell your grandchildren about this little episode.
But touch those triggers and I swear your own *mothers* won't even recognize you.
Clever boys.

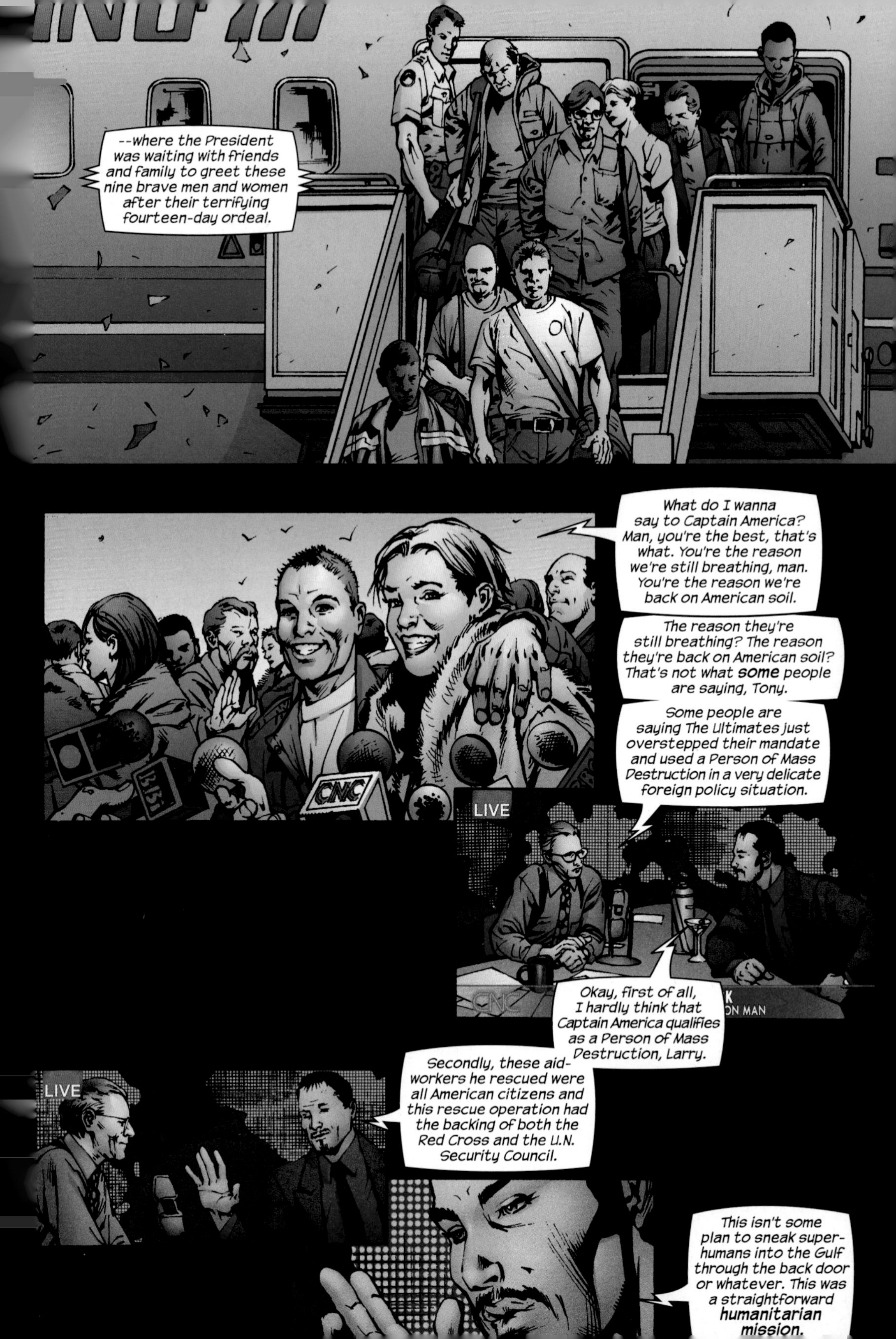
--where the President was waiting with friends and family to greet these nine brave men and women after their terrifying fourteen-day ordeal.
What do I wanna say to Captain America? Man, you're the best, that's what. You're the reason we're still breathing, man. You're the reason we're back on American soil.
CNC
The reason they're still breathing? The reason they're back on American soil? That's not what **some** people are saying, Tony.
Some people are saying The Ultimates just overstepped their mandate and used a Person of Mass Destruction in a very delicate foreign policy situation.
LIVE
Okay, first of all, I hardly think that Captain America qualifies as a Person of Mass Destruction, Larry.
LIVE
Secondly, these aid-workers he rescued were all American citizens and this rescue operation had the backing of both the Red Cross and the U.N. Security Council.
This isn't some plan to sneak super-humans into the Gulf through the back door or whatever. This was a straightforward **humanitarian mission.**

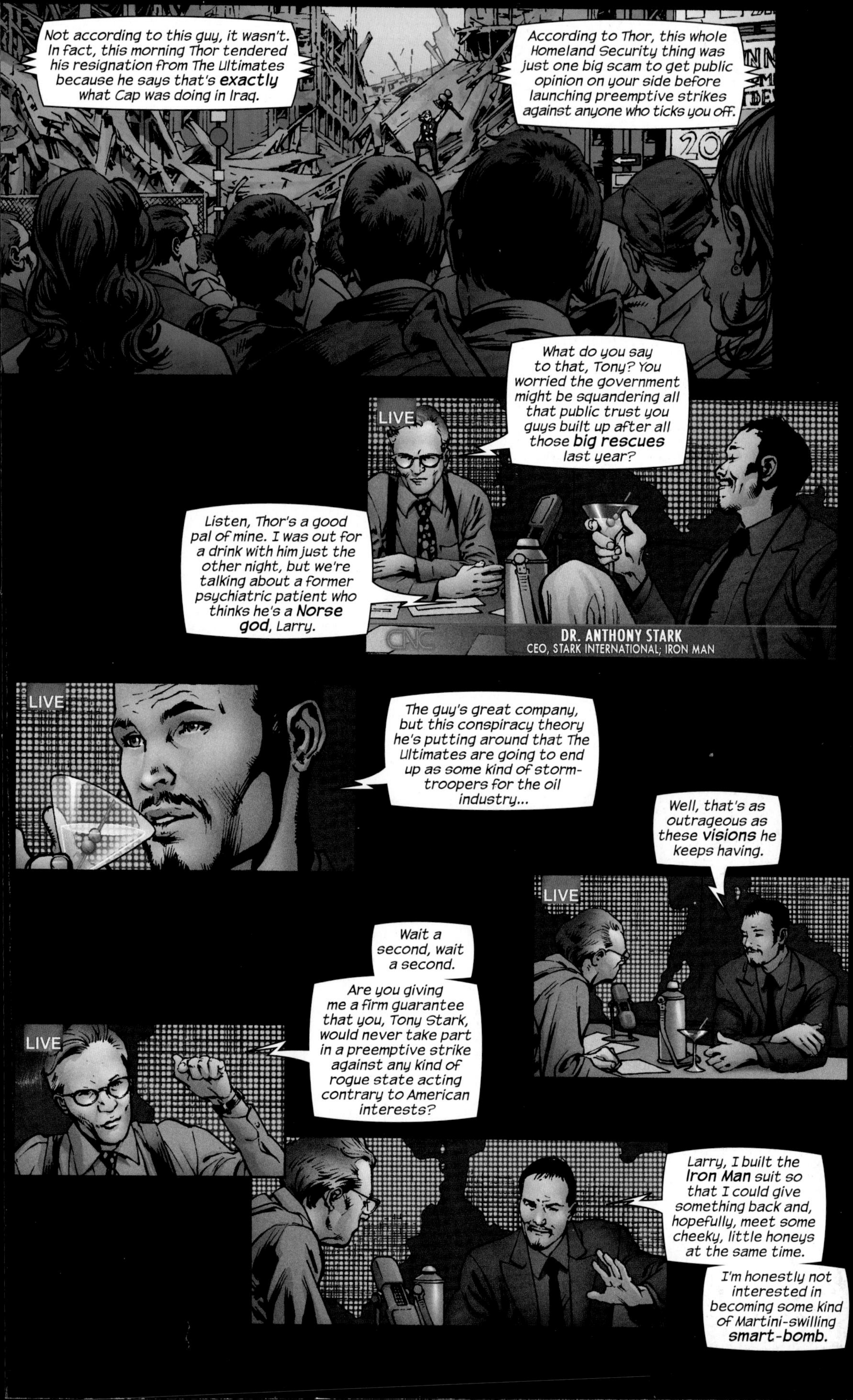

Not according to this guy, it wasn't. In fact, this morning Thor tendered his resignation from The Ultimates because he says that's exactly what Cap was doing in Iraq.
According to Thor, this whole Homeland Security thing was just one big scam to get public opinion on your side before launching preemptive strikes against anyone who ticks you off.
LIVE
What do you say to that, Tony? You worried the government might be squandering all that public trust you guys built up after all those big rescues last year?
Listen, Thor's a good pal of mine. I was out for a drink with him just the other night, but we're talking about a former psychiatric patient who thinks he's a Norse god, Larry.
DR. ANTHONY STARK
CEO, STARK INTERNATIONAL; IRON MAN
LIVE
The guy's great company, but this conspiracy theory he's putting around that The Ultimates are going to end up as some kind of storm-troopers for the oil industry...
Well, that's as outrageous as these visions he keeps having.
LIVE
Wait a second, wait a second.
Are you giving me a firm guarantee that you, Tony Stark, would never take part in a preemptive strike against any kind of rogue state acting contrary to American interests?
LIVE
Larry, I built the Iron Man suit so that I could give something back and, hopefully, meet some cheeky, little honeys at the same time.
I'm honestly not interested in becoming some kind of Martini-swilling smart-bomb.

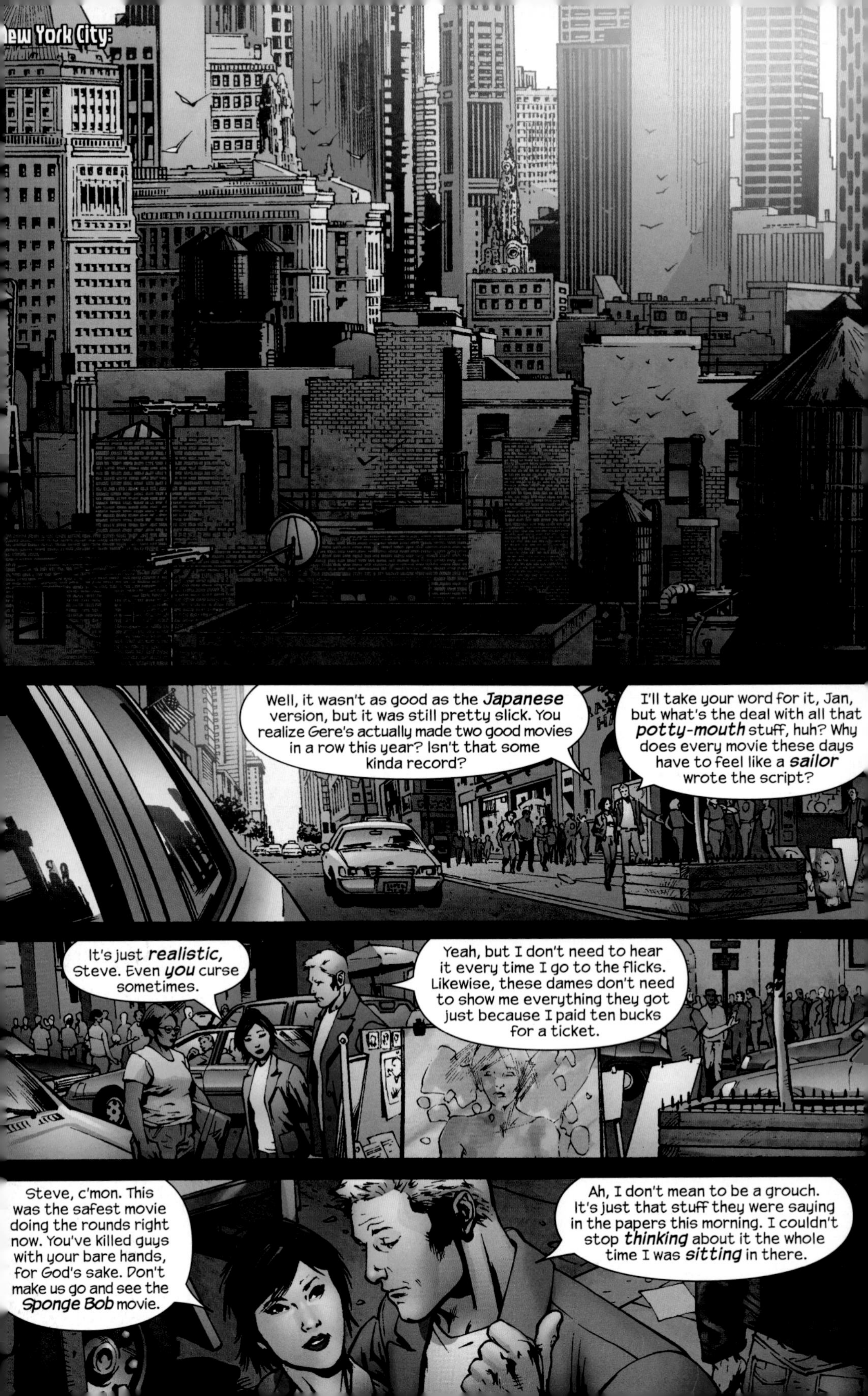
New York City:
Well, it wasn't as good as the Japanese version, but it was still pretty slick. You realize Gere's actually made two good movies in a row this year? Isn't that some kinda record?
I'll take your word for it, Jan, but what's the deal with all that potty-mouth stuff, huh? Why does every movie these days have to feel like a sailor wrote the script?
It's just realistic, Steve. Even you curse sometimes.
Yeah, but I don't need to hear it every time I go to the flicks. Likewise, these dames don't need to show me everything they got just because I paid ten bucks for a ticket.
Steve, c'mon. This was the safest movie doing the rounds right now. You've killed guys with your bare hands, for God's sake. Don't make us go and see the Sponge Bob movie.
Ah, I don't mean to be a grouch. It's just that stuff they were saying in the papers this morning. I couldn't stop thinking about it the whole time I was sitting in there.

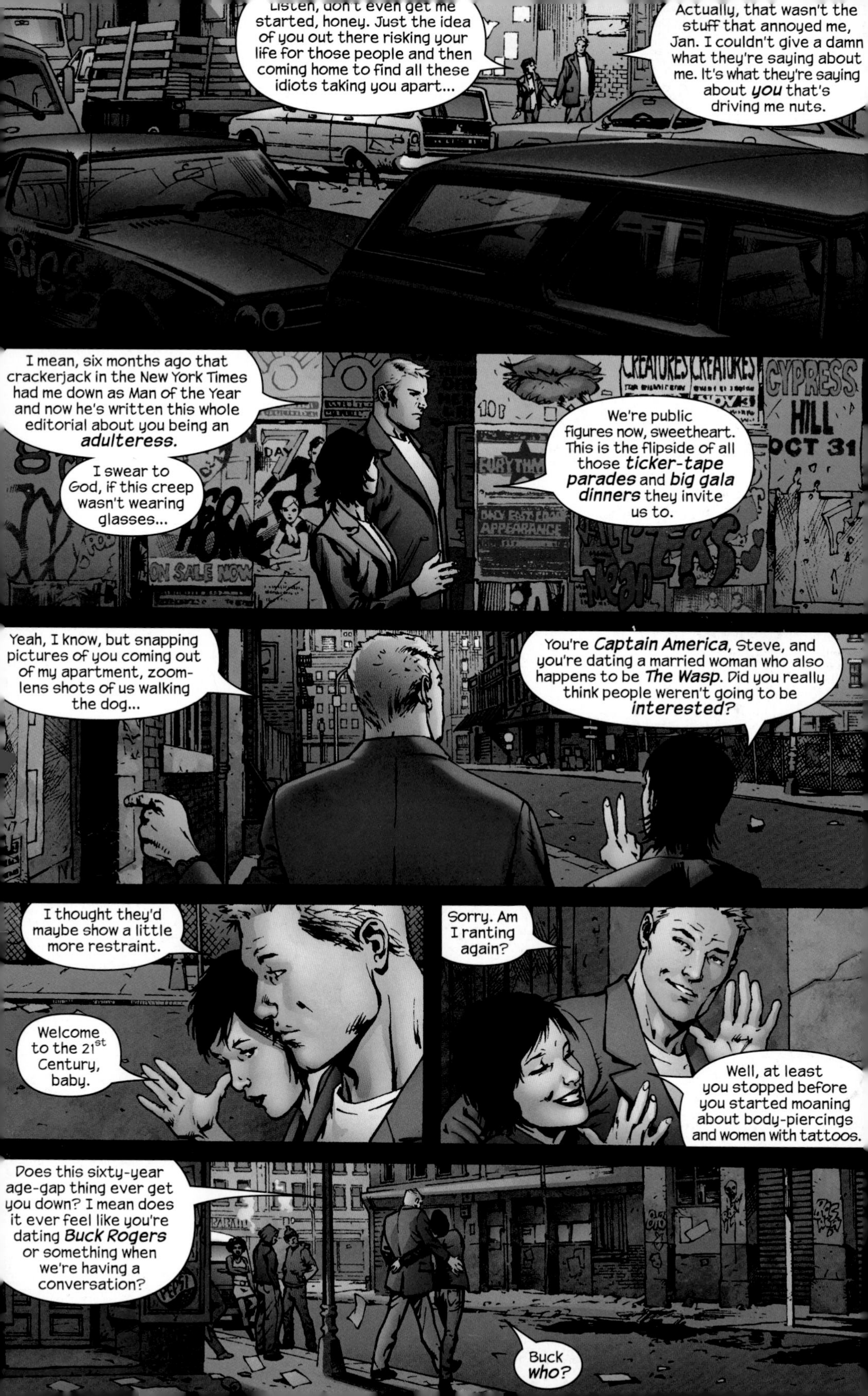
Listen, don't even get me started, honey. Just the idea of you out there risking your life for those people and then coming home to find all these idiots taking you apart...
Actually, that wasn't the stuff that annoyed me, Jan. I couldn't give a damn what they're saying about me. It's what they're saying about *you* that's driving me nuts.
I mean, six months ago that crackerjack in the New York Times had me down as Man of the Year and now he's written this whole editorial about you being an *adulteress.*
I swear to God, if this creep wasn't wearing glasses...
We're public figures now, sweetheart. This is the flipside of all those *ticker-tape parades* and *big gala dinners* they invite us to.
CREATURES CREATURES
CYPRESS HILL OCT 31
ON SALE NOW
APPEARANCE
Yeah, I know, but snapping pictures of you coming out of my apartment, zoom-lens shots of us walking the dog...
You're *Captain America*, Steve, and you're dating a married woman who also happens to be *The Wasp*. Did you really think people weren't going to be *interested?*
I thought they'd maybe show a little more restraint.
Welcome to the 21st Century, baby.
Sorry. Am I ranting again?
Well, at least you stopped before you started moaning about body-piercings and women with tattoos.
Does this sixty-year age-gap thing ever get you down? I mean does it ever feel like you're dating *Buck Rogers* or something when we're having a conversation?
Buck *who?*

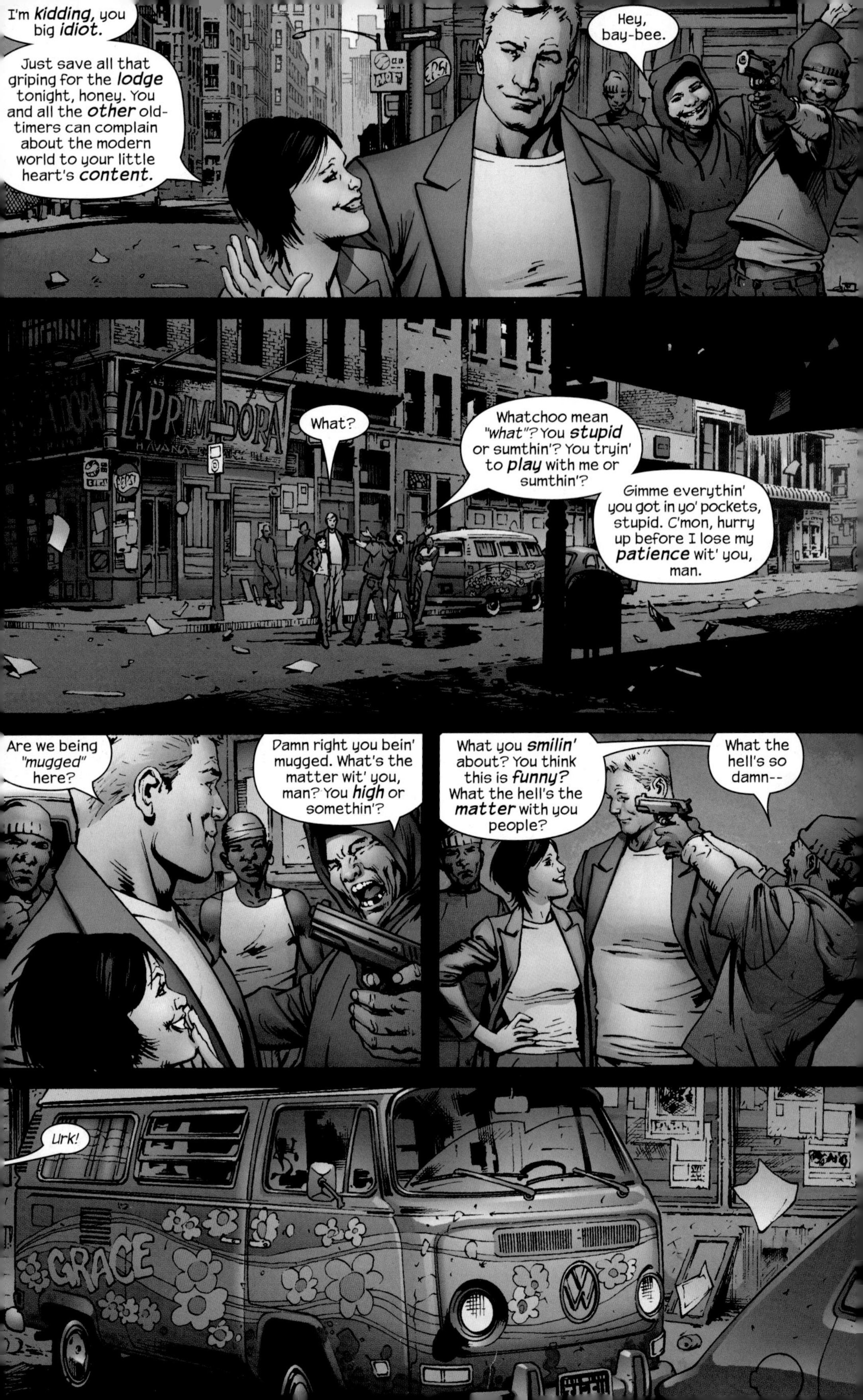
I'm *kidding*, you big *idiot.*
Just save all that griping for the *lodge* tonight, honey. You and all the *other* old-timers can complain about the modern world to your little heart's *content.*
Hey, bay-bee.
What?
Whatchoo mean *"what"*? You *stupid* or sumthin'? You tryin' to *play* with me or sumthin'?
Gimme everythin' you got in yo' pockets, stupid. C'mon, hurry up before I lose my *patience* wit' you, man.
Are we being *"mugged"* here?
Damn right you bein' mugged. What's the matter wit' you, man? You *high* or somethin'?
What you *smilin'* about? You think this is *funny?* What the hell's the *matter* with you people?
What the hell's so damn--
Urk!
GRACE

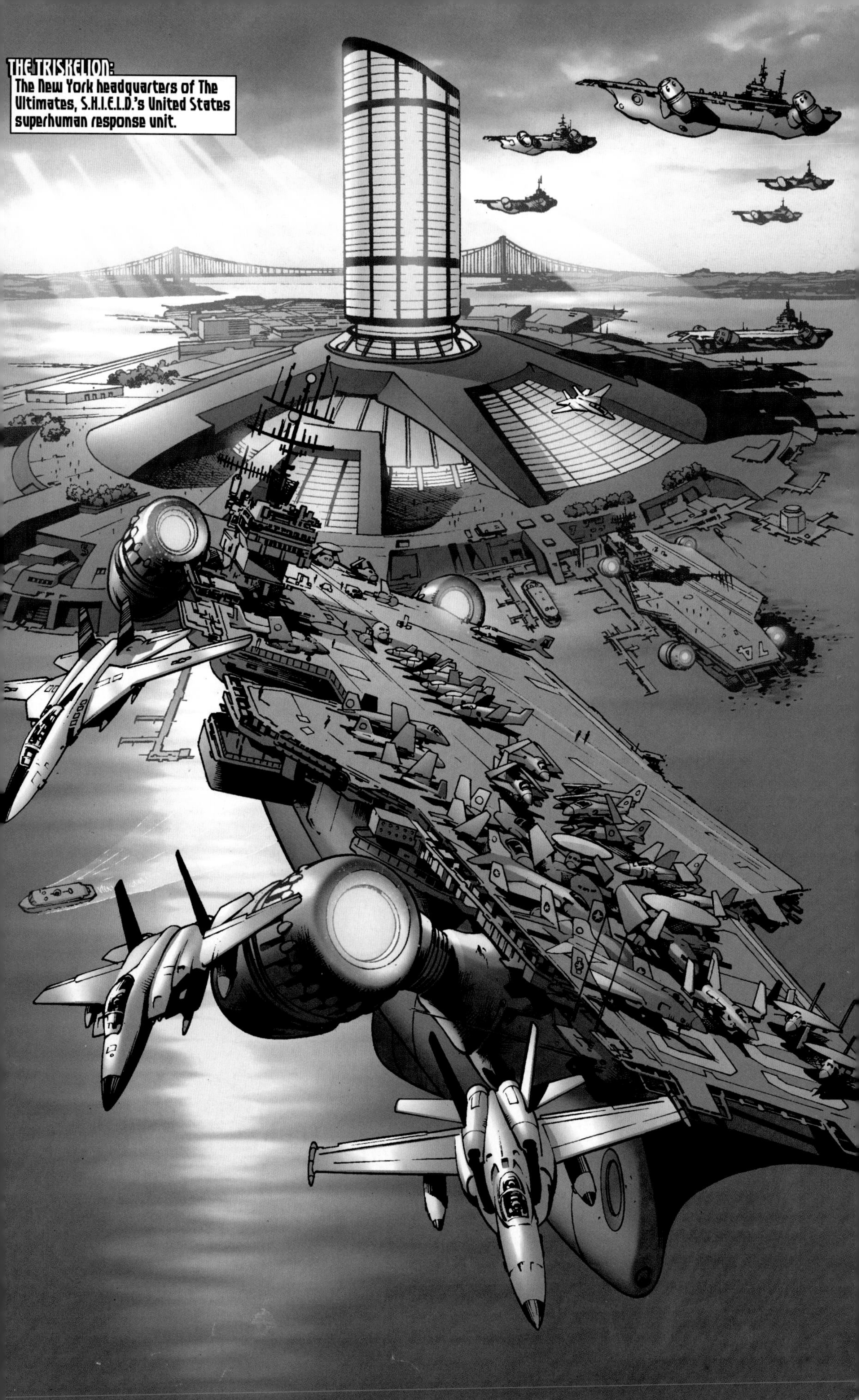
THE TRISKELION:
The New York headquarters of The Ultimates, S.H.I.E.L.D.'s United States superhuman response unit.

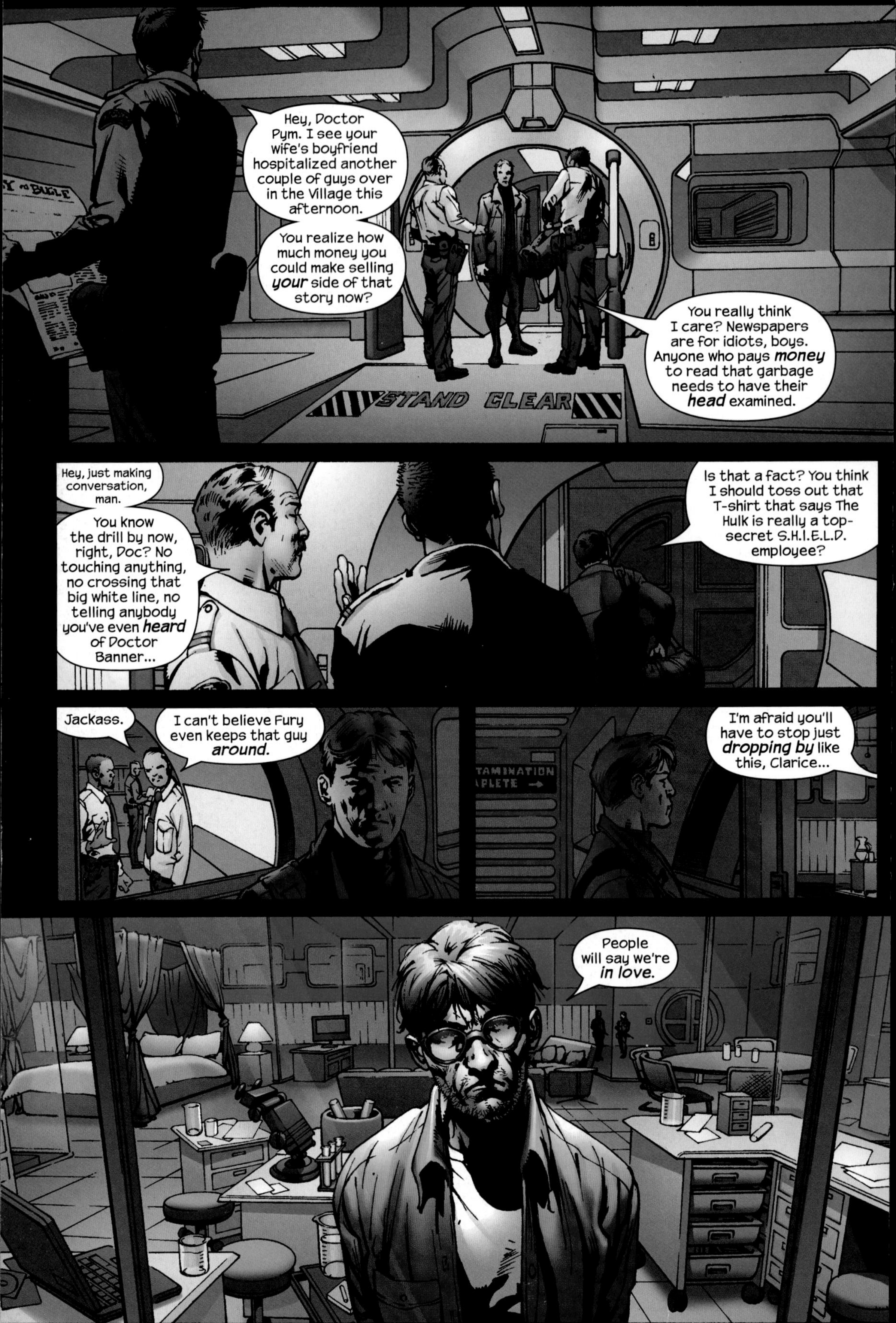

Hey, Doctor Pym. I see your wife's boyfriend hospitalized another couple of guys over in the Village this afternoon.
You realize how much money you could make selling *your* side of that story now?
You really think I care? Newspapers are for idiots, boys. Anyone who pays *money* to read that garbage needs to have their *head* examined.
STAND CLEAR
Hey, just making conversation, man.
You know the drill by now, right, Doc? No touching anything, no crossing that big white line, no telling anybody you've even *heard* of Doctor Banner...
Is that a fact? You think I should toss out that T-shirt that says The Hulk is really a top-secret S.H.I.E.L.D. employee?
Jackass.
I can't believe Fury even keeps that guy *around*.
I'm afraid you'll have to stop just *dropping by* like this, Clarice...
People will say we're *in love*.

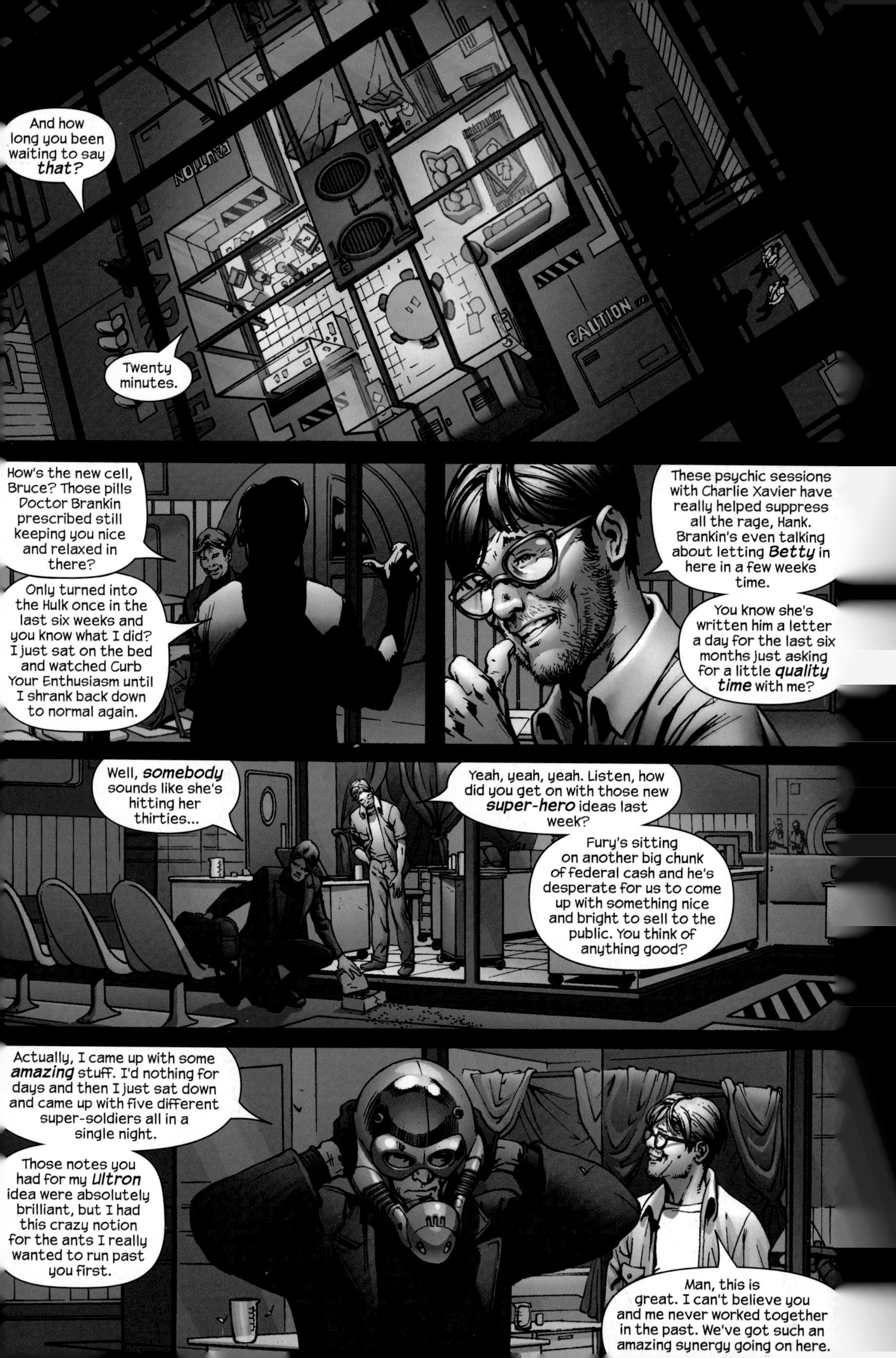
And how long you been waiting to say *that?*
CAUTION
Twenty minutes.
CAUTION
How's the new cell, Bruce? Those pills Doctor Brankin prescribed still keeping you nice and relaxed in there?
Only turned into the Hulk once in the last six weeks and you know what I did? I just sat on the bed and watched Curb Your Enthusiasm until I shrank back down to normal again.
These psychic sessions with Charlie Xavier have really helped suppress all the rage, Hank. Brankin's even talking about letting *Betty* in here in a few weeks time.
You know she's written him a letter a day for the last six months just asking for a little *quality time* with me?
Well, *somebody* sounds like she's hitting her thirties...
Yeah, yeah, yeah. Listen, how did you get on with those new *super-hero* ideas last week?
Fury's sitting on another big chunk of federal cash and he's desperate for us to come up with something nice and bright to sell to the public. You think of anything good?
Actually, I came up with some *amazing* stuff. I'd nothing for days and then I just sat down and came up with five different super-soldiers all in a single night.
Those notes you had for my *Ultron* idea were absolutely brilliant, but I had this crazy notion for the ants I really wanted to run past you first.
Man, this is great. I can't believe you and me never worked together in the past. We've got such an amazing synergy going on here.

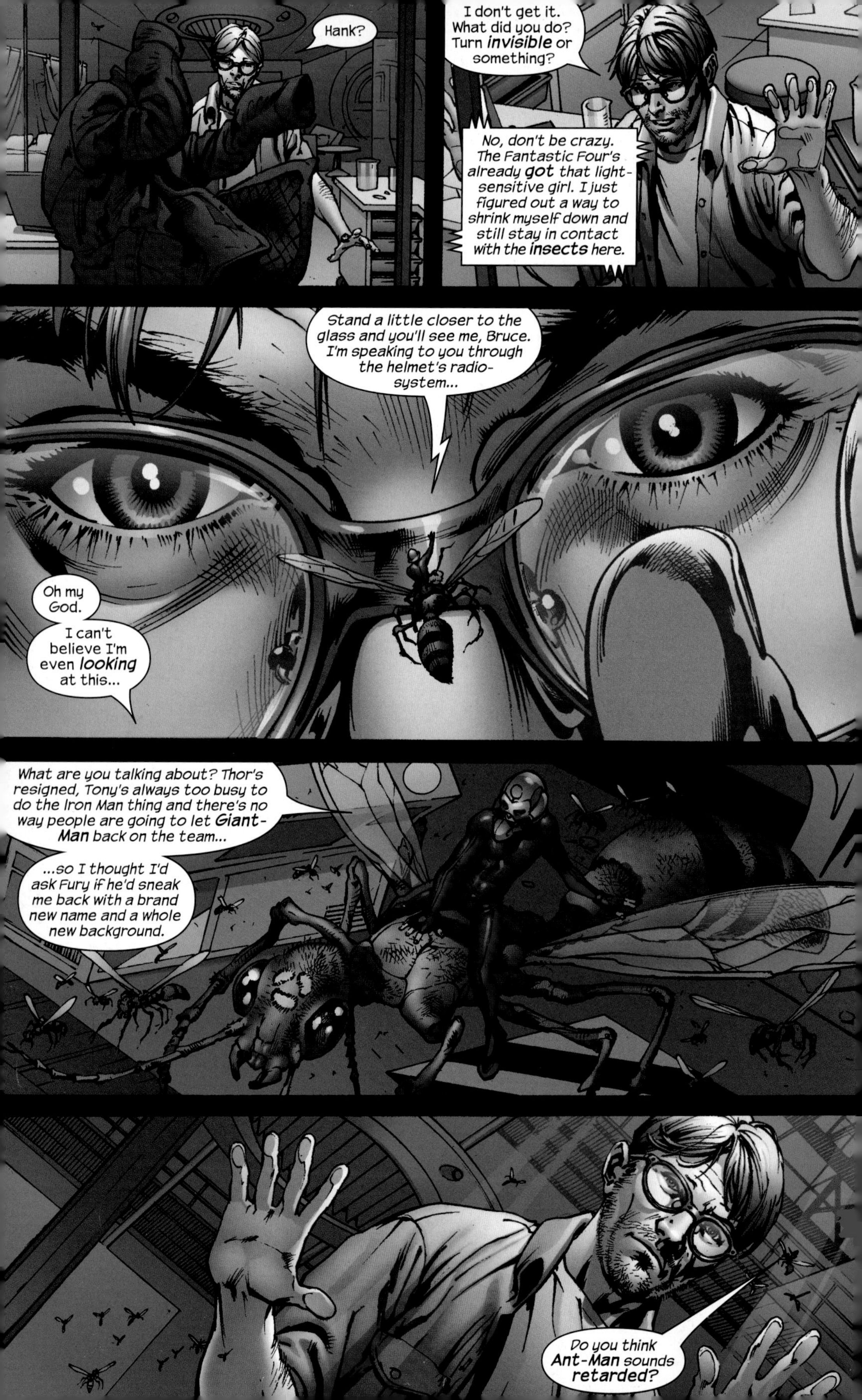
Hank?
I don't get it. What did you do? Turn *invisible* or something?
No, don't be crazy. The Fantastic Four's already **got** that light-sensitive girl. I just figured out a way to shrink myself down and still stay in contact with the **insects** here.
Stand a little closer to the glass and you'll see me, Bruce. I'm speaking to you through the helmet's radio-system...
Oh my God.
I can't believe I'm even *looking* at this...
What are you talking about? Thor's resigned, Tony's always too busy to do the Iron Man thing and there's no way people are going to let **Giant-Man** back on the team...
...so I thought I'd ask Fury if he'd sneak me back with a brand new name and a whole new background.
Do you think **Ant-Man** sounds **retarded?**

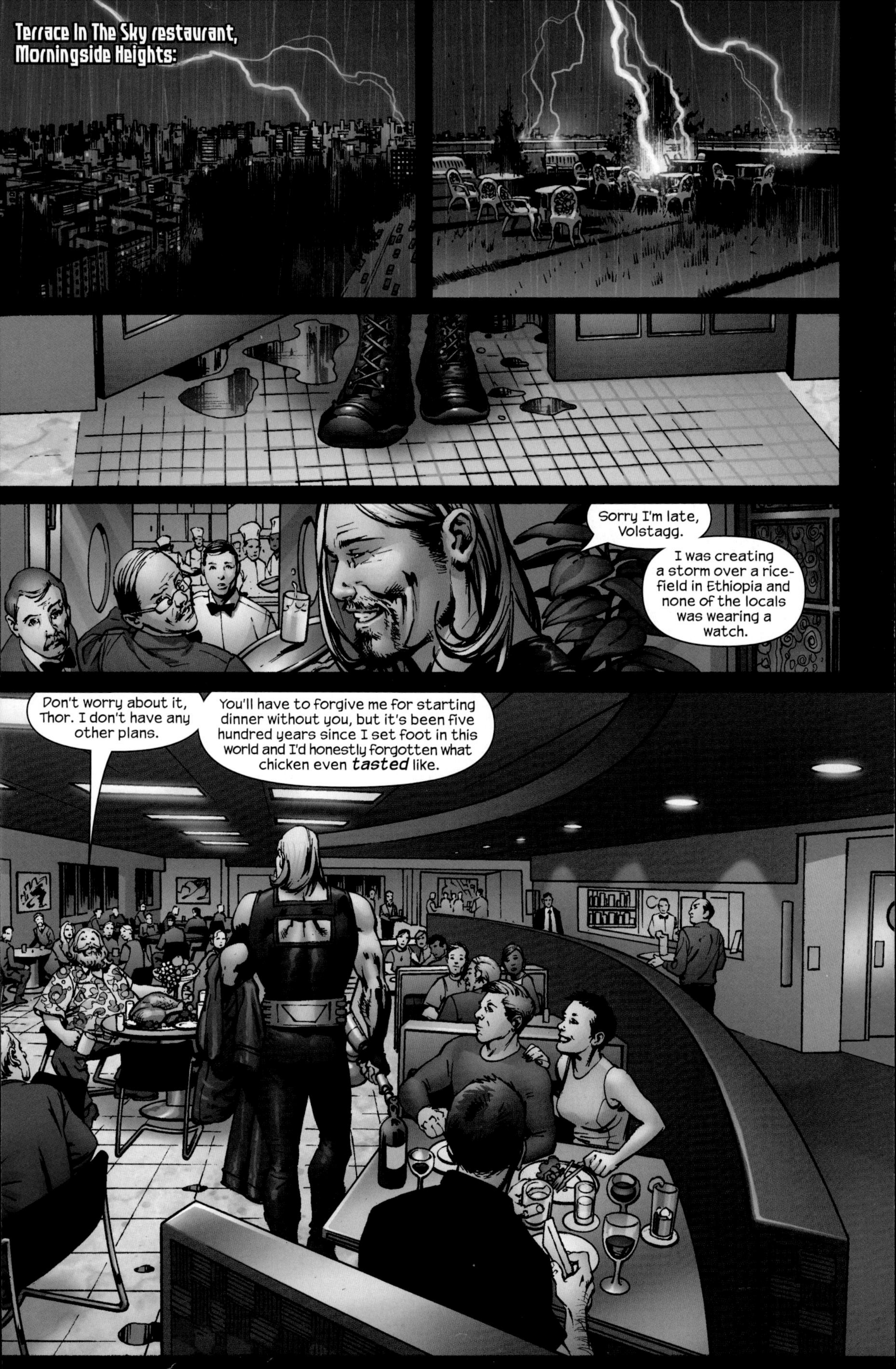
Terrace In The Sky restaurant, Morningside Heights:
Sorry I'm late, Volstagg.
I was creating a storm over a rice-field in Ethiopia and none of the locals was wearing a watch.
Don't worry about it, Thor. I don't have any other plans.
You'll have to forgive me for starting dinner without you, but it's been five hundred years since I set foot in this world and I'd honestly forgotten what chicken even *tasted* like.

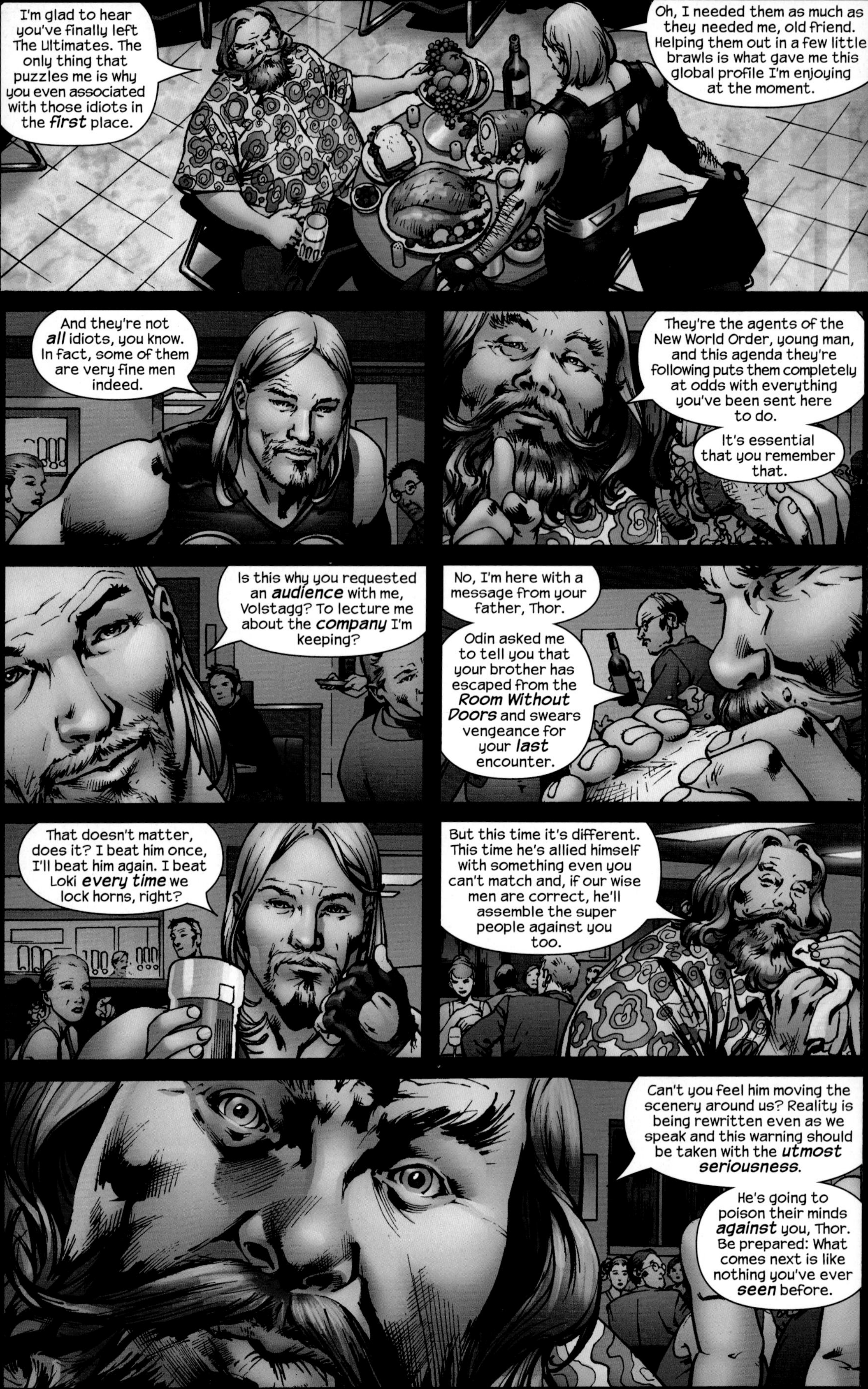
I'm glad to hear you've finally left The Ultimates. The only thing that puzzles me is why you even associated with those idiots in the *first* place.
Oh, I needed them as much as they needed me, old friend. Helping them out in a few little brawls is what gave me this global profile I'm enjoying at the moment.
And they're not *all* idiots, you know. In fact, some of them are very fine men indeed.
They're the agents of the New World Order, young man, and this agenda they're following puts them completely at odds with everything you've been sent here to do.
It's essential that you remember that.
Is this why you requested an *audience* with me, Volstagg? To lecture me about the *company* I'm keeping?
No, I'm here with a message from your father, Thor.
Odin asked me to tell you that your brother has escaped from the *Room Without Doors* and swears vengeance for your *last* encounter.
That doesn't matter, does it? I beat him once, I'll beat him again. I beat Loki *every time* we lock horns, right?
But this time it's different. This time he's allied himself with something even you can't match and, if our wise men are correct, he'll assemble the super people against you too.
Can't you feel him moving the scenery around us? Reality is being rewritten even as we speak and this warning should be taken with the *utmost seriousness*.
He's going to poison their minds *against* you, Thor. Be prepared: What comes next is like nothing you've ever *seen* before.

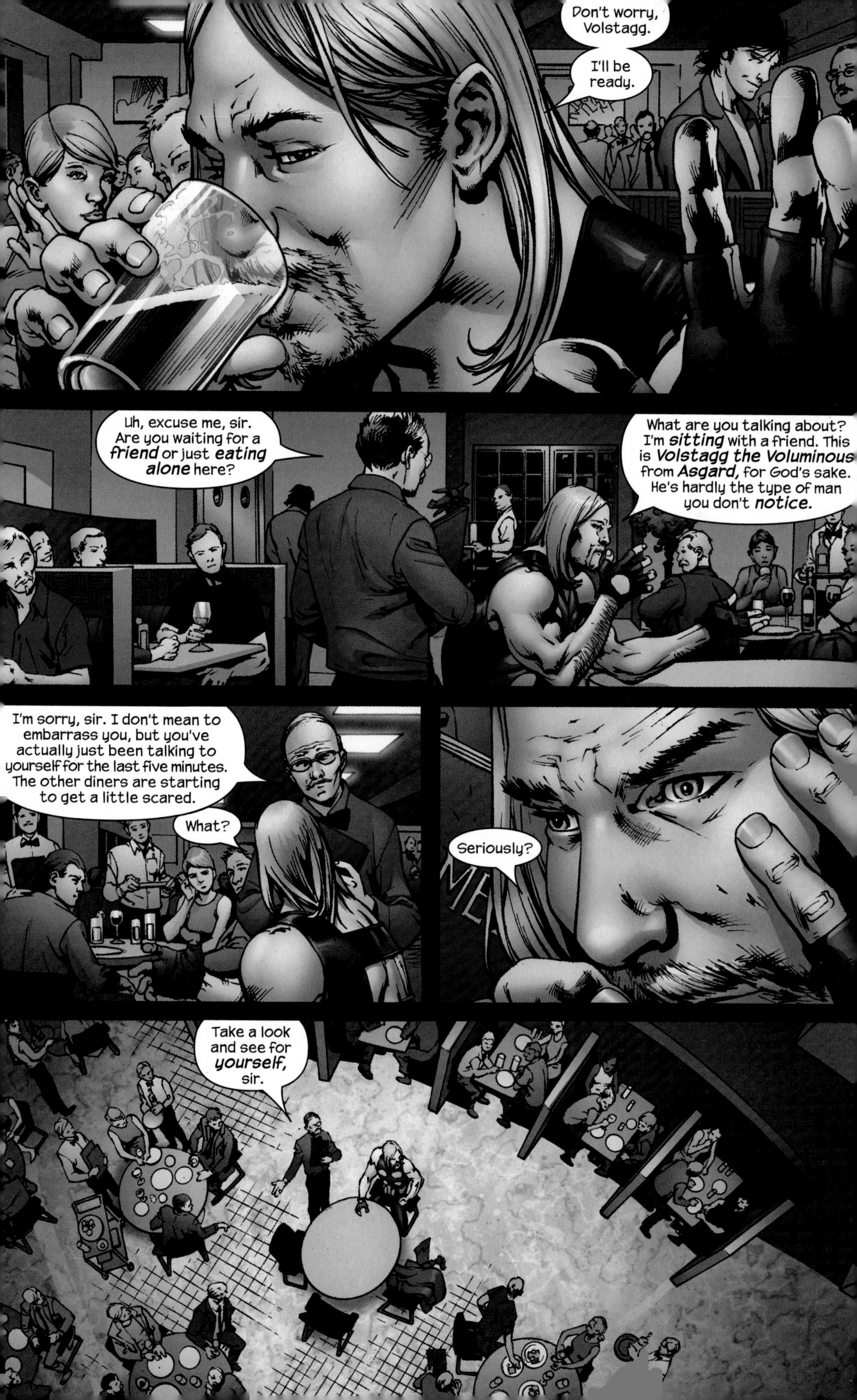
Don't worry, Volstagg.
I'll be ready.
Uh, excuse me, sir. Are you waiting for a friend or just eating alone here?
What are you talking about? I'm sitting with a friend. This is Volstagg the Voluminous from Asgard, for God's sake. He's hardly the type of man you don't notice.
I'm sorry, sir. I don't mean to embarrass you, but you've actually just been talking to yourself for the last five minutes. The other diners are starting to get a little scared.
What?
Seriously?
Take a look and see for yourself, sir.

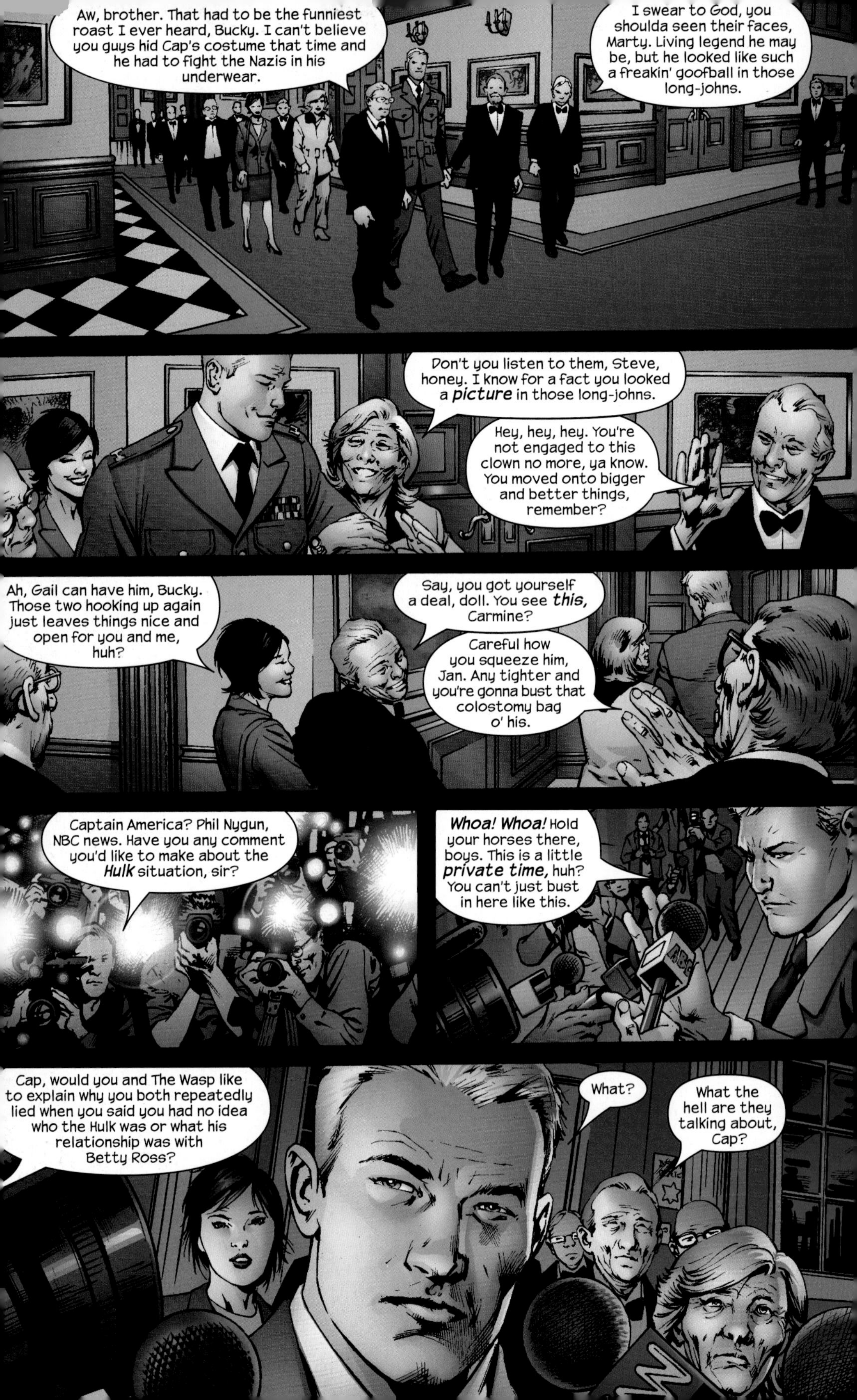
Aw, brother. That had to be the funniest roast I ever heard, Bucky. I can't believe you guys hid Cap's costume that time and he had to fight the Nazis in his underwear.
I swear to God, you shoulda seen their faces, Marty. Living legend he may be, but he looked like such a freakin' goofball in those long-johns.
Don't you listen to them, Steve, honey. I know for a fact you looked a picture in those long-johns.
Hey, hey, hey. You're not engaged to this clown no more, ya know. You moved onto bigger and better things, remember?
Ah, Gail can have him, Bucky. Those two hooking up again just leaves things nice and open for you and me, huh?
Say, you got yourself a deal, doll. You see this, Carmine?
Careful how you squeeze him, Jan. Any tighter and you're gonna bust that colostomy bag o' his.
Captain America? Phil Nygun, NBC news. Have you any comment you'd like to make about the Hulk situation, sir?
Whoa! Whoa! Hold your horses there, boys. This is a little private time, huh? You can't just bust in here like this.
Cap, would you and The Wasp like to explain why you both repeatedly lied when you said you had no idea who the Hulk was or what his relationship was with Betty Ross?
What?
What the hell are they talking about, Cap?

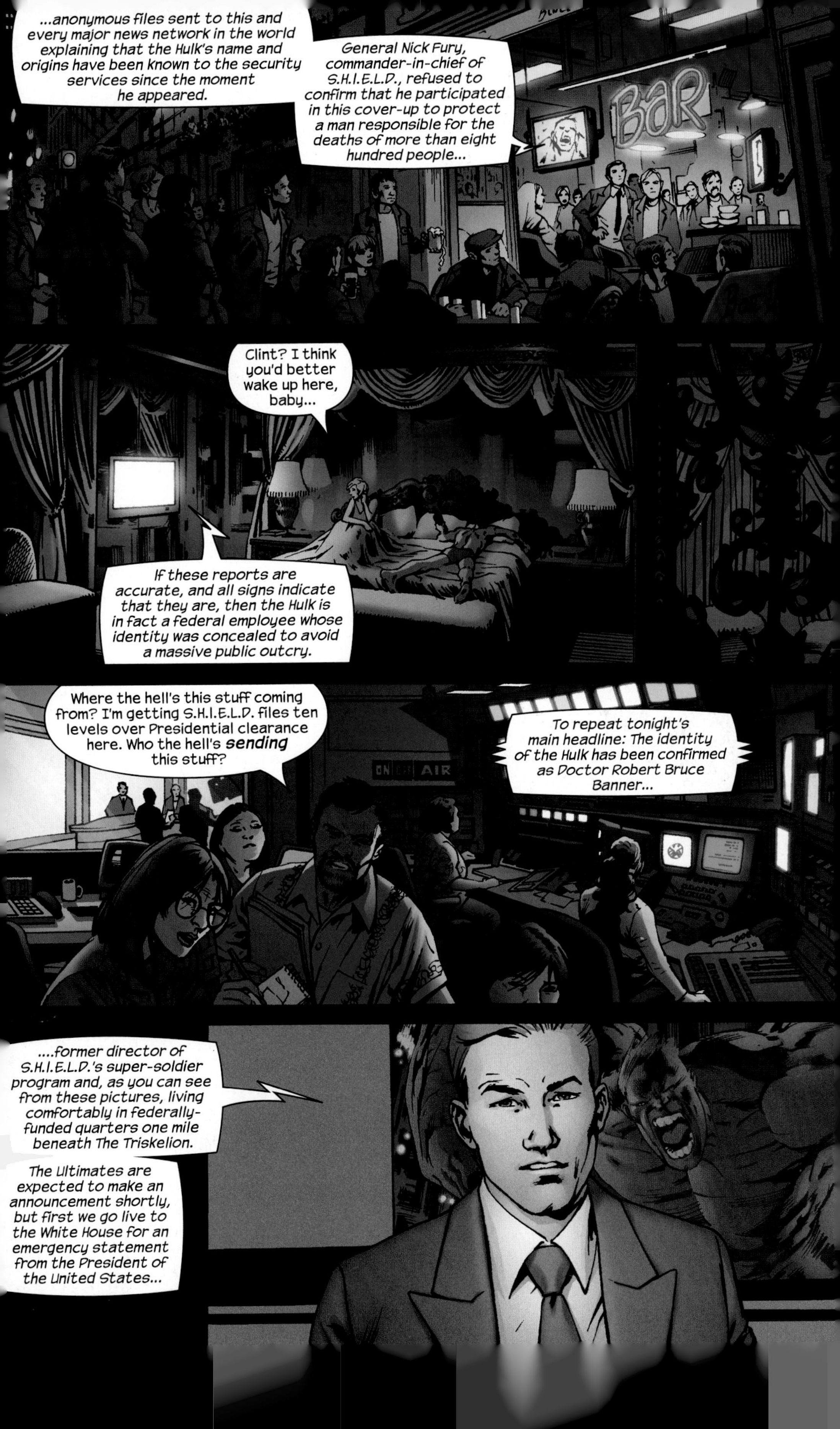
...anonymous files sent to this and every major news network in the world explaining that the Hulk's name and origins have been known to the security services since the moment he appeared.
General Nick Fury, commander-in-chief of S.H.I.E.L.D., refused to confirm that he participated in this cover-up to protect a man responsible for the deaths of more than eight hundred people...
BAR
Clint? I think you'd better wake up here, baby...
If these reports are accurate, and all signs indicate that they are, then the Hulk is in fact a federal employee whose identity was concealed to avoid a massive public outcry.
Where the hell's this stuff coming from? I'm getting S.H.I.E.L.D. files ten levels over Presidential clearance here. Who the hell's **sending** this stuff?
To repeat tonight's main headline: The identity of the Hulk has been confirmed as Doctor Robert Bruce Banner...
ON AIR
....former director of S.H.I.E.L.D.'s super-soldier program and, as you can see from these pictures, living comfortably in federally-funded quarters one mile beneath The Triskelion.
The Ultimates are expected to make an announcement shortly, but first we go live to the White House for an emergency statement from the President of the United States...

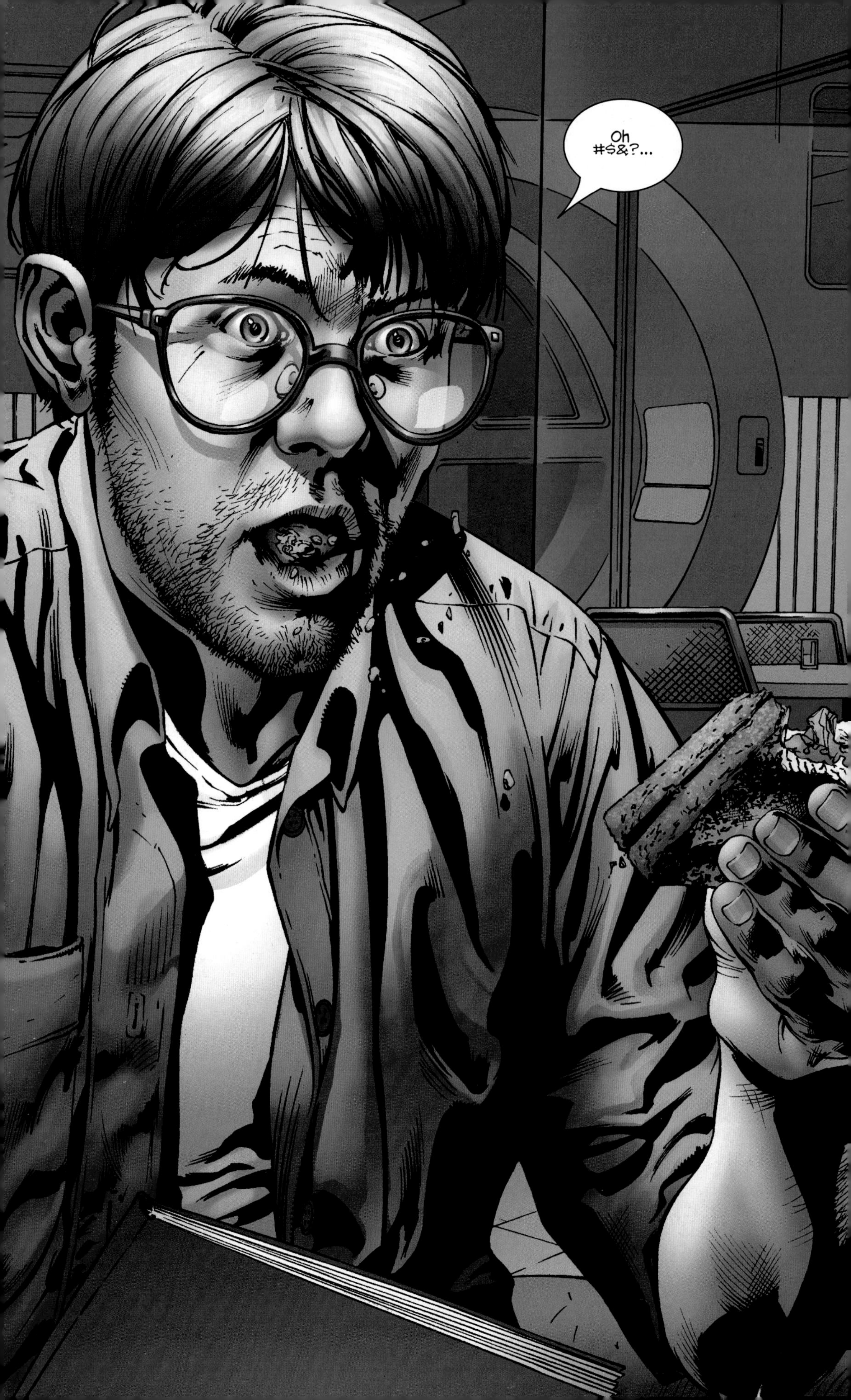
Oh #$&?...

DEAD MAN WALKING

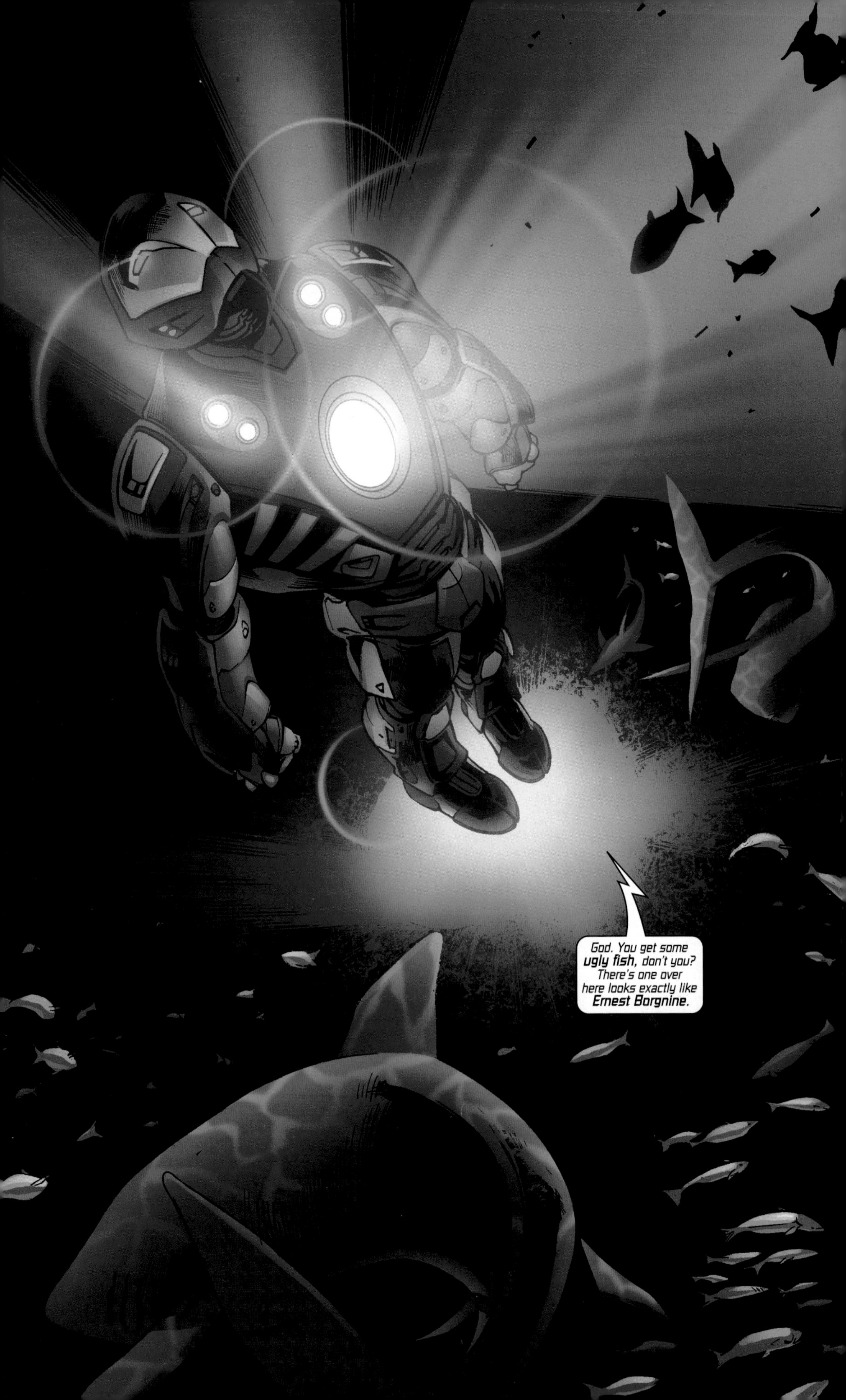
God. You get some **ugly fish**, don't you? There's one over here looks exactly like **Ernest Borgnine**.

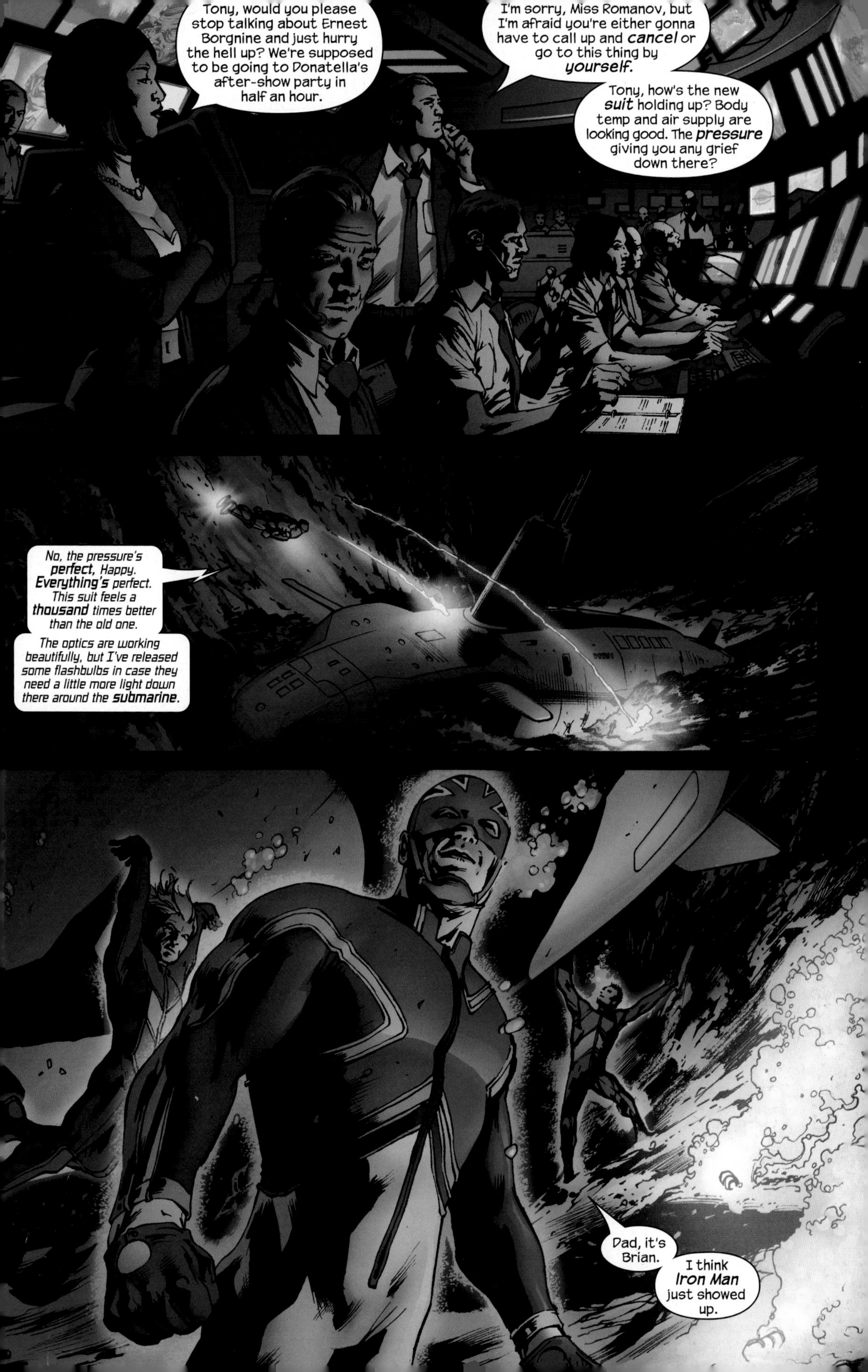
Tony, would you please stop talking about Ernest Borgnine and just hurry the hell up? We're supposed to be going to Donatella's after-show party in half an hour.
I'm sorry, Miss Romanov, but I'm afraid you're either gonna have to call up and cancel or go to this thing by yourself.
Tony, how's the new suit holding up? Body temp and air supply are looking good. The pressure giving you any grief down there?
No, the pressure's perfect, Happy. Everything's perfect. This suit feels a thousand times better than the old one.
The optics are working beautifully, but I've released some flashbulbs in case they need a little more light down there around the submarine.
Dad, it's Brian.
I think Iron Man just showed up.

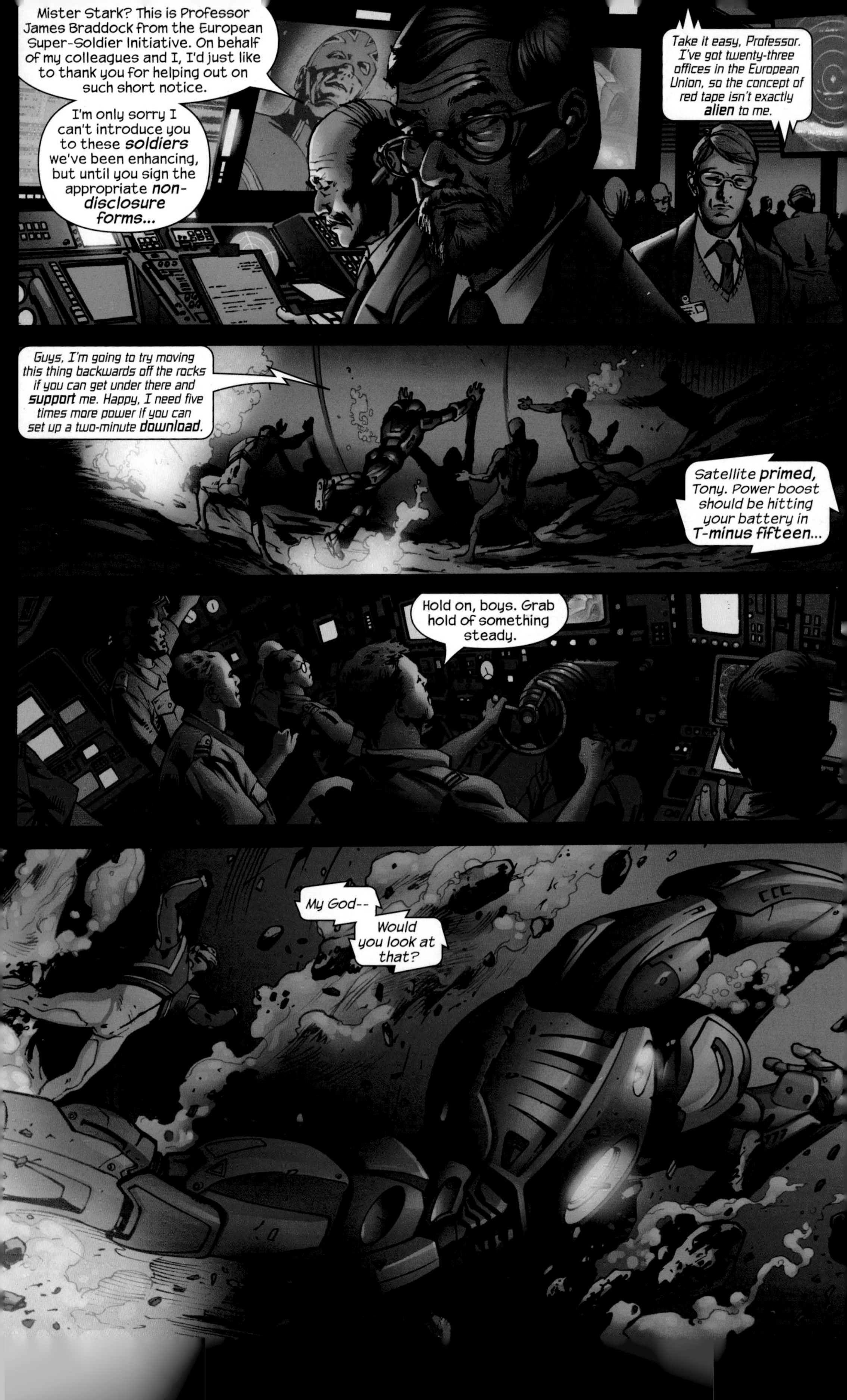
Mister Stark? This is Professor James Braddock from the European Super-Soldier Initiative. On behalf of my colleagues and I, I'd just like to thank you for helping out on such short notice.
I'm only sorry I can't introduce you to these soldiers we've been enhancing, but until you sign the appropriate non-disclosure forms...
Take it easy, Professor. I've got twenty-three offices in the European Union, so the concept of red tape isn't exactly alien to me.
Guys, I'm going to try moving this thing backwards off the rocks if you can get under there and support me. Happy, I need five times more power if you can set up a two-minute download.
Satellite primed, Tony. Power boost should be hitting your battery in T-minus fifteen...
Hold on, boys. Grab hold of something steady.
My God--
Would you look at that?

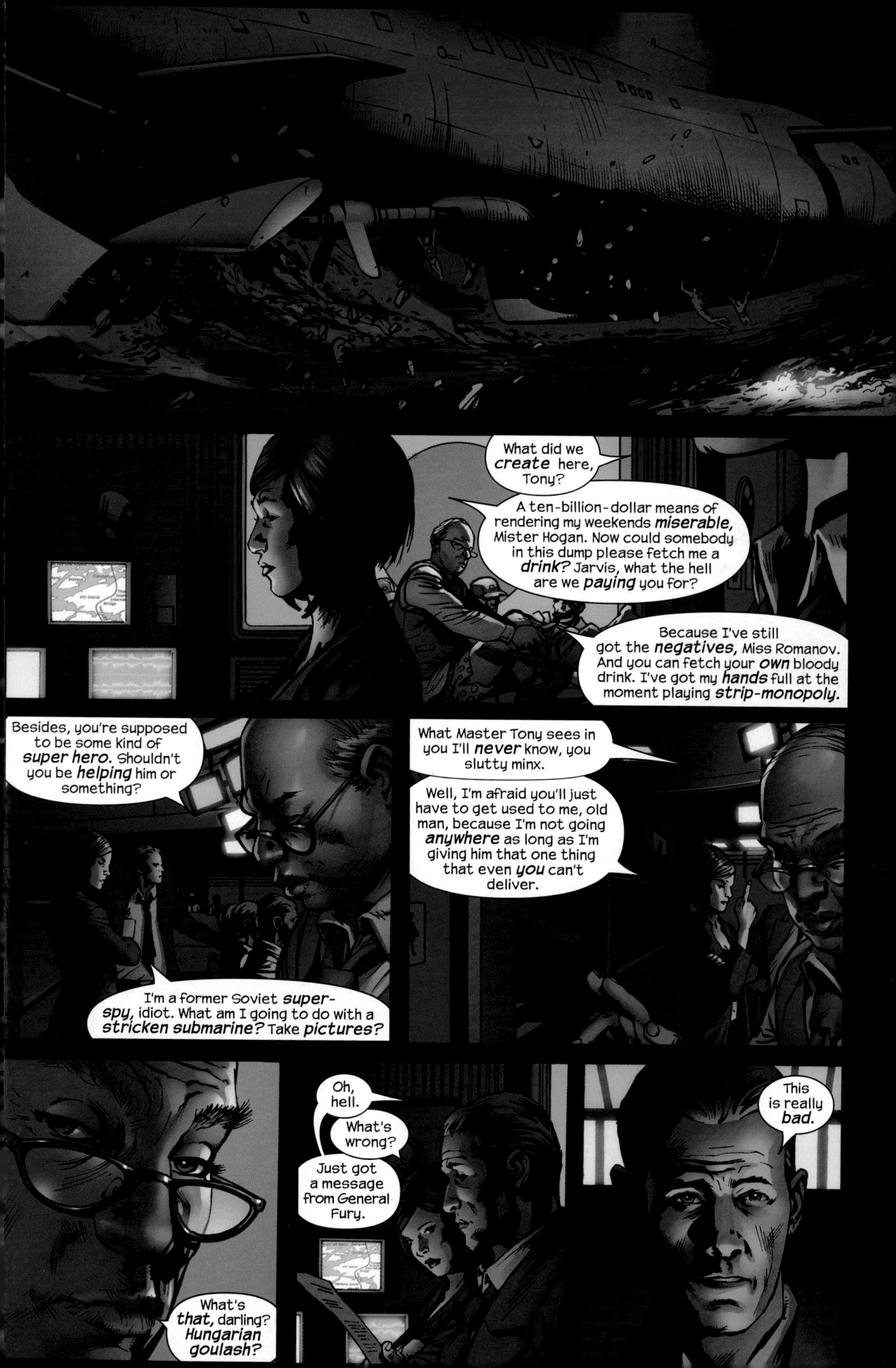
What did we create here, Tony?
A ten-billion-dollar means of rendering my weekends miserable, Mister Hogan. Now could somebody in this dump please fetch me a drink? Jarvis, what the hell are we paying you for?
Because I've still got the negatives, Miss Romanov. And you can fetch your own bloody drink. I've got my hands full at the moment playing strip-monopoly.
Besides, you're supposed to be some kind of super hero. Shouldn't you be helping him or something?
I'm a former Soviet super-spy, idiot. What am I going to do with a stricken submarine? Take pictures?
What Master Tony sees in you I'll never know, you slutty minx.
Well, I'm afraid you'll just have to get used to me, old man, because I'm not going anywhere as long as I'm giving him that one thing that even you can't deliver.
What's that, darling? Hungarian goulash?
Oh, hell.
What's wrong?
Just got a message from General Fury.
This is really bad.

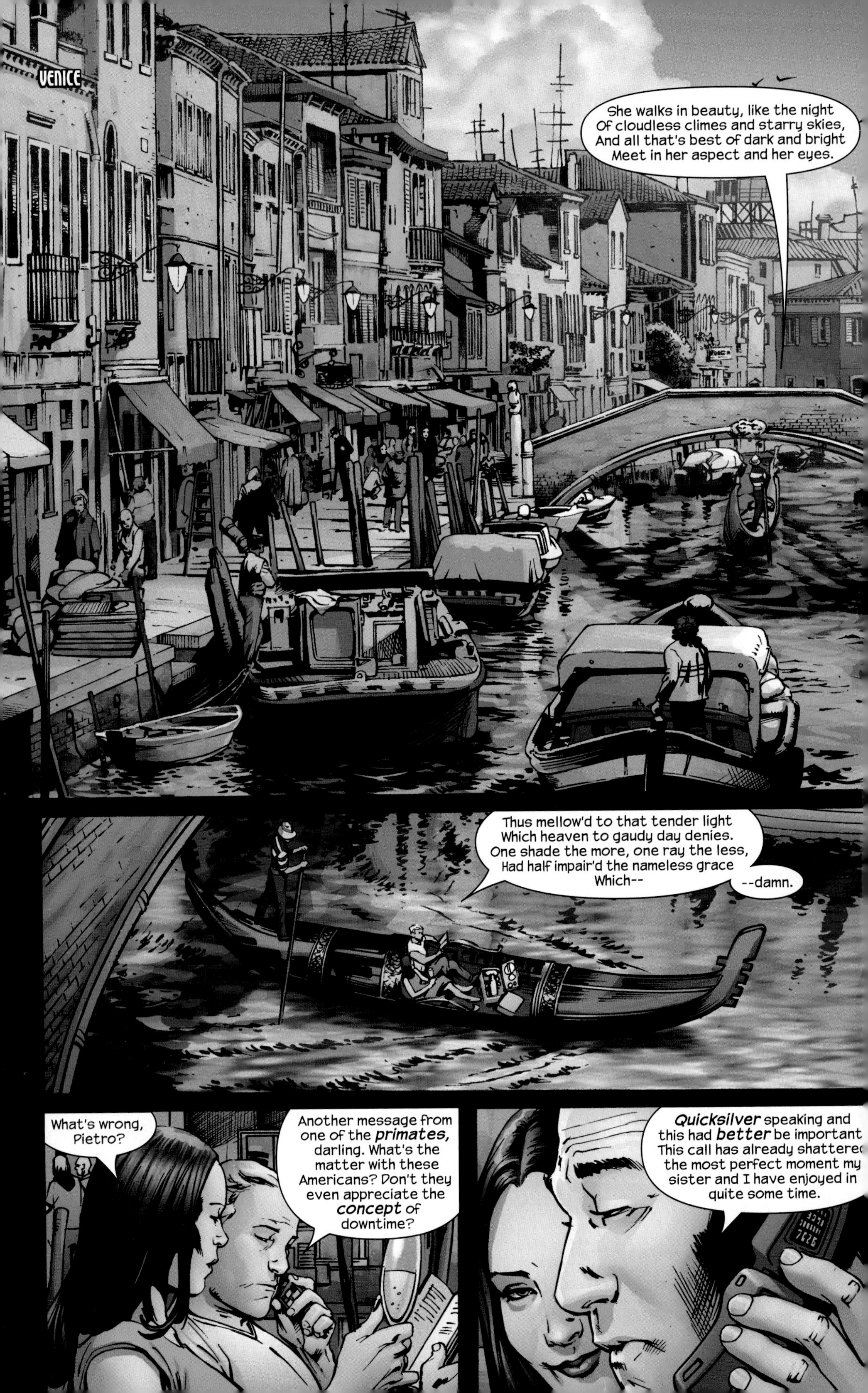

VENICE
She walks in beauty, like the night
Of cloudless climes and starry skies,
And all that's best of dark and bright
Meet in her aspect and her eyes.
Thus mellow'd to that tender light
Which heaven to gaudy day denies.
One shade the more, one ray the less,
Had half impair'd the nameless grace
Which--
--damn.
What's wrong, Pietro?
Another message from one of the *primates,* darling. What's the matter with these Americans? Don't they even appreciate the *concept* of downtime?
Quicksilver speaking and this had *better* be important. This call has already shattered the most perfect moment my sister and I have enjoyed in quite some time.

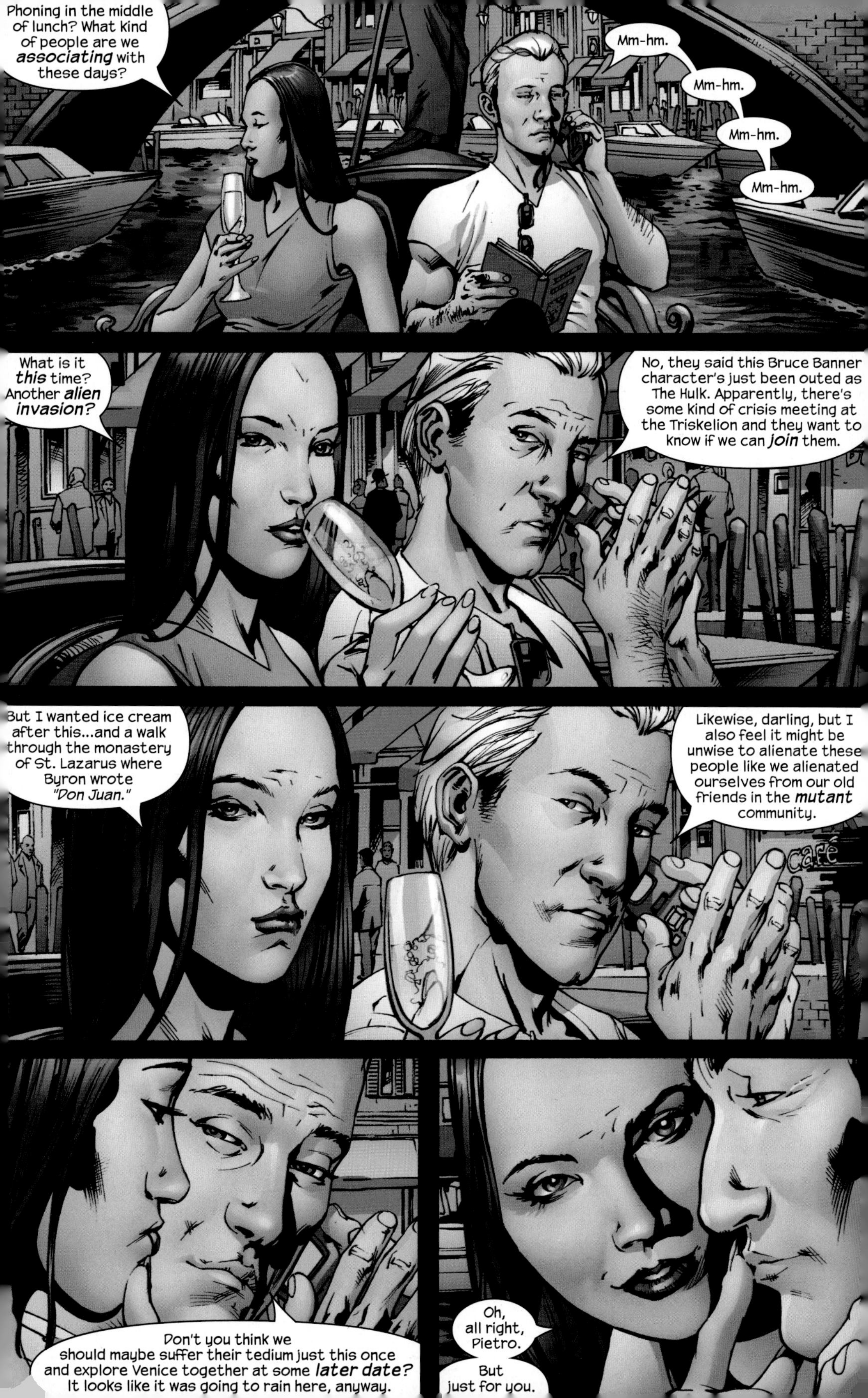

Phoning in the middle of lunch? What kind of people are we *associating* with these days?
Mm-hm.
Mm-hm.
Mm-hm.
Mm-hm.
What is it *this* time? Another *alien invasion?*
No, they said this Bruce Banner character's just been outed as The Hulk. Apparently, there's some kind of crisis meeting at the Triskelion and they want to know if we can *join* them.
But I wanted ice cream after this...and a walk through the monastery of St. Lazarus where Byron wrote *"Don Juan."*
Likewise, darling, but I also feel it might be unwise to alienate these people like we alienated ourselves from our old friends in the *mutant* community.
Don't you think we should maybe suffer their tedium just this once and explore Venice together at some *later date?* It looks like it was going to rain here, anyway.
Oh, all right, Pietro.
But just for you.

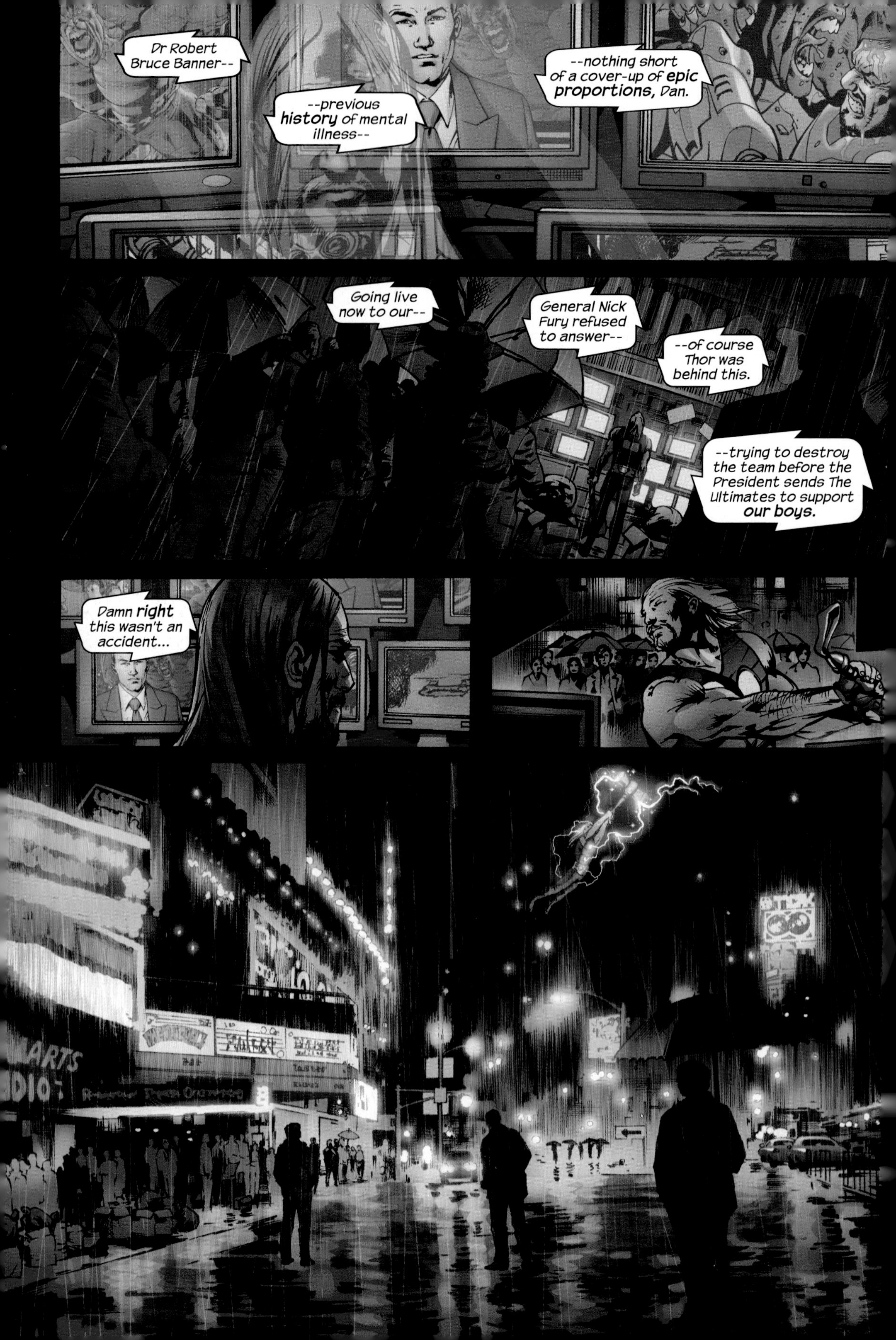
Dr Robert Bruce Banner--
--previous history of mental illness--
--nothing short of a cover-up of epic proportions, Dan.
Going live now to our--
General Nick Fury refused to answer--
--of course Thor was behind this.
--trying to destroy the team before the President sends The Ultimates to support our boys.
Damn right this wasn't an accident...

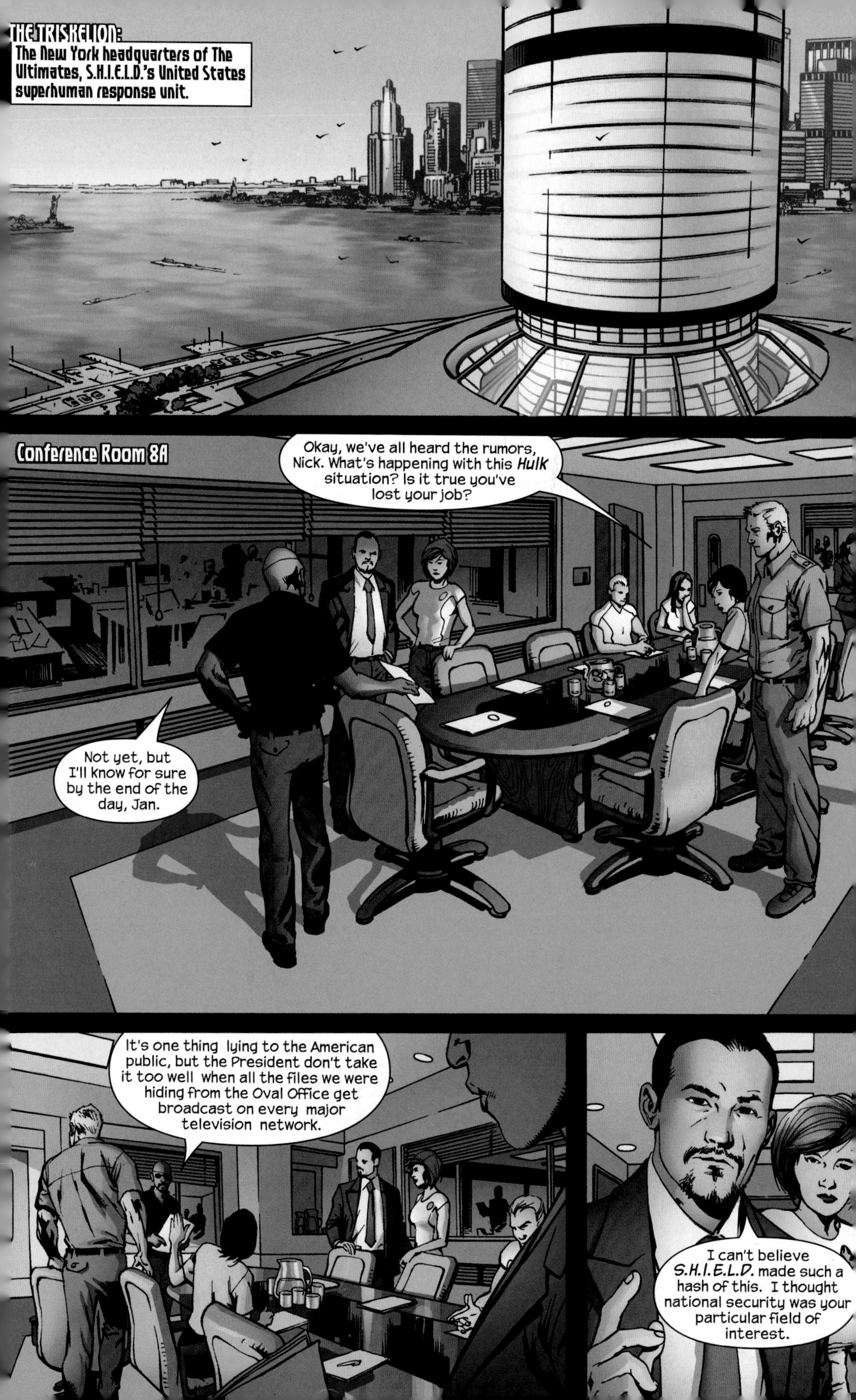
THE TRISKELION:
The New York headquarters of The Ultimates, S.H.I.E.L.D.'s United States superhuman response unit.
Conference Room 8A
Okay, we've all heard the rumors, Nick. What's happening with this *Hulk* situation? Is it true you've lost your job?
Not yet, but I'll know for sure by the end of the day, Jan.
It's one thing lying to the American public, but the President don't take it too well when all the files we were hiding from the Oval Office get broadcast on every major television network.
I can't believe *S.H.I.E.L.D.* made such a hash of this. I thought national security was your particular field of interest.

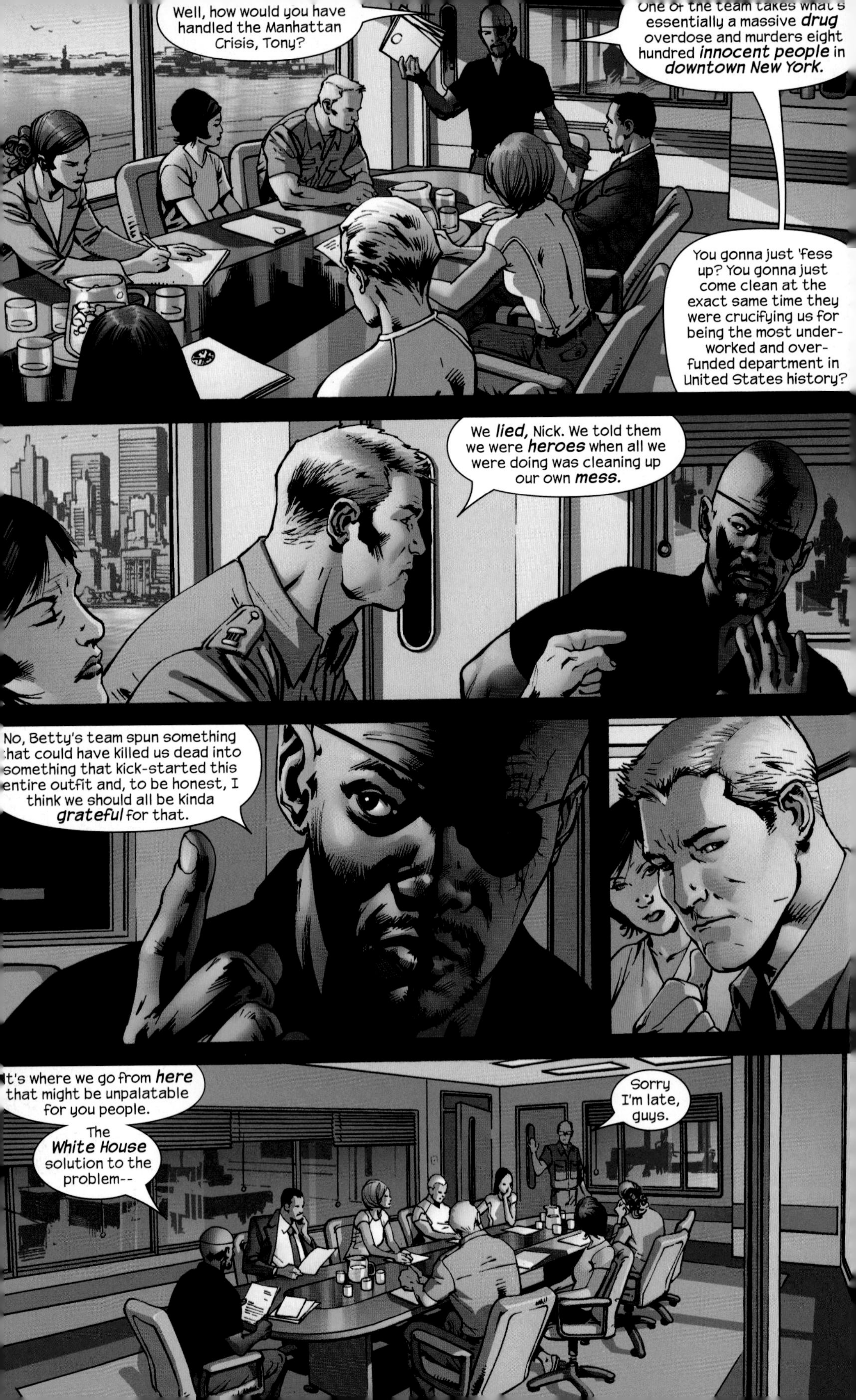

Well, how would you have handled the Manhattan Crisis, Tony?
One of the team takes what's essentially a massive drug overdose and murders eight hundred innocent people in downtown New York.
You gonna just 'fess up? You gonna just come clean at the exact same time they were crucifying us for being the most under-worked and over-funded department in United States history?
We lied, Nick. We told them we were heroes when all we were doing was cleaning up our own mess.
No, Betty's team spun something that could have killed us dead into something that kick-started this entire outfit and, to be honest, I think we should all be kinda grateful for that.
It's where we go from here that might be unpalatable for you people.
The White House solution to the problem--
Sorry I'm late, guys.

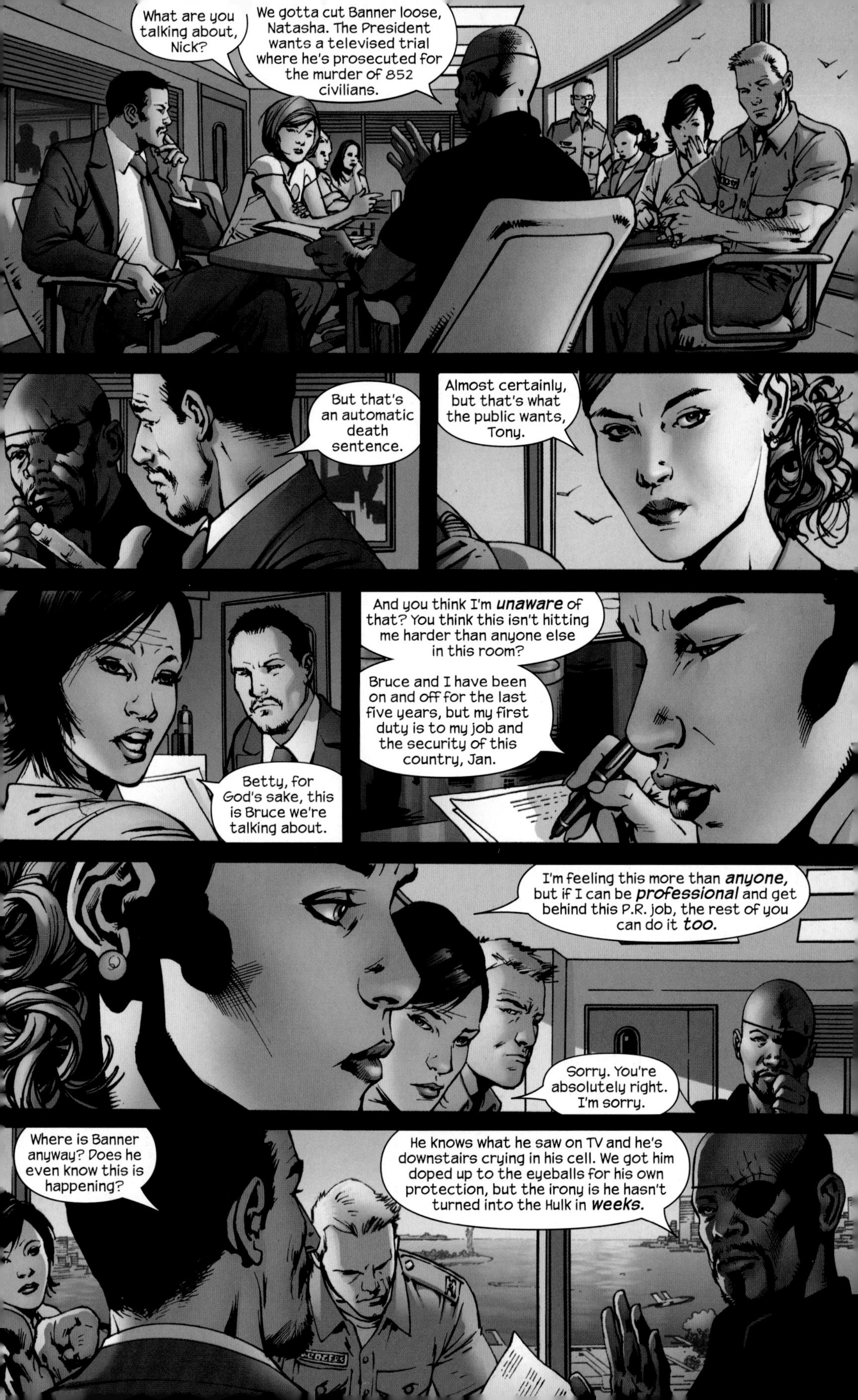
What are you talking about, Nick?
We gotta cut Banner loose, Natasha. The President wants a televised trial where he's prosecuted for the murder of 852 civilians.
But that's an automatic death sentence.
Almost certainly, but that's what the public wants, Tony.
Betty, for God's sake, this is Bruce we're talking about.
And you think I'm *unaware* of that? You think this isn't hitting me harder than anyone else in this room?
Bruce and I have been on and off for the last five years, but my first duty is to my job and the security of this country, Jan.
I'm feeling this more than *anyone*, but if I can be *professional* and get behind this P.R. job, the rest of you can do it *too.*
Sorry. You're absolutely right. I'm sorry.
Where is Banner anyway? Does he even know this is happening?
He knows what he saw on TV and he's downstairs crying in his cell. We got him doped up to the eyeballs for his own protection, but the irony is he hasn't turned into the Hulk in *weeks.*

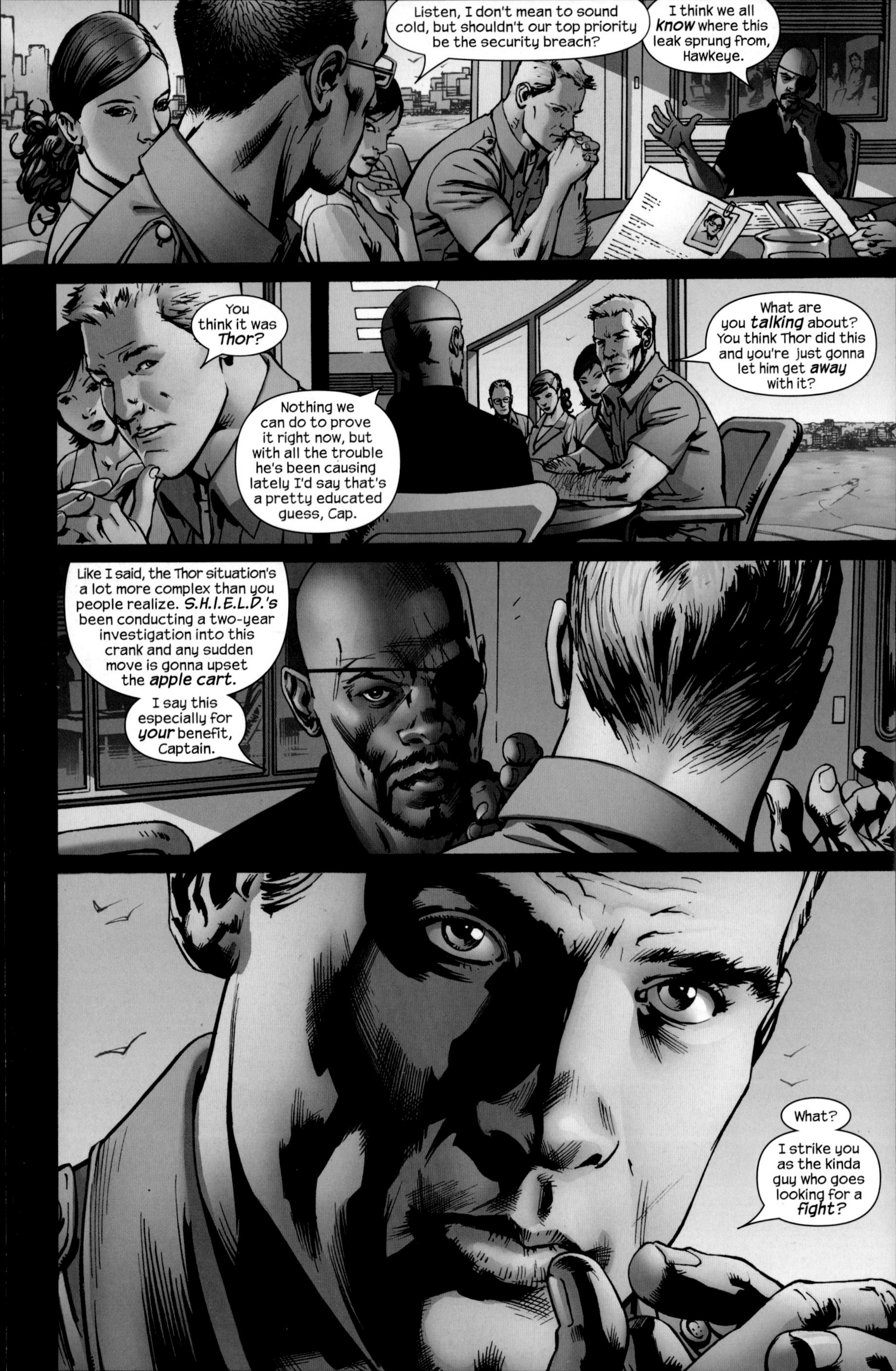

Listen, I don't mean to sound cold, but shouldn't our top priority be the security breach?
I think we all know where this leak sprung from, Hawkeye.
You think it was Thor?
Nothing we can do to prove it right now, but with all the trouble he's been causing lately I'd say that's a pretty educated guess, Cap.
What are you talking about? You think Thor did this and you're just gonna let him get away with it?
Like I said, the Thor situation's a lot more complex than you people realize. S.H.I.E.L.D.'s been conducting a two-year investigation into this crank and any sudden move is gonna upset the apple cart.
I say this especially for your benefit, Captain.
What?
I strike you as the kinda guy who goes looking for a fight?

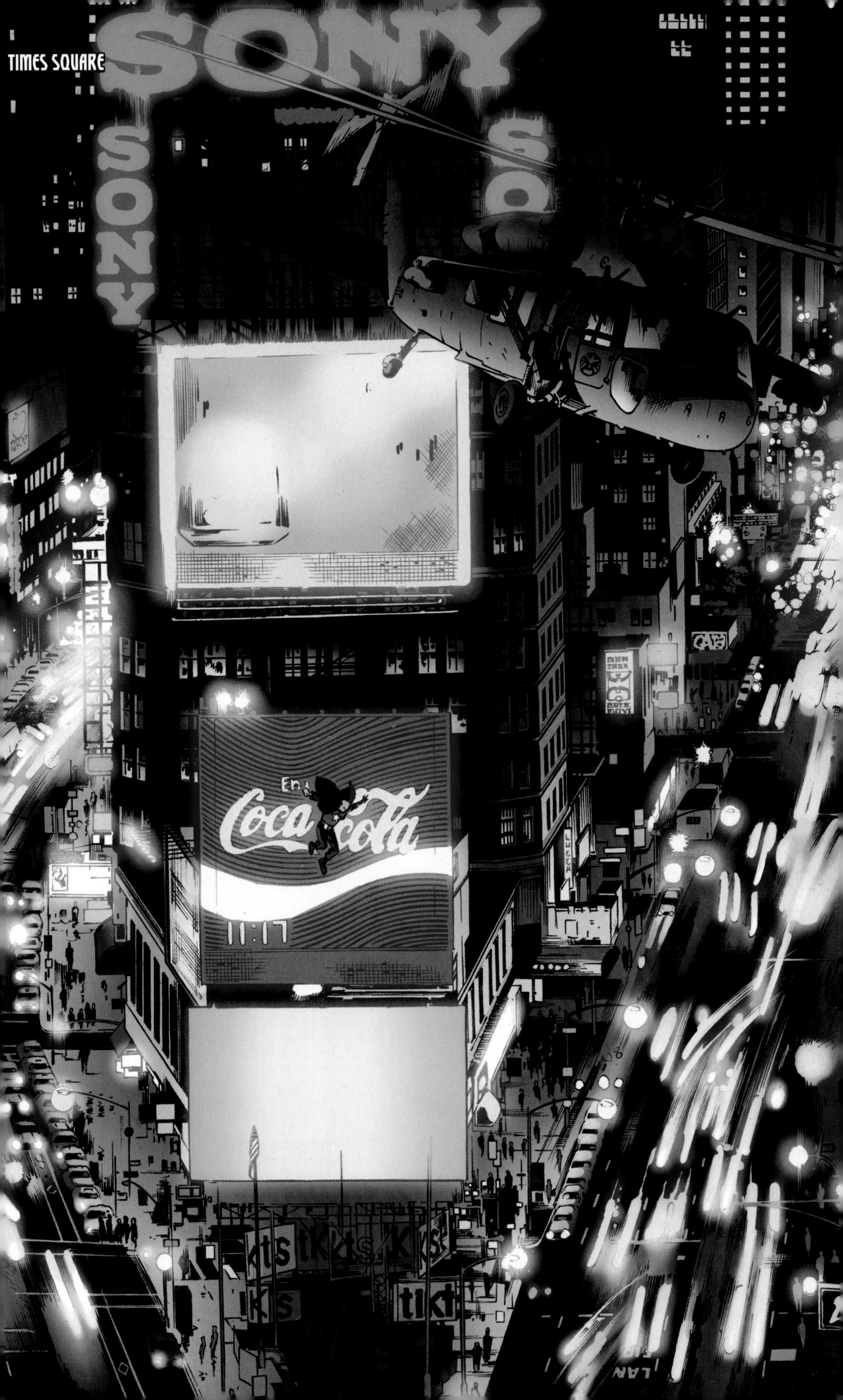
TIMES SQUARE
SONY
SONY
Coca-Cola
11:17

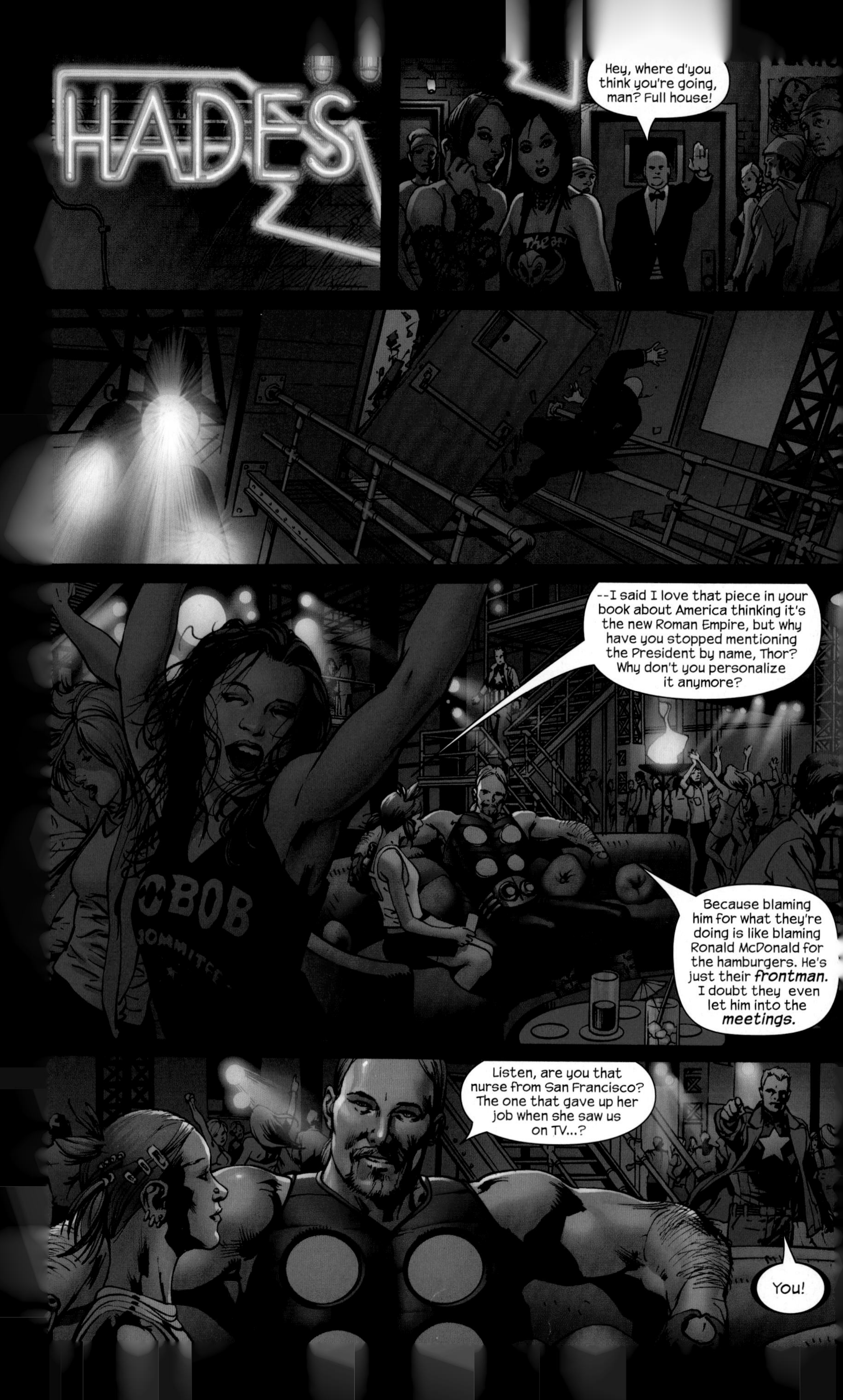
HADES
Hey, where d'you think you're going, man? Full house!
--I said I love that piece in your book about America thinking it's the new Roman Empire, but why have you stopped mentioning the President by name, Thor? Why don't you personalize it anymore?
Because blaming him for what they're doing is like blaming Ronald McDonald for the hamburgers. He's just their *frontman.* I doubt they even let him into the *meetings.*
Listen, are you that nurse from San Francisco? The one that gave up her job when she saw us on TV...?
You!

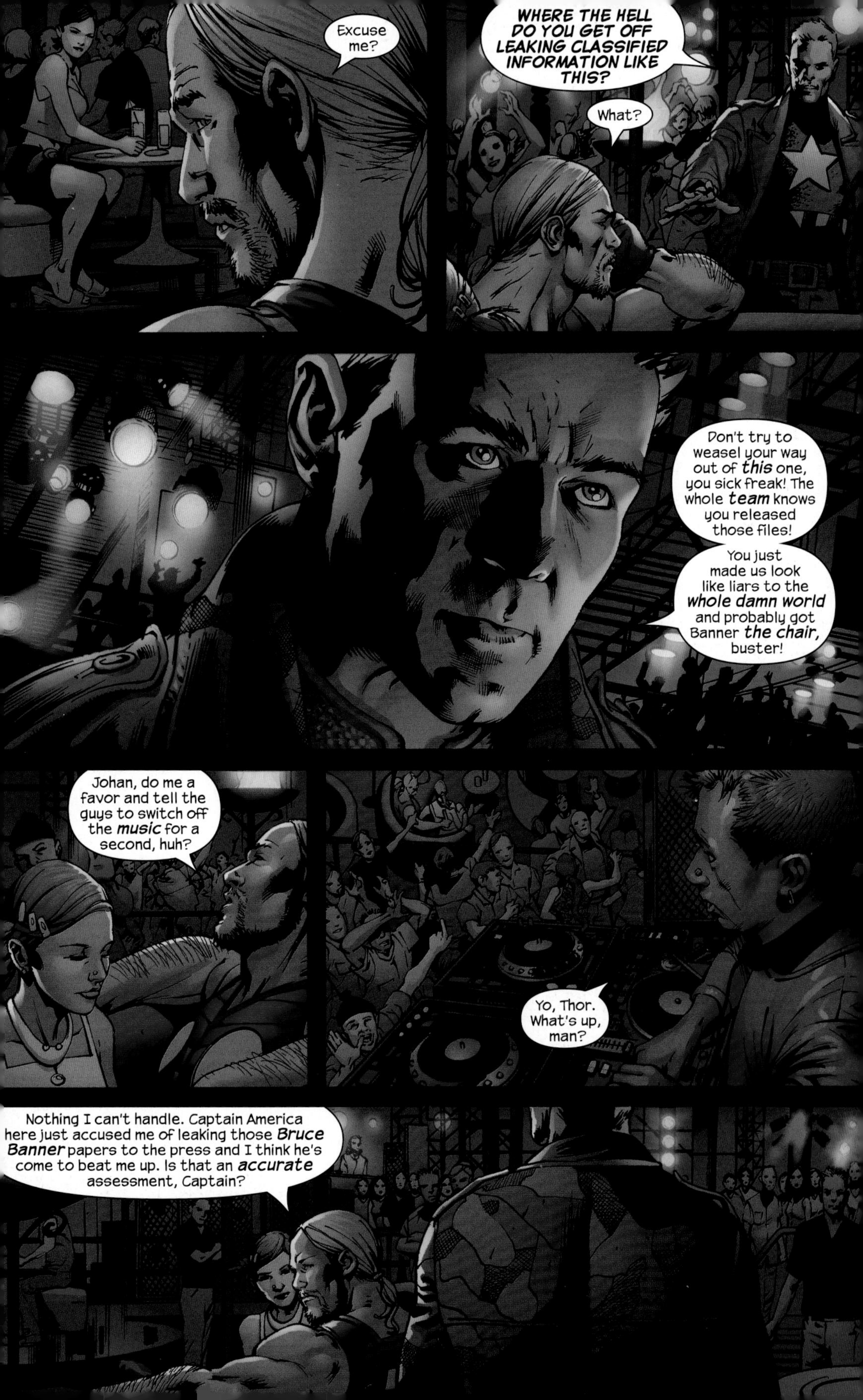
Excuse me?
WHERE THE HELL DO YOU GET OFF LEAKING CLASSIFIED INFORMATION LIKE THIS?
What?
Don't try to weasel your way out of *this* one, you sick freak! The whole *team* knows you released those files!
You just made us look like liars to the *whole damn world* and probably got Banner *the chair,* buster!
Johan, do me a favor and tell the guys to switch off the *music* for a second, huh?
Yo, Thor. What's up, man?
Nothing I can't handle. Captain America here just accused me of leaking those *Bruce Banner* papers to the press and I think he's come to beat me up. Is that an *accurate* assessment, Captain?

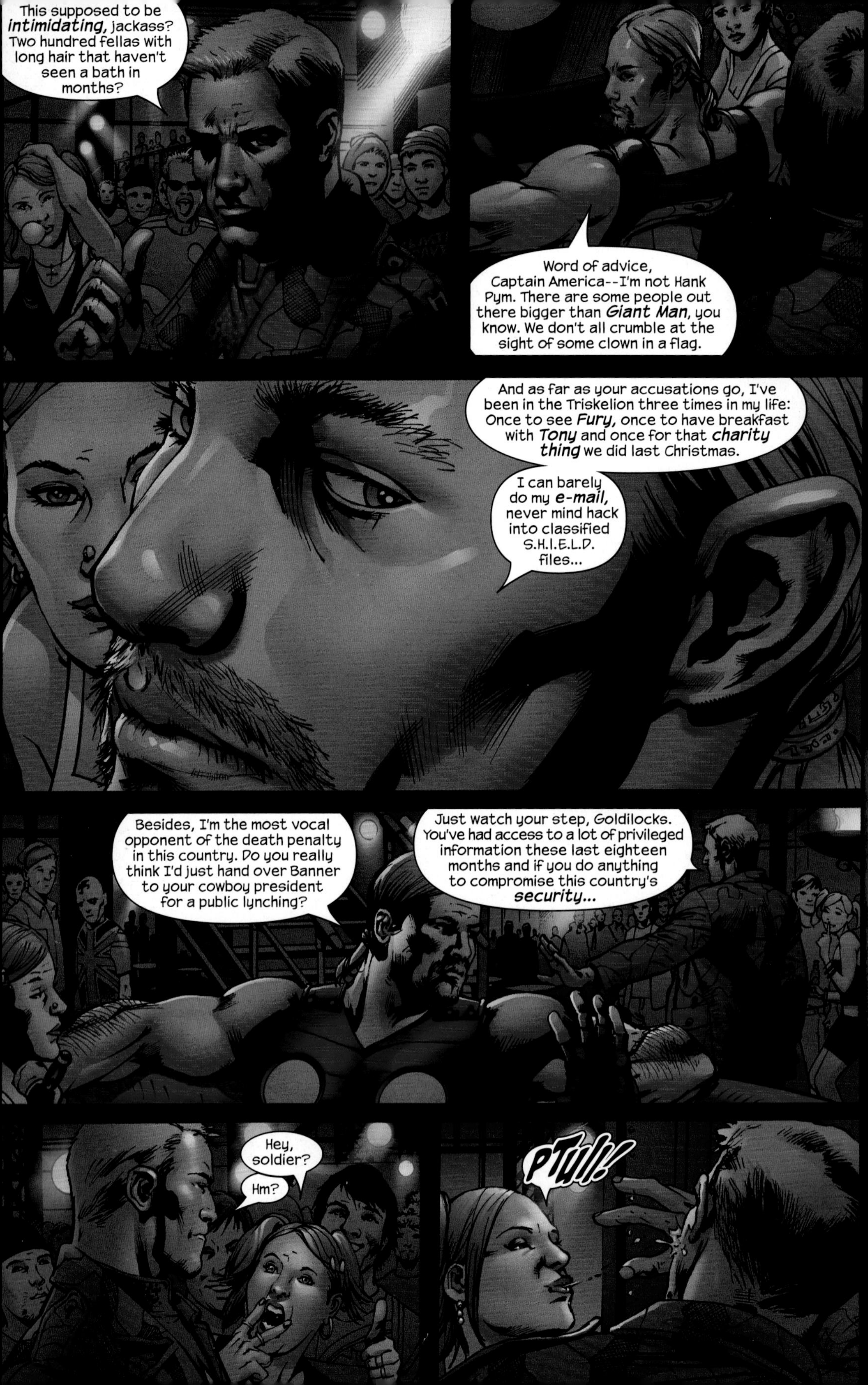
This supposed to be *intimidating,* jackass? Two hundred fellas with long hair that haven't seen a bath in months?
Word of advice, Captain America--I'm not Hank Pym. There are some people out there bigger than *Giant Man*, you know. We don't all crumble at the sight of some clown in a flag.
And as far as your accusations go, I've been in the Triskelion three times in my life: Once to see *Fury,* once to have breakfast with *Tony* and once for that *charity thing* we did last Christmas.
I can barely do my *e-mail,* never mind hack into classified S.H.I.E.L.D. files...
Besides, I'm the most vocal opponent of the death penalty in this country. Do you really think I'd just hand over Banner to your cowboy president for a public lynching?
Just watch your step, Goldilocks. You've had access to a lot of privileged information these last eighteen months and if you do anything to compromise this country's *security...*
Hey, soldier?
Hm?
PTUI!

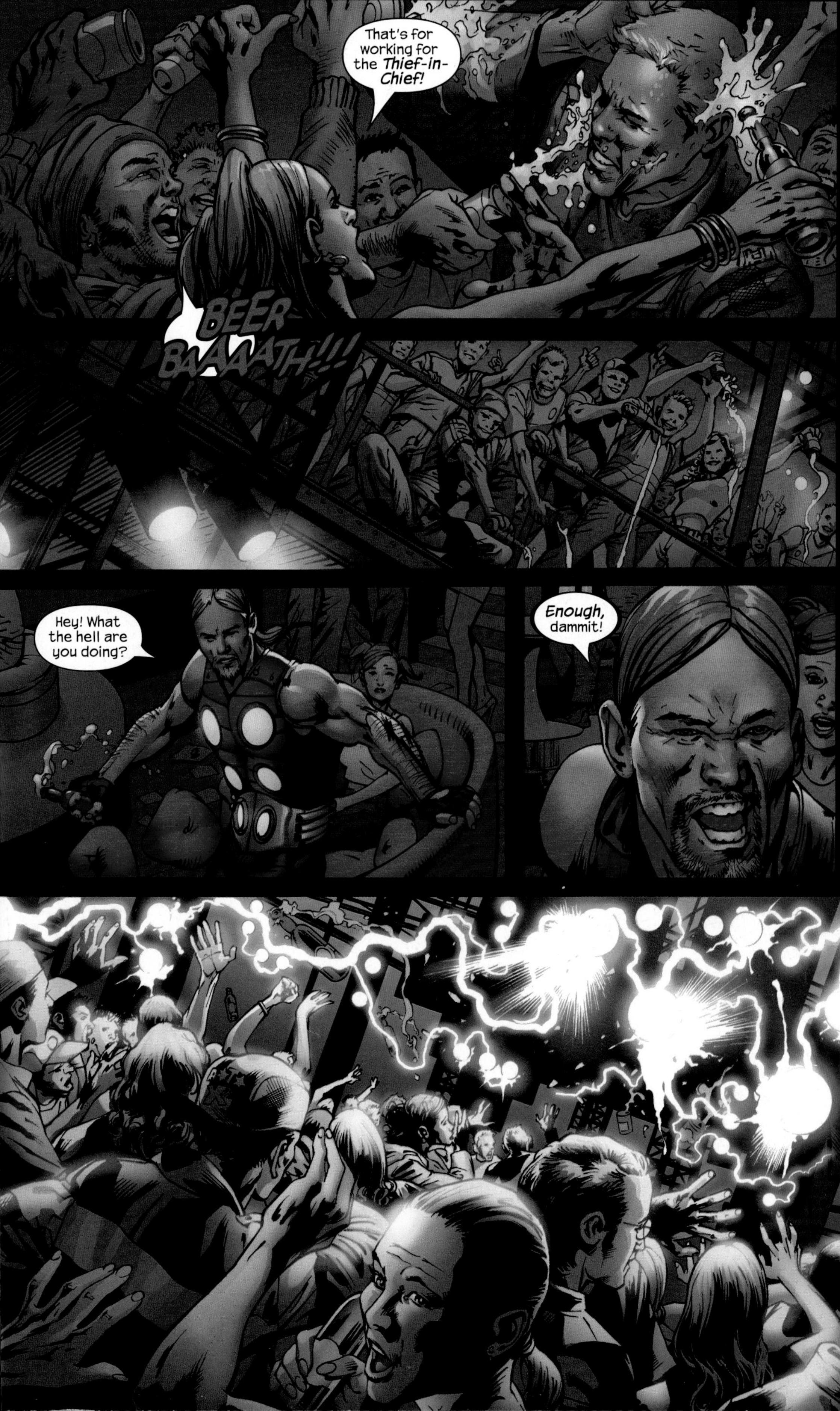
That's for working for the *Thief-in-Chief!*
BEER BAAAATH!!!
Hey! What the hell are you doing?
Enough, dammit!

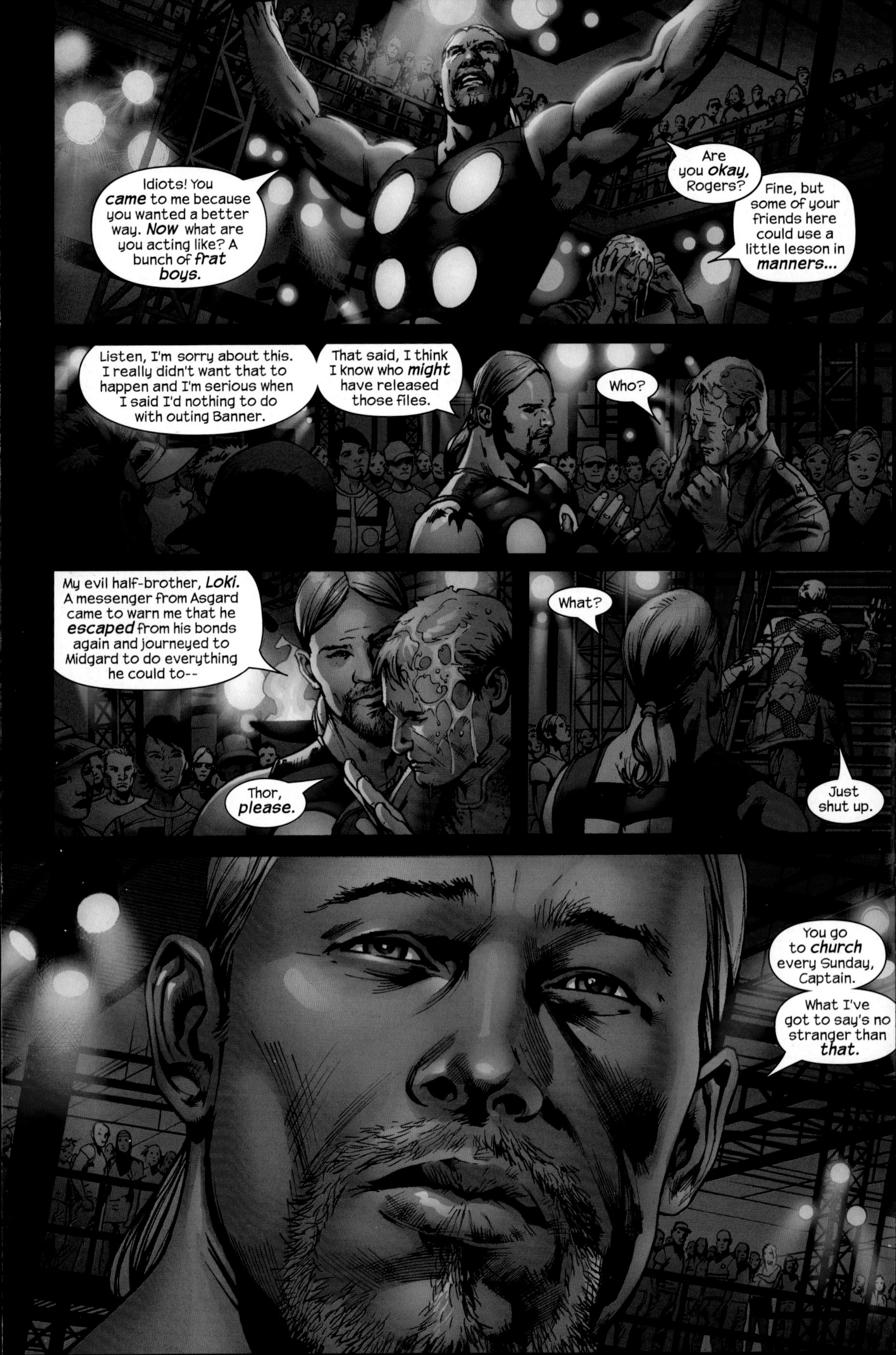
Idiots! You came to me because you wanted a better way. Now what are you acting like? A bunch of frat boys.
Are you okay, Rogers?
Fine, but some of your friends here could use a little lesson in manners...
Listen, I'm sorry about this. I really didn't want that to happen and I'm serious when I said I'd nothing to do with outing Banner.
That said, I think I know who might have released those files.
Who?
My evil half-brother, Loki. A messenger from Asgard came to warn me that he escaped from his bonds again and journeyed to Midgard to do everything he could to--
Thor, please.
What?
Just shut up.
You go to church every Sunday, Captain.
What I've got to say's no stranger than that.

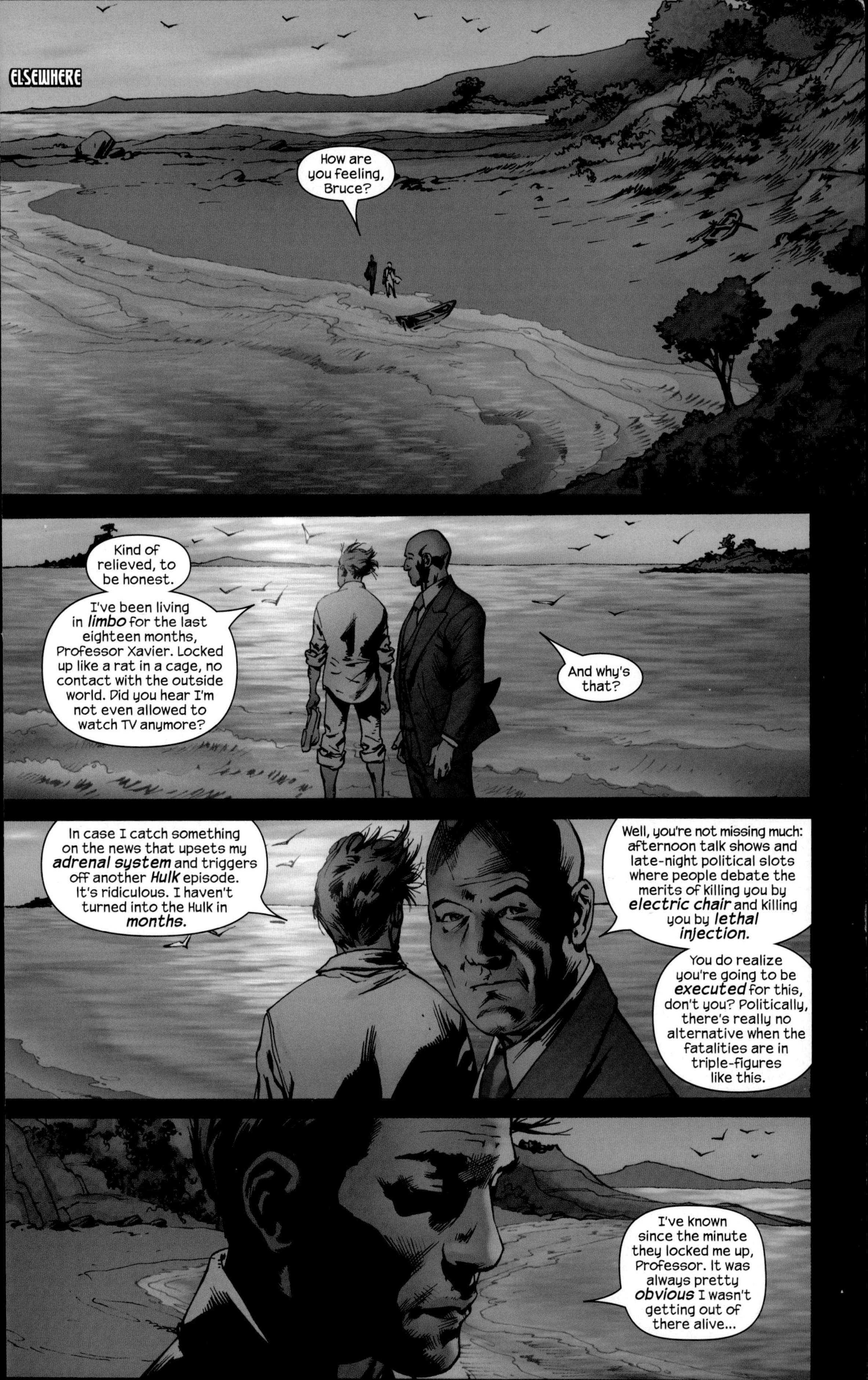
ELSEWHERE
How are you feeling, Bruce?
Kind of relieved, to be honest.
I've been living in *limbo* for the last eighteen months, Professor Xavier. Locked up like a rat in a cage, no contact with the outside world. Did you hear I'm not even allowed to watch TV anymore?
And why's that?
In case I catch something on the news that upsets my *adrenal system* and triggers off another *Hulk* episode. It's ridiculous. I haven't turned into the Hulk in *months.*
Well, you're not missing much: afternoon talk shows and late-night political slots where people debate the merits of killing you by *electric chair* and killing you by *lethal injection.*
You do realize you're going to be *executed* for this, don't you? Politically, there's really no alternative when the fatalities are in triple-figures like this.
I've known since the minute they locked me up, Professor. It was always pretty *obvious* I wasn't getting out of there alive...

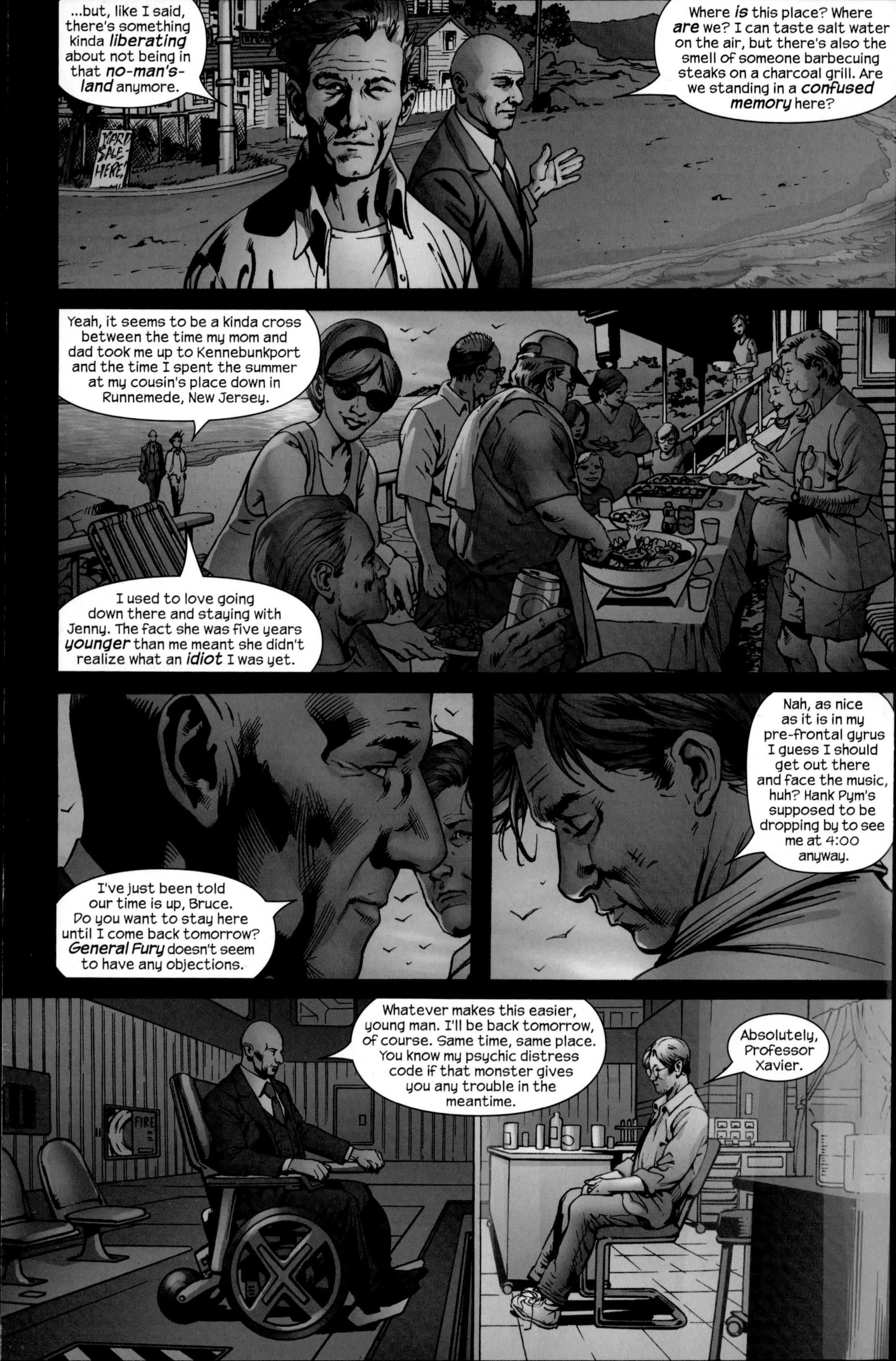

...but, like I said, there's something kinda liberating about not being in that no-man's-land anymore.
Where is this place? Where are we? I can taste salt water on the air, but there's also the smell of someone barbecuing steaks on a charcoal grill. Are we standing in a confused memory here?
YARD SALE HERE!
Yeah, it seems to be a kinda cross between the time my mom and dad took me up to Kennebunkport and the time I spent the summer at my cousin's place down in Runnemede, New Jersey.
I used to love going down there and staying with Jenny. The fact she was five years younger than me meant she didn't realize what an idiot I was yet.
I've just been told our time is up, Bruce. Do you want to stay here until I come back tomorrow? General Fury doesn't seem to have any objections.
Nah, as nice as it is in my pre-frontal gyrus I guess I should get out there and face the music, huh? Hank Pym's supposed to be dropping by to see me at 4:00 anyway.
Whatever makes this easier, young man. I'll be back tomorrow, of course. Same time, same place. You know my psychic distress code if that monster gives you any trouble in the meantime.
Absolutely, Professor Xavier.
FIRE

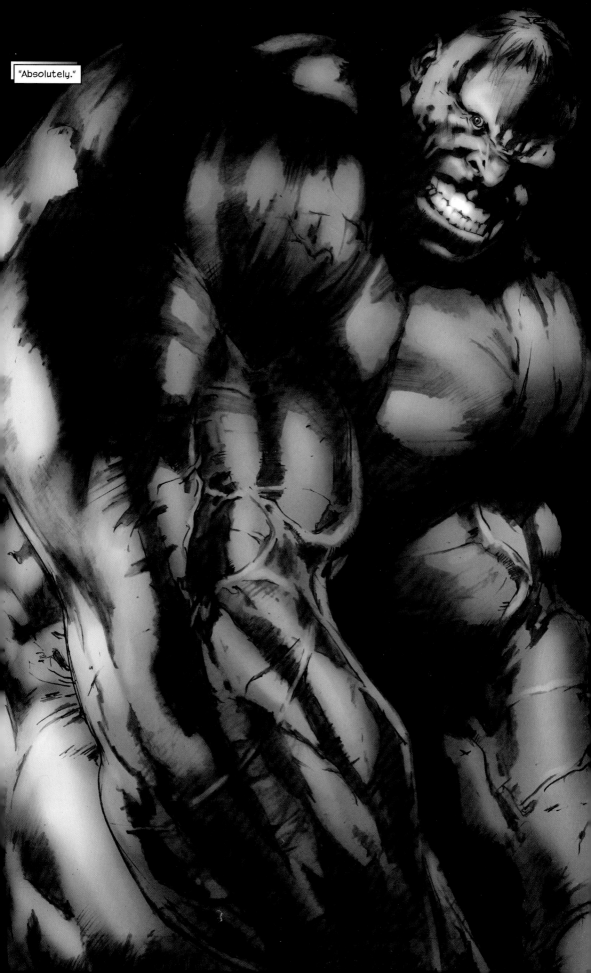

"Absolutely."

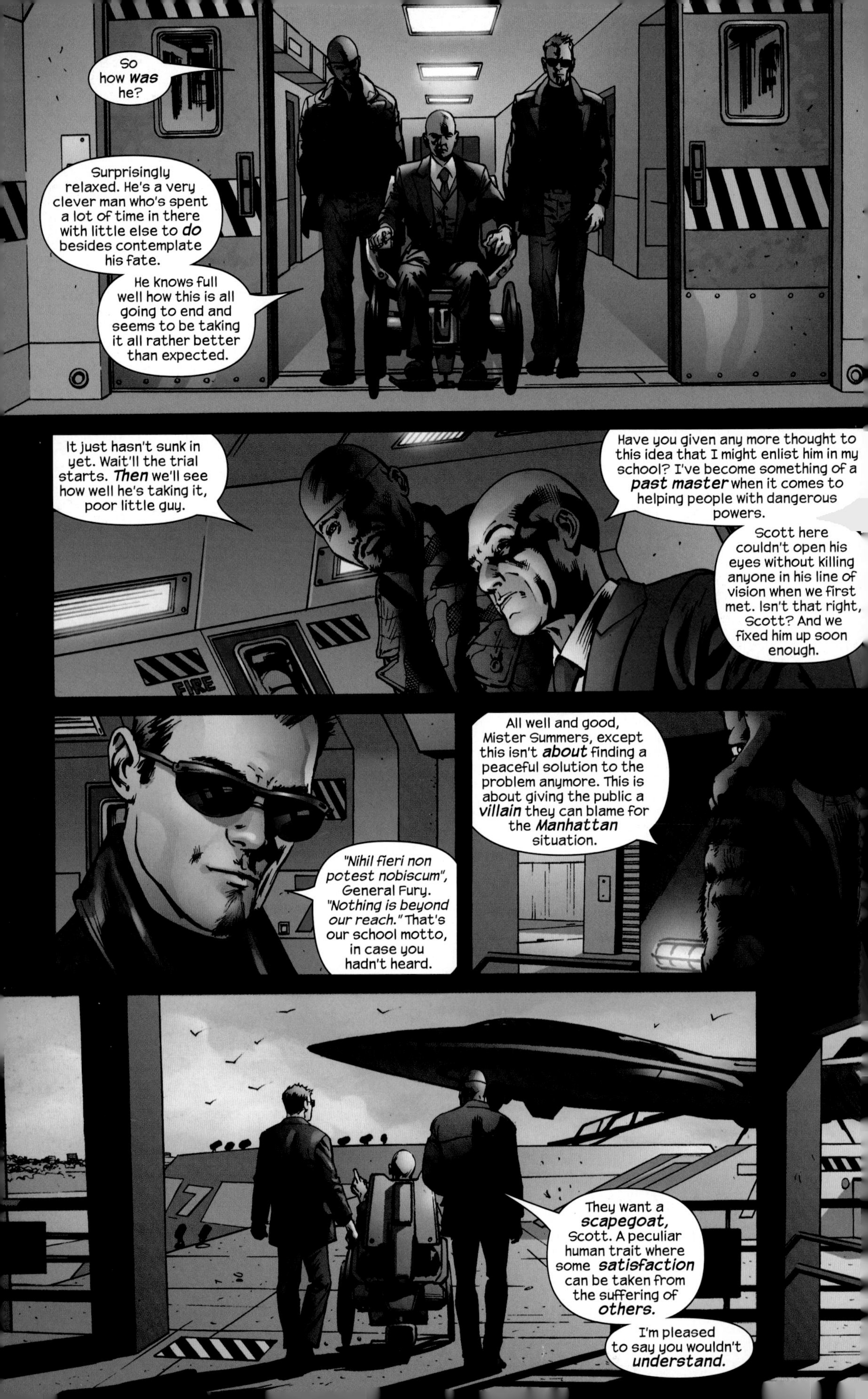
So how *was* he?
Surprisingly relaxed. He's a very clever man who's spent a lot of time in there with little else to *do* besides contemplate his fate.
He knows full well how this is all going to end and seems to be taking it all rather better than expected.
It just hasn't sunk in yet. Wait'll the trial starts. *Then* we'll see how well he's taking it, poor little guy.
Have you given any more thought to this idea that I might enlist him in my school? I've become something of a *past master* when it comes to helping people with dangerous powers.
Scott here couldn't open his eyes without killing anyone in his line of vision when we first met. Isn't that right, Scott? And we fixed him up soon enough.
FIRE
"Nihil fieri non potest nobiscum", General Fury. "Nothing is beyond our reach." That's our school motto, in case you hadn't heard.
All well and good, Mister Summers, except this isn't *about* finding a peaceful solution to the problem anymore. This is about giving the public a *villain* they can blame for the *Manhattan* situation.
They want a *scapegoat,* Scott. A peculiar human trait where some *satisfaction* can be taken from the suffering of *others.*
I'm pleased to say you wouldn't *understand.*

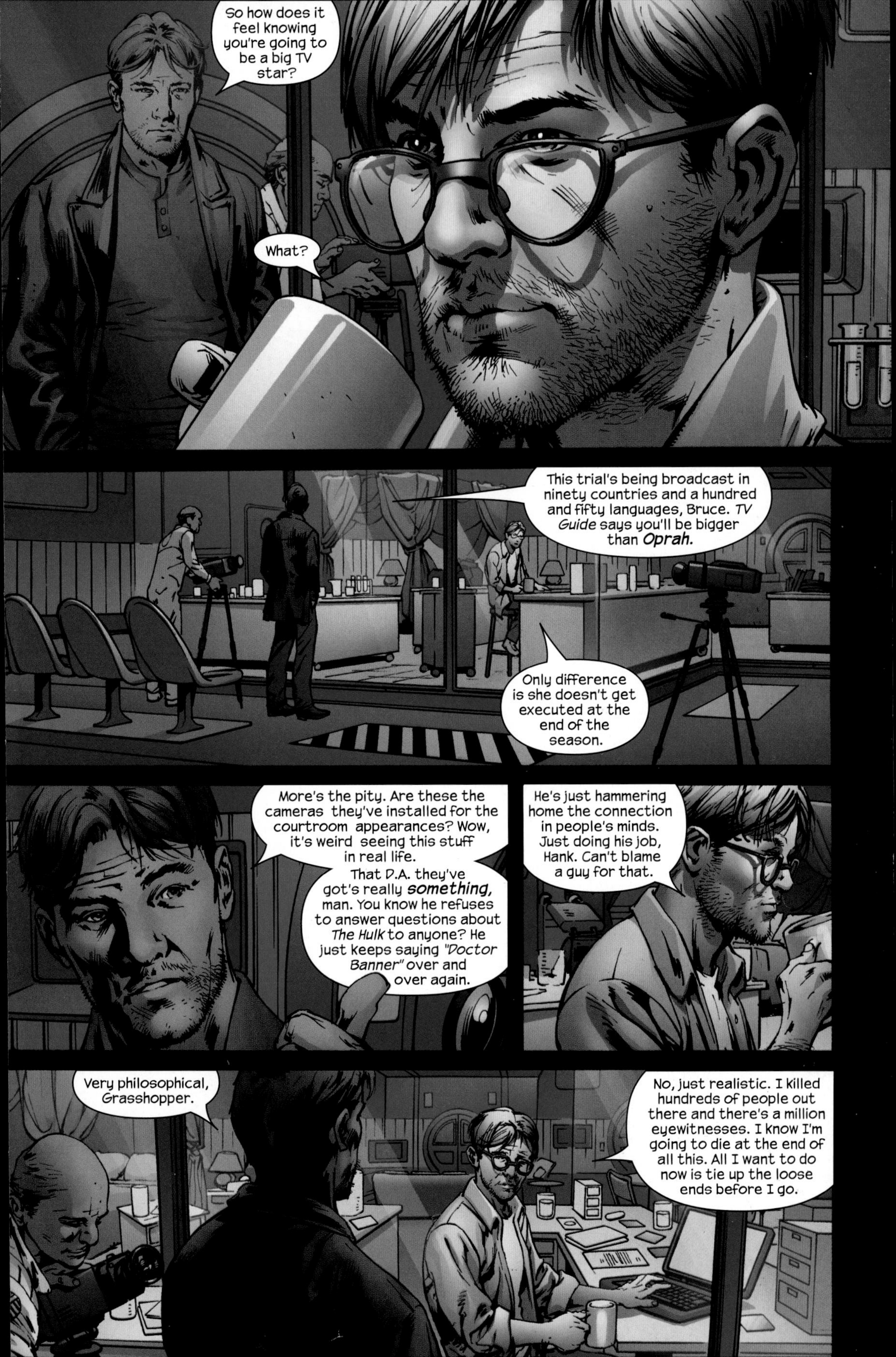
So how does it feel knowing you're going to be a big TV star?
What?
This trial's being broadcast in ninety countries and a hundred and fifty languages, Bruce. *TV Guide* says you'll be bigger than **Oprah.**
Only difference is she doesn't get executed at the end of the season.
More's the pity. Are these the cameras they've installed for the courtroom appearances? Wow, it's weird seeing this stuff in real life.
That D.A. they've got's really **something,** man. You know he refuses to answer questions about *The Hulk* to anyone? He just keeps saying *"Doctor Banner"* over and over again.
He's just hammering home the connection in people's minds. Just doing his job, Hank. Can't blame a guy for that.
Very philosophical, Grasshopper.
No, just realistic. I killed hundreds of people out there and there's a million eyewitnesses. I know I'm going to die at the end of all this. All I want to do now is tie up the loose ends before I go.

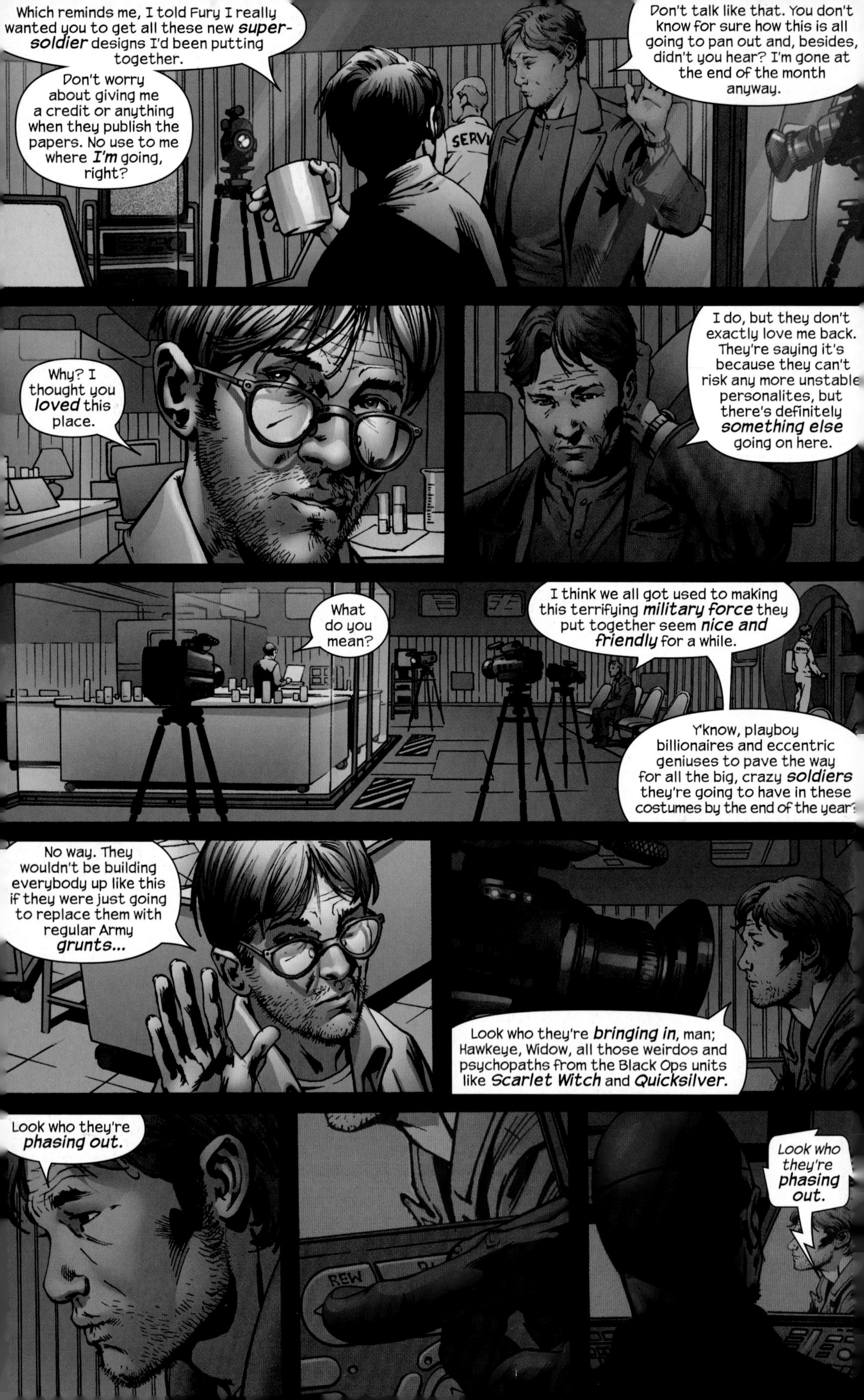
Which reminds me, I told Fury I really wanted you to get all these new super-soldier designs I'd been putting together.
Don't worry about giving me a credit or anything when they publish the papers. No use to me where I'm going, right?
Don't talk like that. You don't know for sure how this is all going to pan out and, besides, didn't you hear? I'm gone at the end of the month anyway.
SERV
Why? I thought you loved this place.
I do, but they don't exactly love me back. They're saying it's because they can't risk any more unstable personalites, but there's definitely something else going on here.
What do you mean?
I think we all got used to making this terrifying military force they put together seem nice and friendly for a while.
Y'know, playboy billionaires and eccentric geniuses to pave the way for all the big, crazy soldiers they're going to have in these costumes by the end of the year?
No way. They wouldn't be building everybody up like this if they were just going to replace them with regular Army grunts...
Look who they're bringing in, man; Hawkeye, Widow, all those weirdos and psychopaths from the Black Ops units like Scarlet Witch and Quicksilver.
Look who they're phasing out.
REW
Look who they're phasing out.

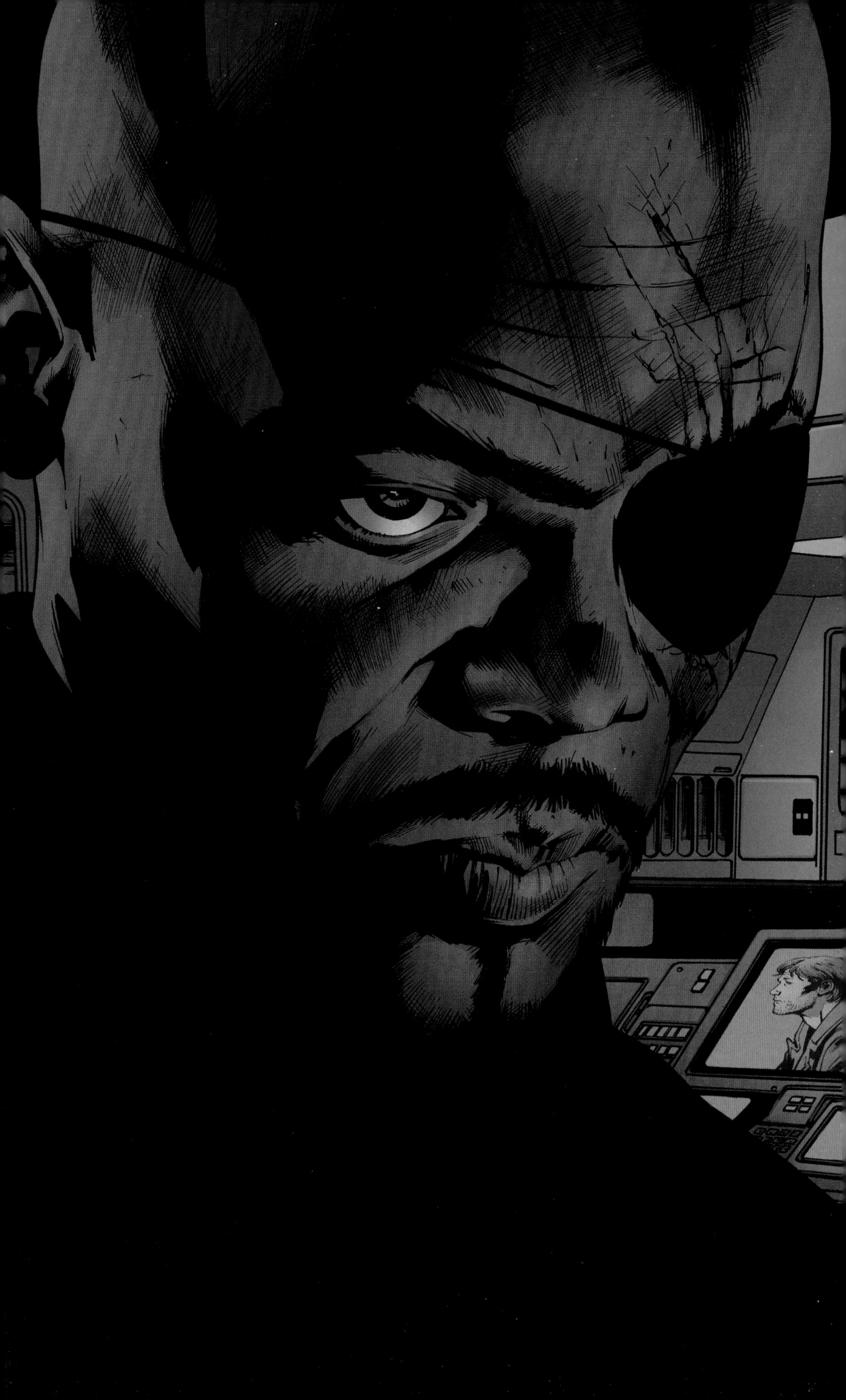

TRIAL OF THE INCREDIBLE HULK

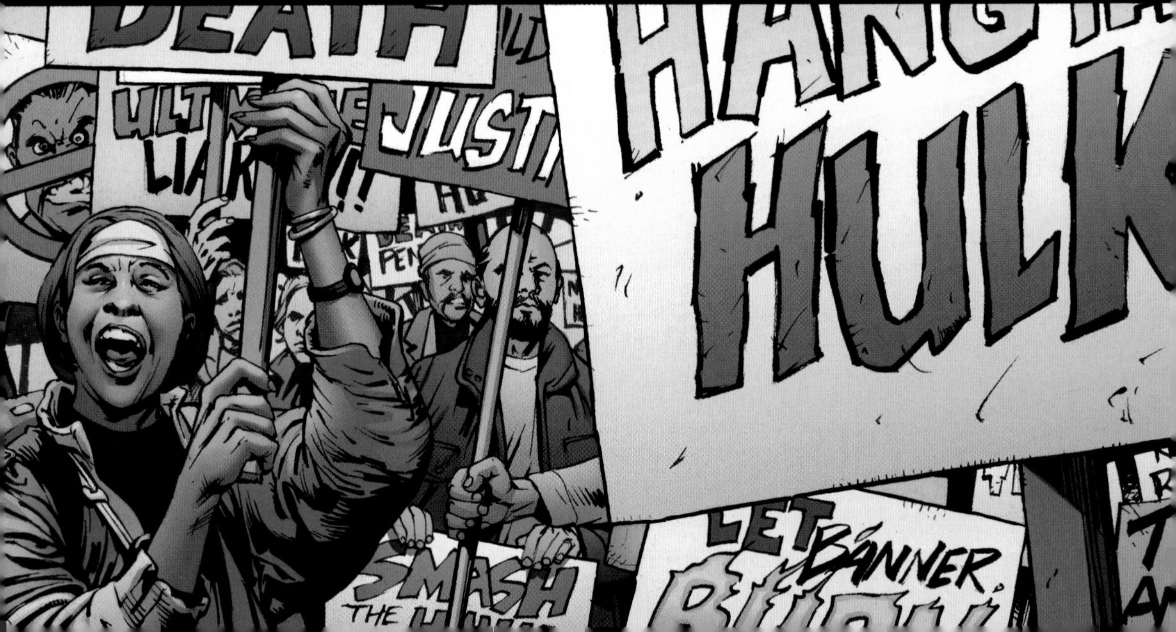
DEATH
LET BANNER
SMASH
THE

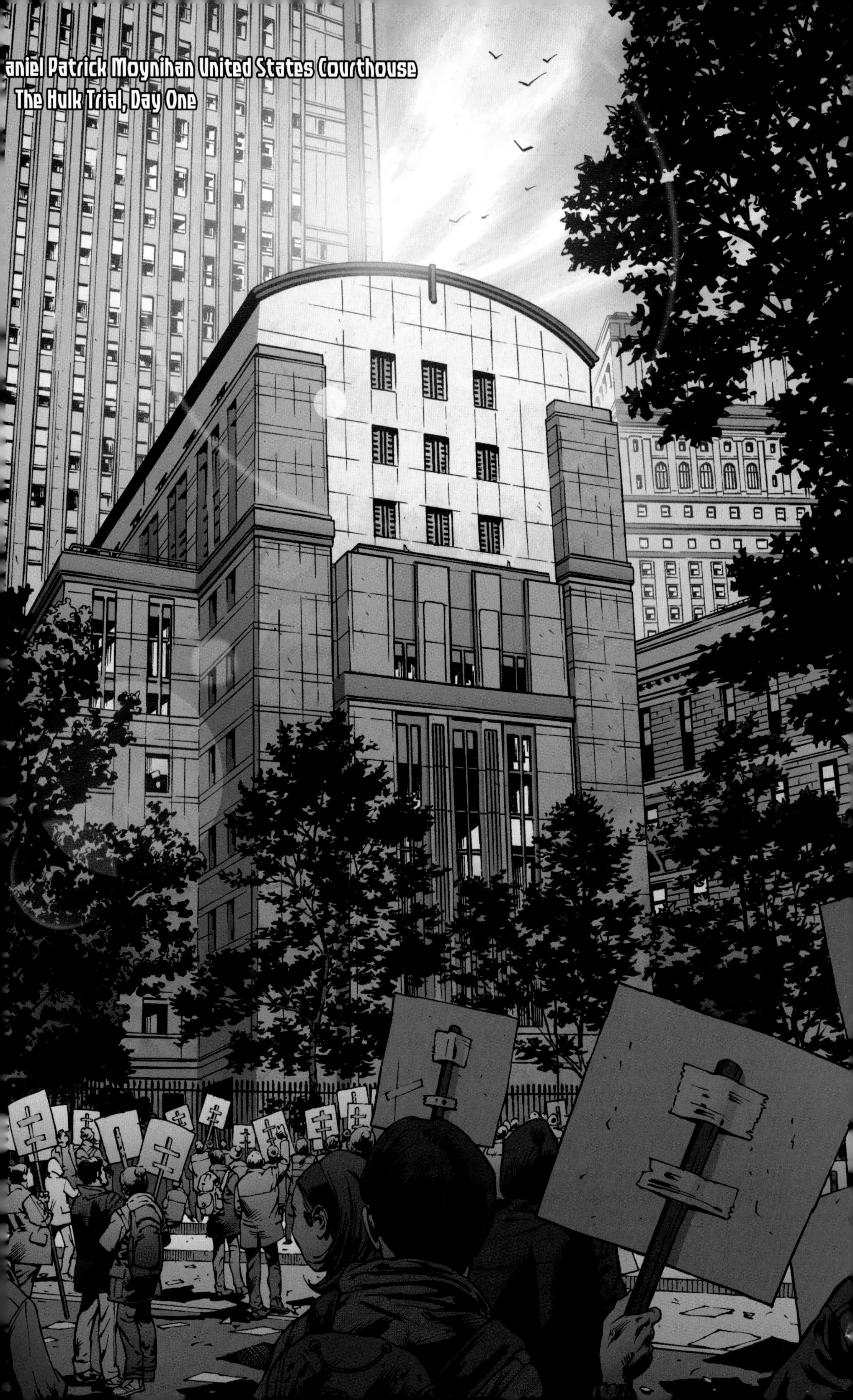
aniel Patrick Moynihan United States Courthouse
The Hulk Trial, Day One

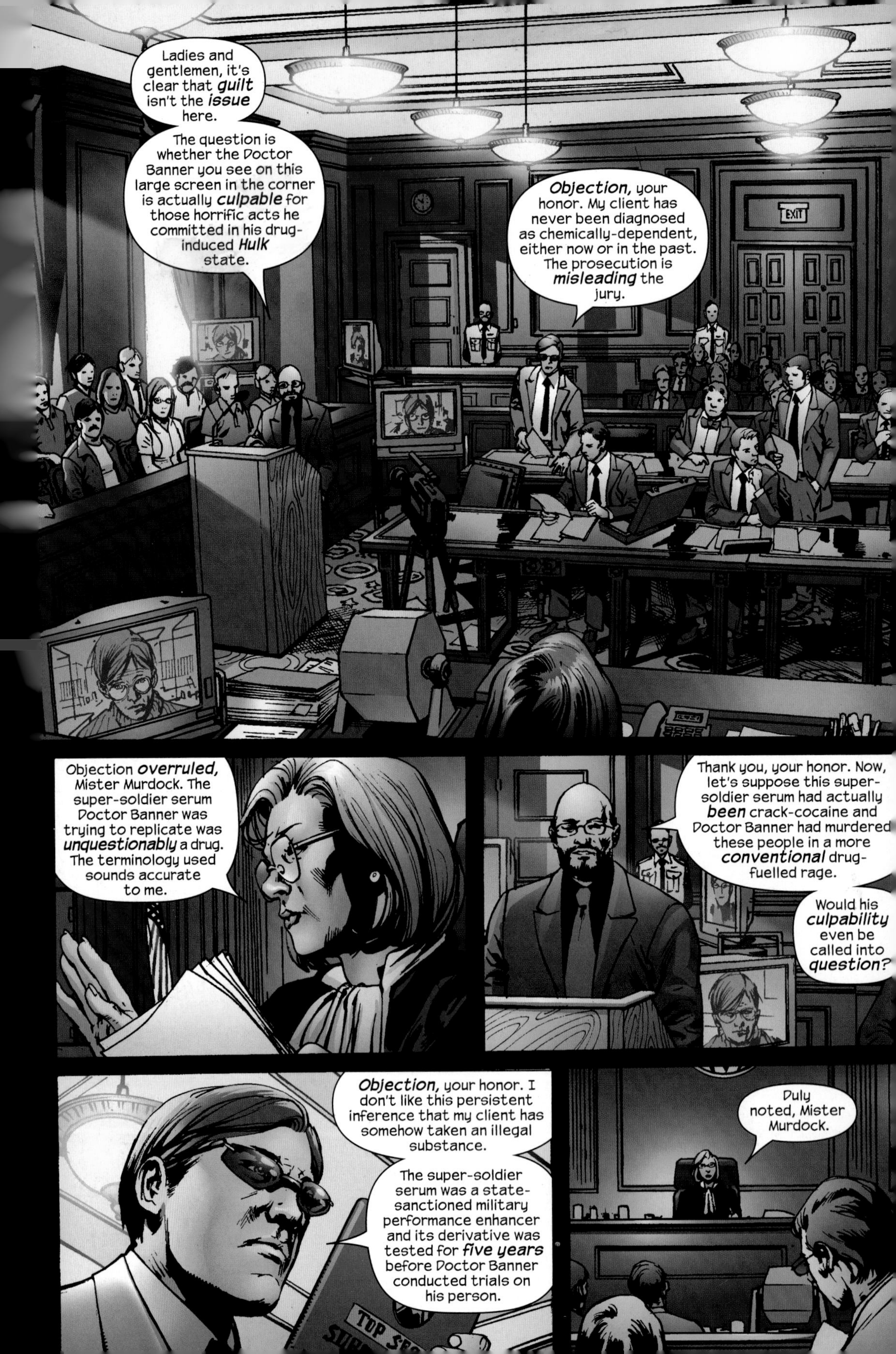

Ladies and gentlemen, it's clear that *guilt* isn't the *issue* here.
The question is whether the Doctor Banner you see on this large screen in the corner is actually *culpable* for those horrific acts he committed in his drug-induced *Hulk* state.
EXIT
Objection, your honor. My client has never been diagnosed as chemically-dependent, either now or in the past. The prosecution is *misleading* the jury.
Objection *overruled,* Mister Murdock. The super-soldier serum Doctor Banner was trying to replicate was *unquestionably* a drug. The terminology used sounds accurate to me.
Thank you, your honor. Now, let's suppose this super-soldier serum had actually *been* crack-cocaine and Doctor Banner had murdered these people in a more *conventional* drug-fuelled rage.
Would his *culpability* even be called into *question?*
Objection, your honor. I don't like this persistent inference that my client has somehow taken an illegal substance.
The super-soldier serum was a state-sanctioned military performance enhancer and its derivative was tested for *five years* before Doctor Banner conducted trials on his person.
Duly noted, Mister Murdock.

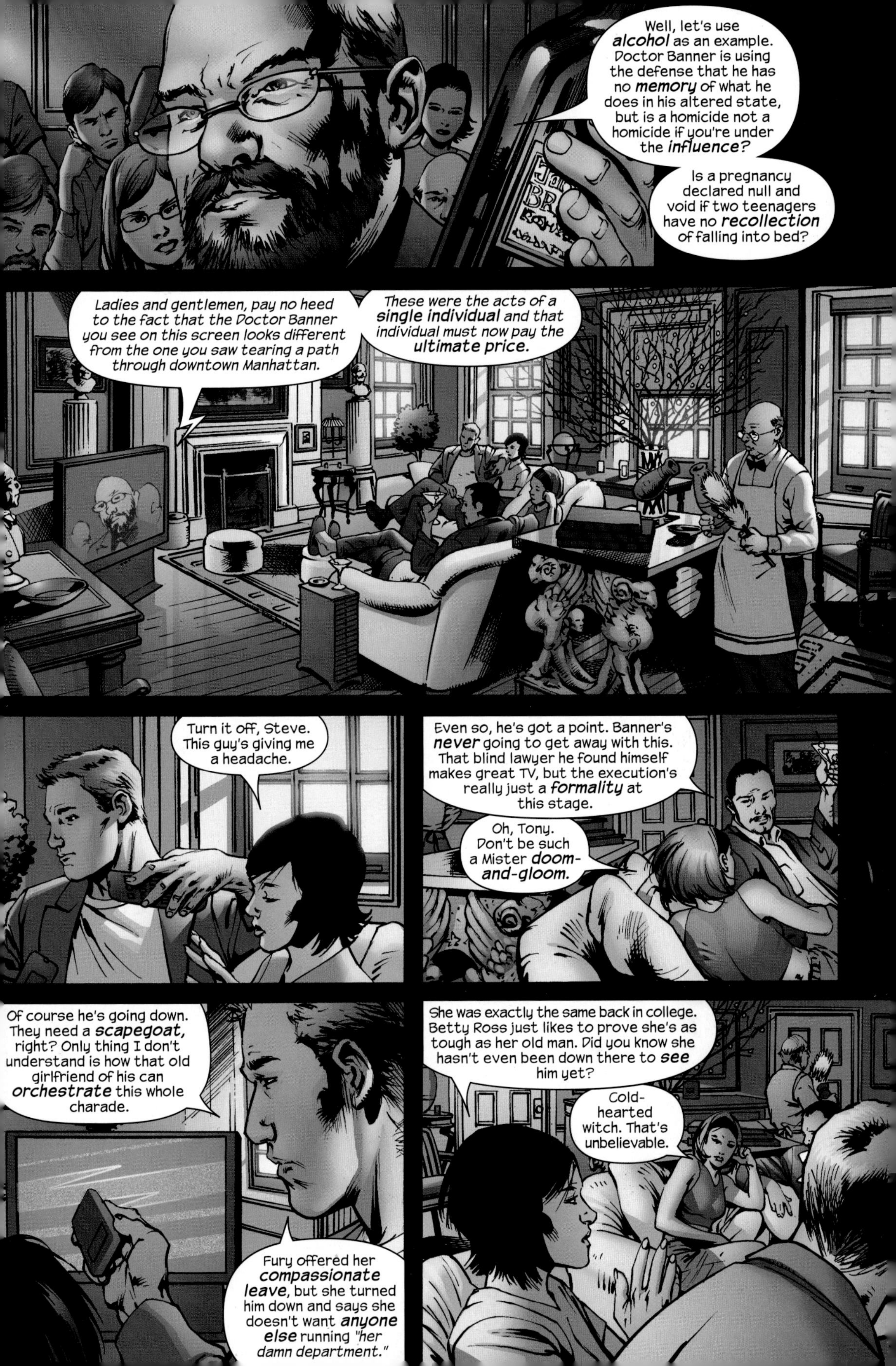
Well, let's use alcohol as an example. Doctor Banner is using the defense that he has no memory of what he does in his altered state, but is a homicide not a homicide if you're under the influence?
Is a pregnancy declared null and void if two teenagers have no recollection of falling into bed?
Ladies and gentlemen, pay no heed to the fact that the Doctor Banner you see on this screen looks different from the one you saw tearing a path through downtown Manhattan.
These were the acts of a single individual and that individual must now pay the ultimate price.
Turn it off, Steve. This guy's giving me a headache.
Even so, he's got a point. Banner's never going to get away with this. That blind lawyer he found himself makes great TV, but the execution's really just a formality at this stage.
Oh, Tony. Don't be such a Mister doom-and-gloom.
Of course he's going down. They need a scapegoat, right? Only thing I don't understand is how that old girlfriend of his can orchestrate this whole charade.
Fury offered her compassionate leave, but she turned him down and says she doesn't want anyone else running "her damn department."
She was exactly the same back in college. Betty Ross just likes to prove she's as tough as her old man. Did you know she hasn't even been down there to see him yet?
Cold-hearted witch. That's unbelievable.

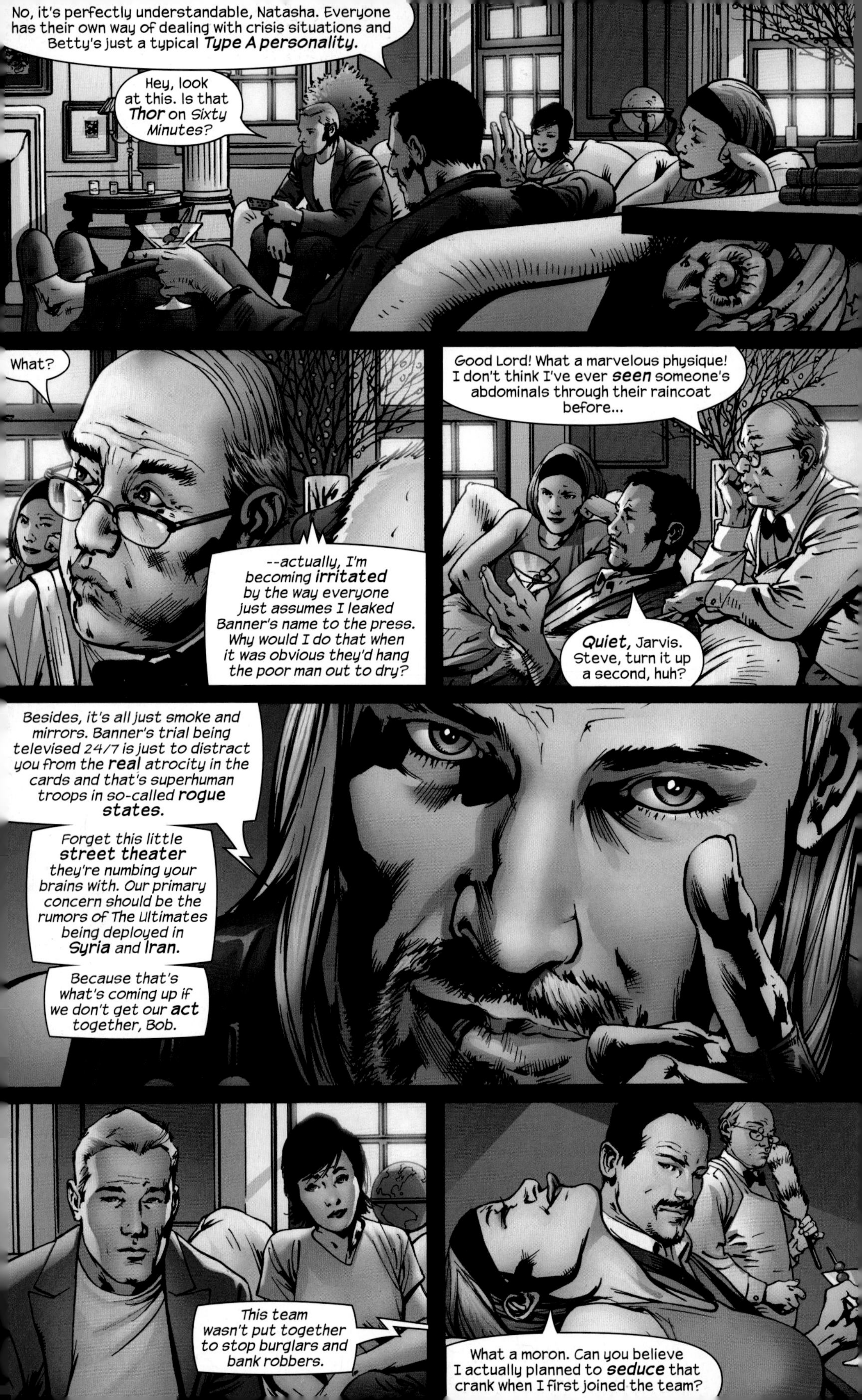
No, it's perfectly understandable, Natasha. Everyone has their own way of dealing with crisis situations and Betty's just a typical *Type A personality.*
Hey, look at this. Is that *Thor* on Sixty Minutes?
What?
--actually, I'm becoming *irritated* by the way everyone just assumes I leaked Banner's name to the press. Why would I do that when it was obvious they'd hang the poor man out to dry?
Good Lord! What a marvelous physique! I don't think I've ever *seen* someone's abdominals through their raincoat before...
Quiet, Jarvis. Steve, turn it up a second, huh?
Besides, it's all just smoke and mirrors. Banner's trial being televised 24/7 is just to distract you from the *real* atrocity in the cards and that's superhuman troops in so-called *rogue states.*
Forget this little *street theater* they're numbing your brains with. Our primary concern should be the rumors of The Ultimates being deployed in *Syria* and *Iran.*
Because that's what's coming up if we don't get our *act* together, Bob.
This team wasn't put together to stop burglars and bank robbers.
What a moron. Can you believe I actually planned to *seduce* that crank when I first joined the team?

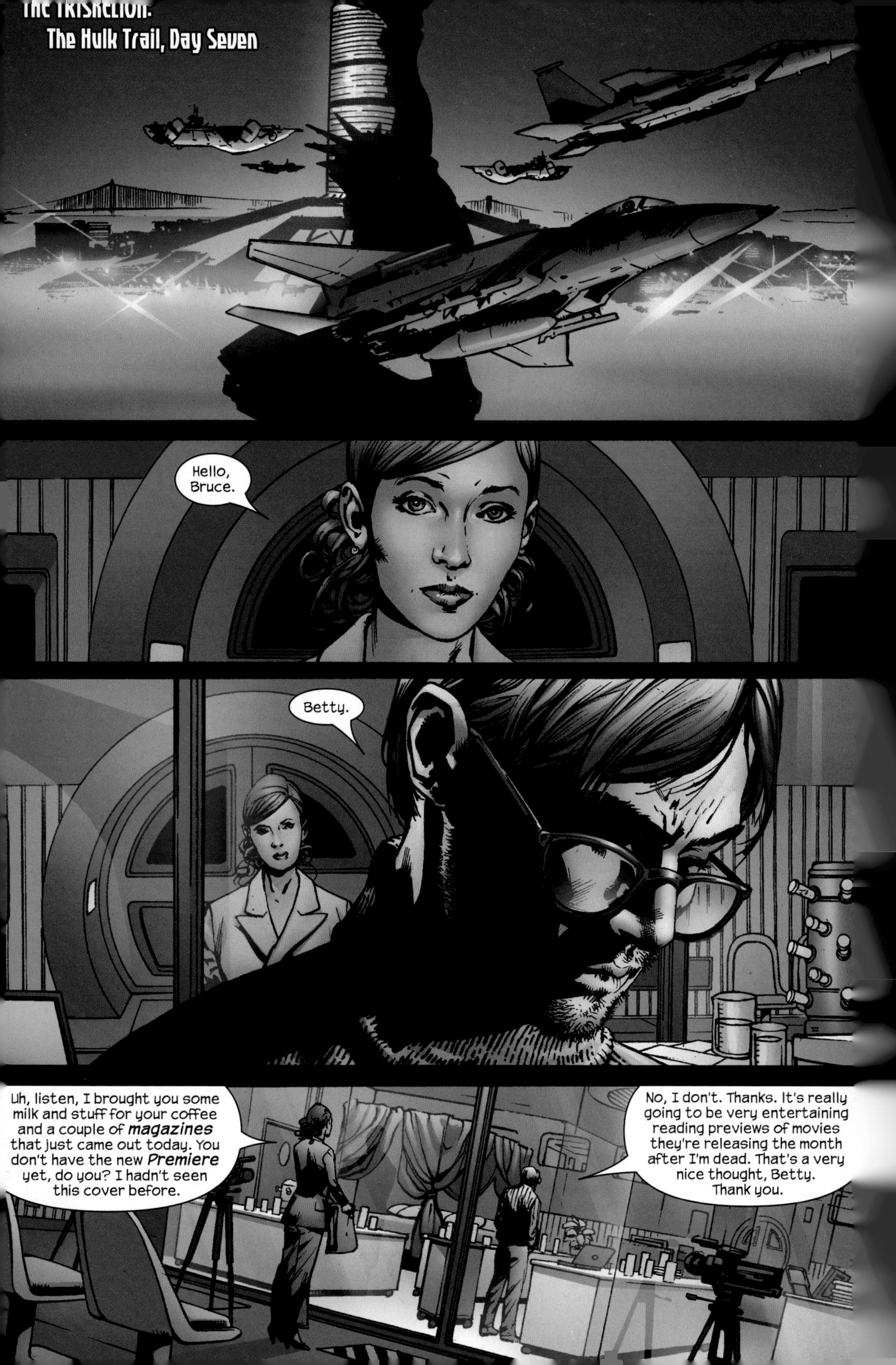
The Triskelion:
The Hulk Trail, Day Seven
Hello, Bruce.
Betty.
Uh, listen, I brought you some milk and stuff for your coffee and a couple of *magazines* that just came out today. You don't have the new *Premiere* yet, do you? I hadn't seen this cover before.
No, I don't. Thanks. It's really going to be very entertaining reading previews of movies they're releasing the month after I'm dead. That's a very nice thought, Betty. Thank you.

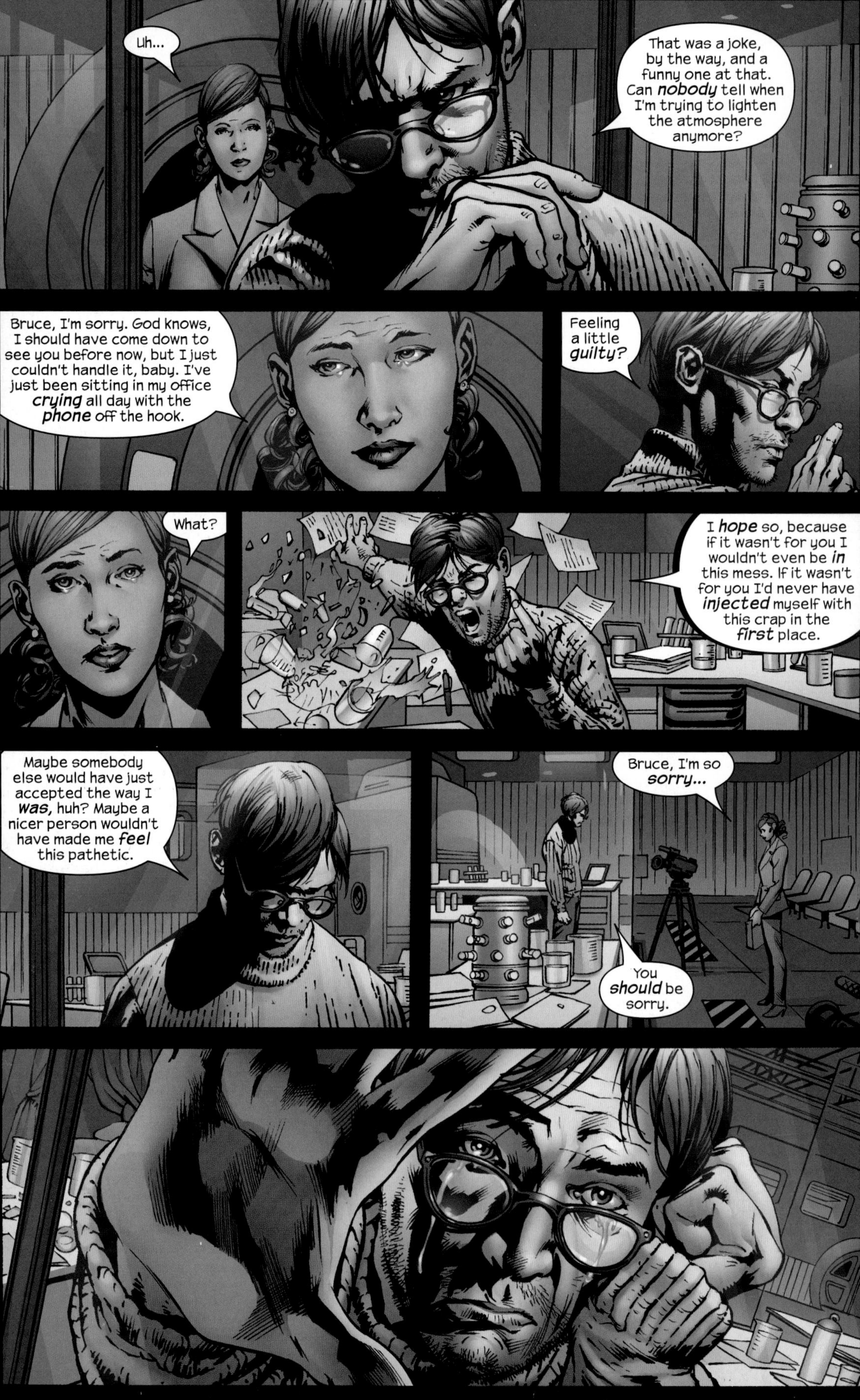
Uh...
That was a joke, by the way, and a funny one at that. Can nobody tell when I'm trying to lighten the atmosphere anymore?
Bruce, I'm sorry. God knows, I should have come down to see you before now, but I just couldn't handle it, baby. I've just been sitting in my office crying all day with the phone off the hook.
Feeling a little guilty?
What?
I hope so, because if it wasn't for you I wouldn't even be in this mess. If it wasn't for you I'd never have injected myself with this crap in the first place.
Maybe somebody else would have just accepted the way I was, huh? Maybe a nicer person wouldn't have made me feel this pathetic.
Bruce, I'm so sorry...
You should be sorry.

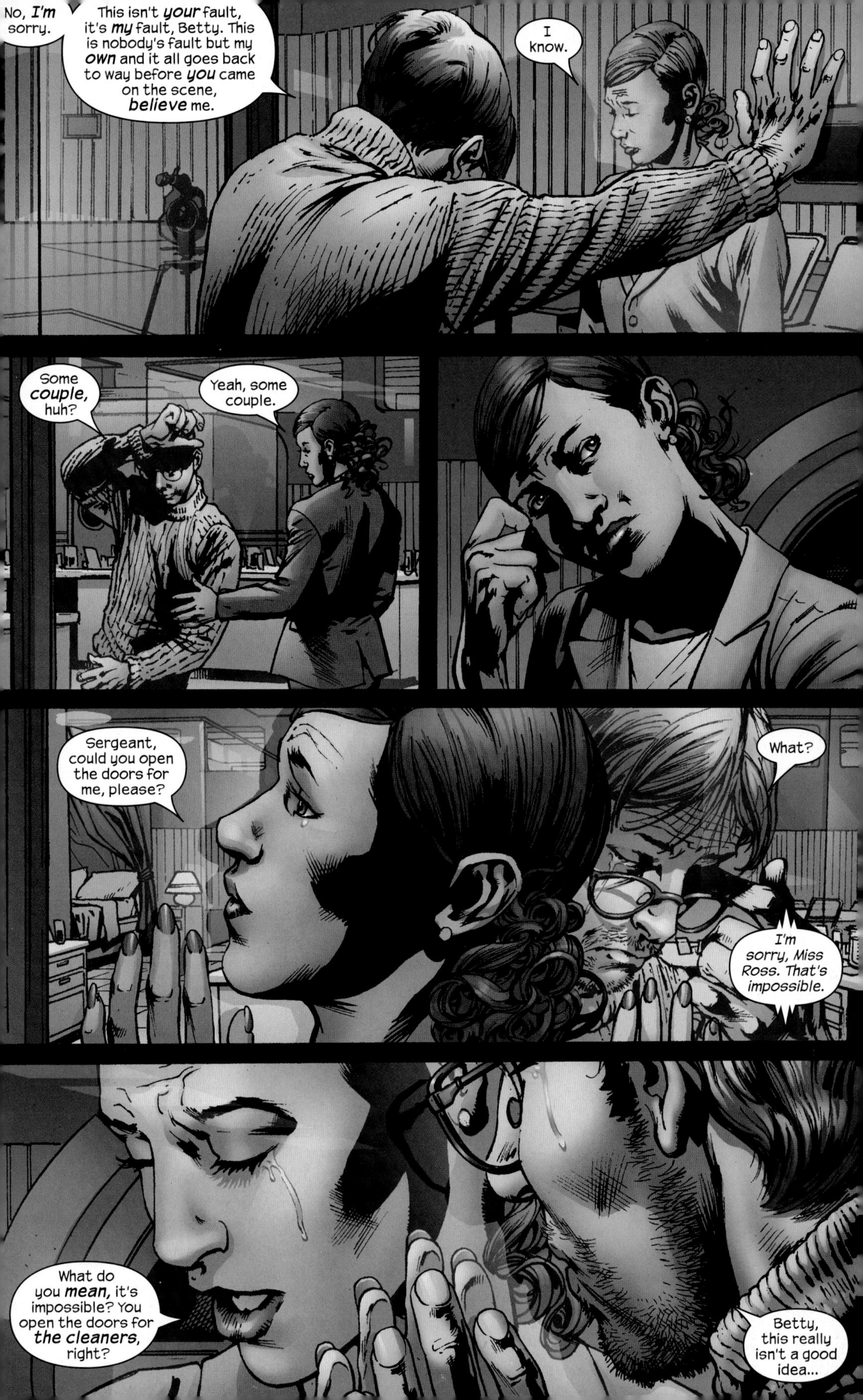
No, *I'm* sorry.
This isn't *your* fault, it's *my* fault, Betty. This is nobody's fault but my *own* and it all goes back to way before *you* came on the scene, *believe* me.
I know.
Some *couple*, huh?
Yeah, some couple.
Sergeant, could you open the doors for me, please?
What?
I'm sorry, Miss Ross. That's impossible.
What do you *mean*, it's impossible? You open the doors for *the cleaners*, right?
Betty, this really isn't a good idea...

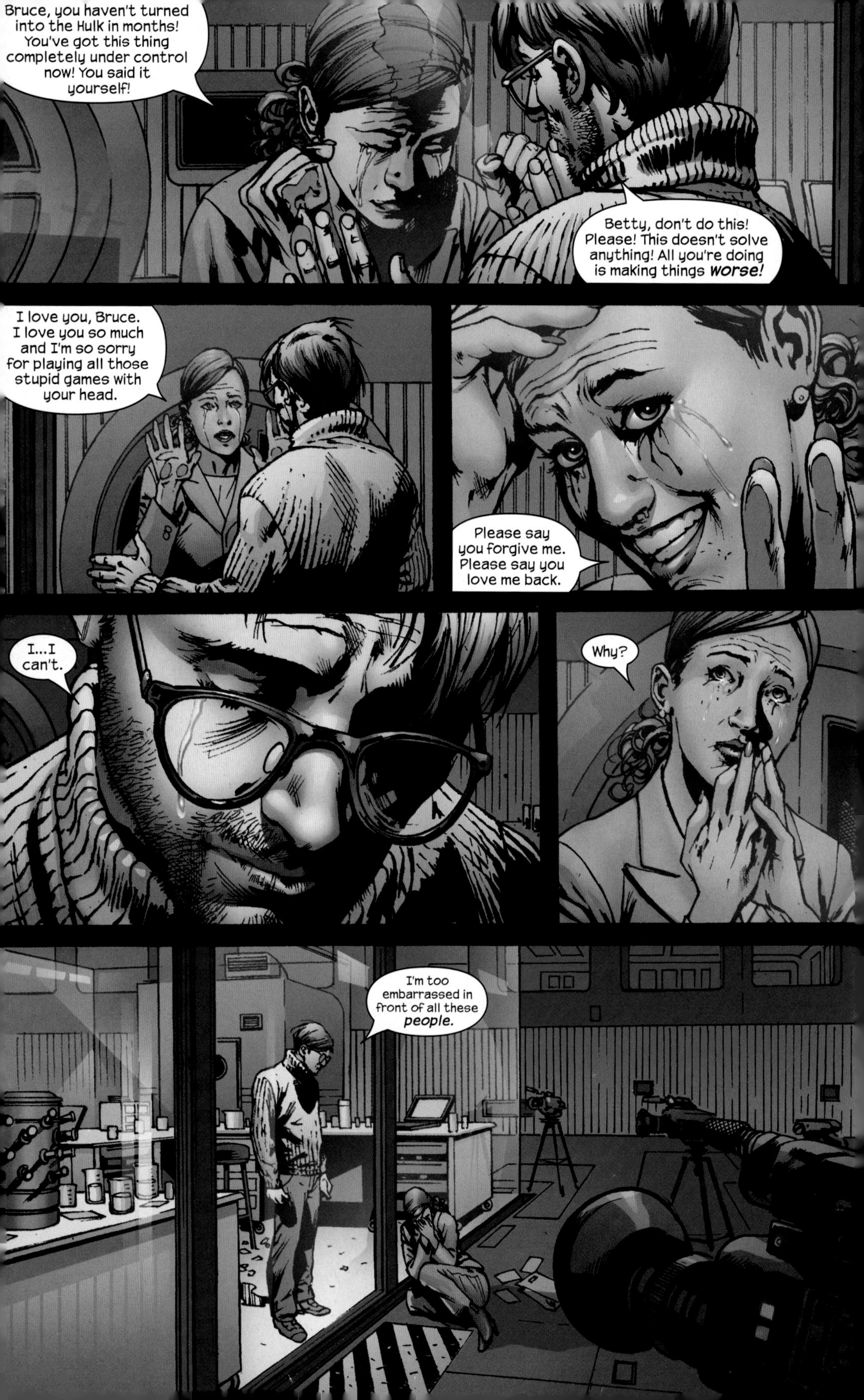
Bruce, you haven't turned into the Hulk in months! You've got this thing completely under control now! You said it yourself!
Betty, don't do this! Please! This doesn't solve anything! All you're doing is making things *worse!*
I love you, Bruce. I love you so much and I'm so sorry for playing all those stupid games with your head.
Please say you forgive me. Please say you love me back.
I...I can't.
Why?
I'm too embarrassed in front of all these *people.*

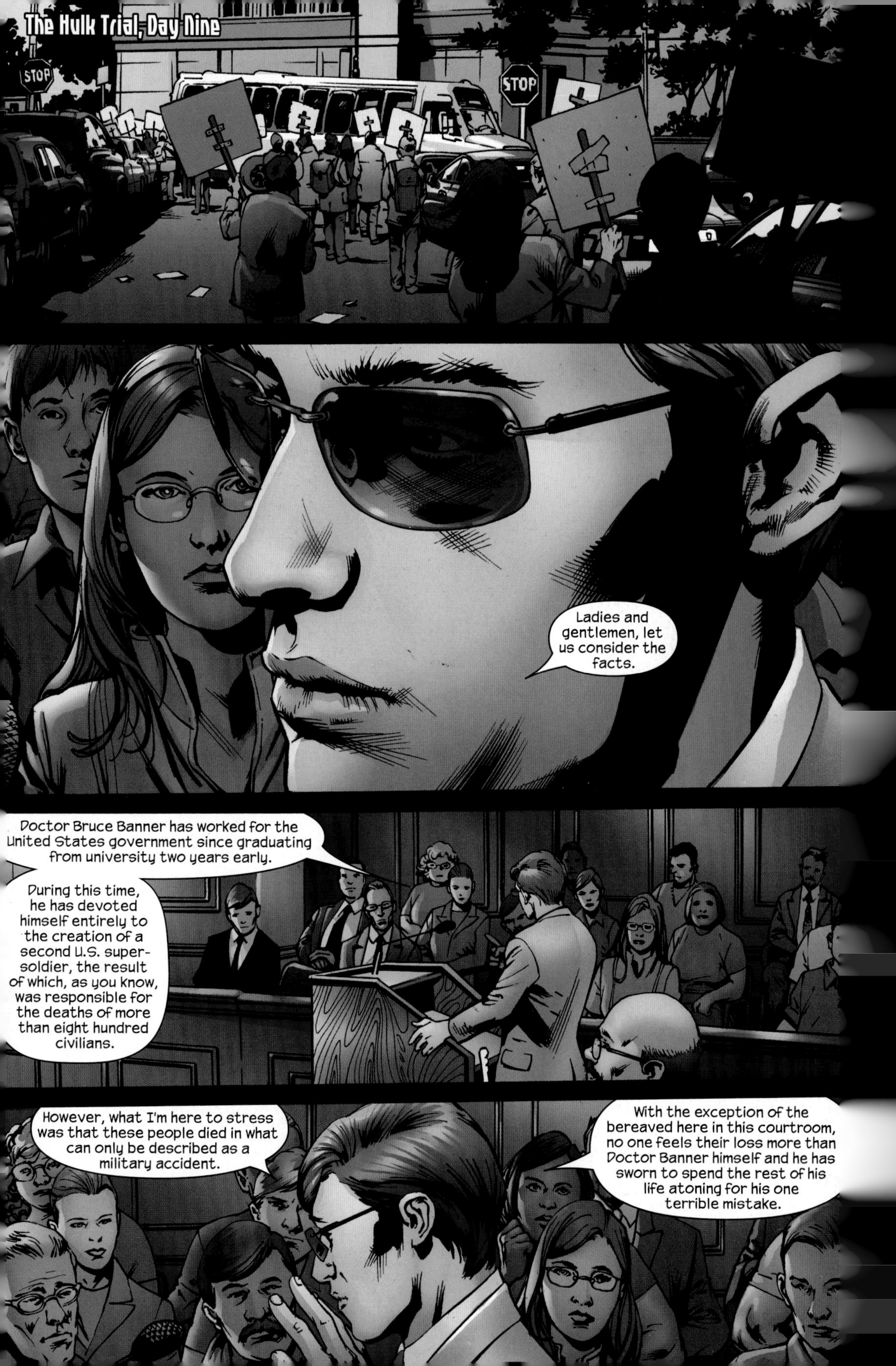
The Hulk Trial, Day Nine
STOP
STOP
Ladies and gentlemen, let us consider the facts.
Doctor Bruce Banner has worked for the United States government since graduating from university two years early.
During this time, he has devoted himself entirely to the creation of a second U.S. super-soldier, the result of which, as you know, was responsible for the deaths of more than eight hundred civilians.
However, what I'm here to stress was that these people died in what can only be described as a military accident.
With the exception of the bereaved here in this courtroom, no one feels their loss more than Doctor Banner himself and he has sworn to spend the rest of his life atoning for his one terrible mistake.

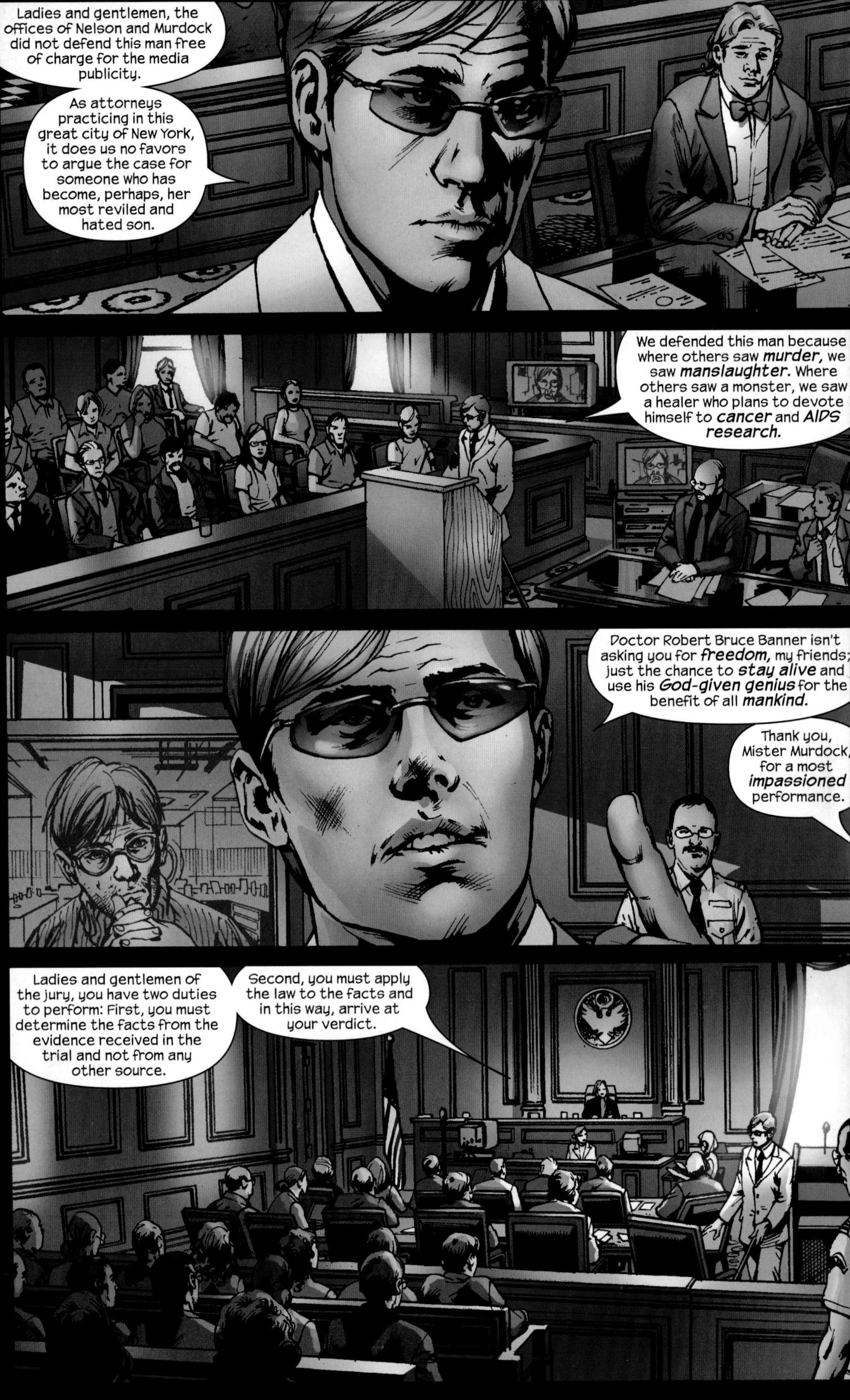
Ladies and gentlemen, the offices of Nelson and Murdock did not defend this man free of charge for the media publicity.
As attorneys practicing in this great city of New York, it does us no favors to argue the case for someone who has become, perhaps, her most reviled and hated son.
We defended this man because where others saw *murder,* we saw *manslaughter.* Where others saw a monster, we saw a healer who plans to devote himself to *cancer* and *AIDS research.*
Doctor Robert Bruce Banner isn't asking you for *freedom,* my friends; just the chance to *stay alive* and use his *God-given genius* for the benefit of all *mankind.*
Thank you, Mister Murdock, for a most *impassioned* performance.
Ladies and gentlemen of the jury, you have two duties to perform: First, you must determine the facts from the evidence received in the trial and not from any other source.
Second, you must apply the law to the facts and in this way, arrive at your verdict.

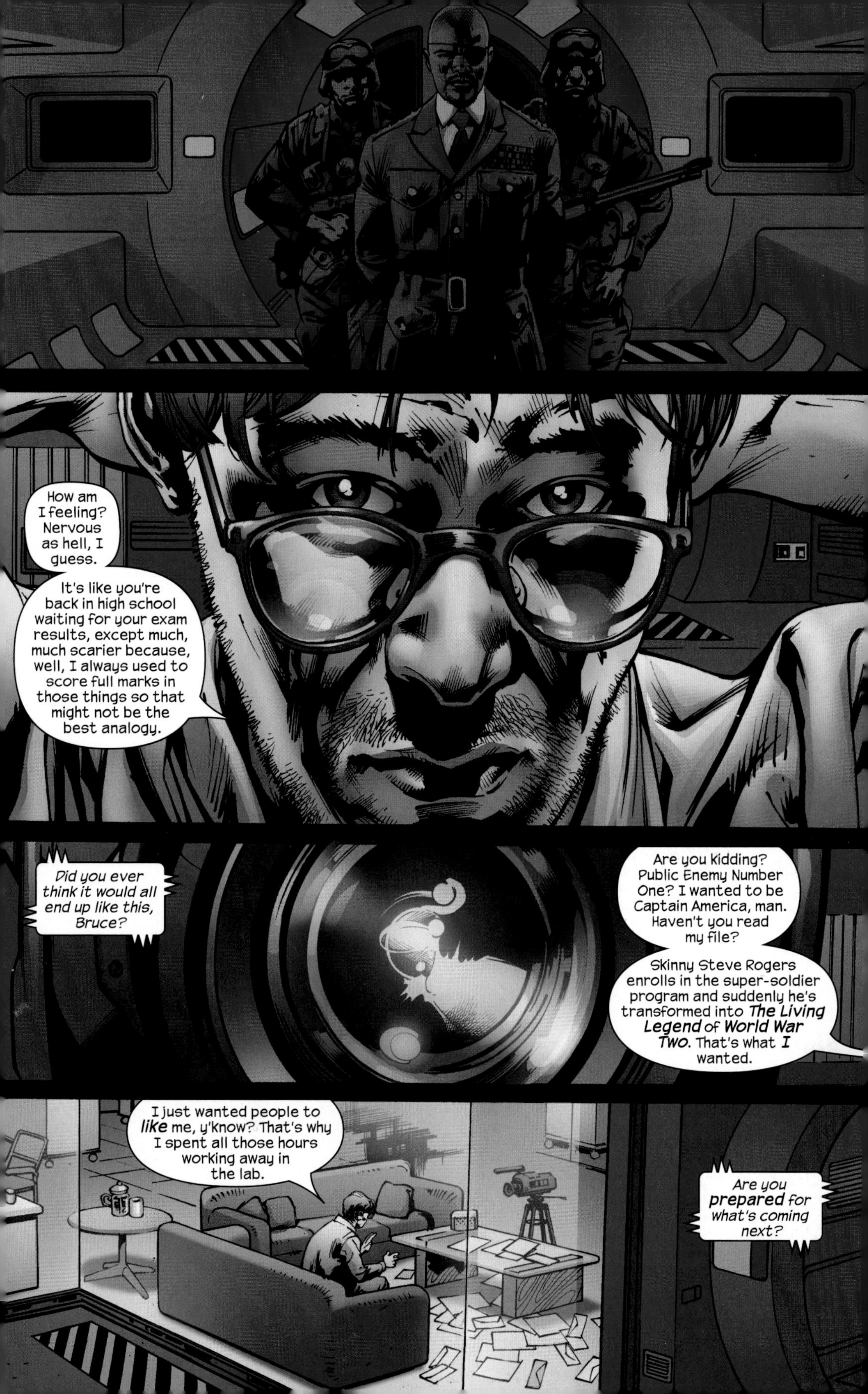
How am I feeling? Nervous as hell, I guess.
It's like you're back in high school waiting for your exam results, except much, much scarier because, well, I always used to score full marks in those things so that might not be the best analogy.
Did you ever think it would all end up like this, Bruce?
Are you kidding? Public Enemy Number One? I wanted to be Captain America, man. Haven't you read my file?
Skinny Steve Rogers enrolls in the super-soldier program and suddenly he's transformed into The Living Legend of World War Two. That's what I wanted.
I just wanted people to like me, y'know? That's why I spent all those hours working away in the lab.
Are you prepared for what's coming next?

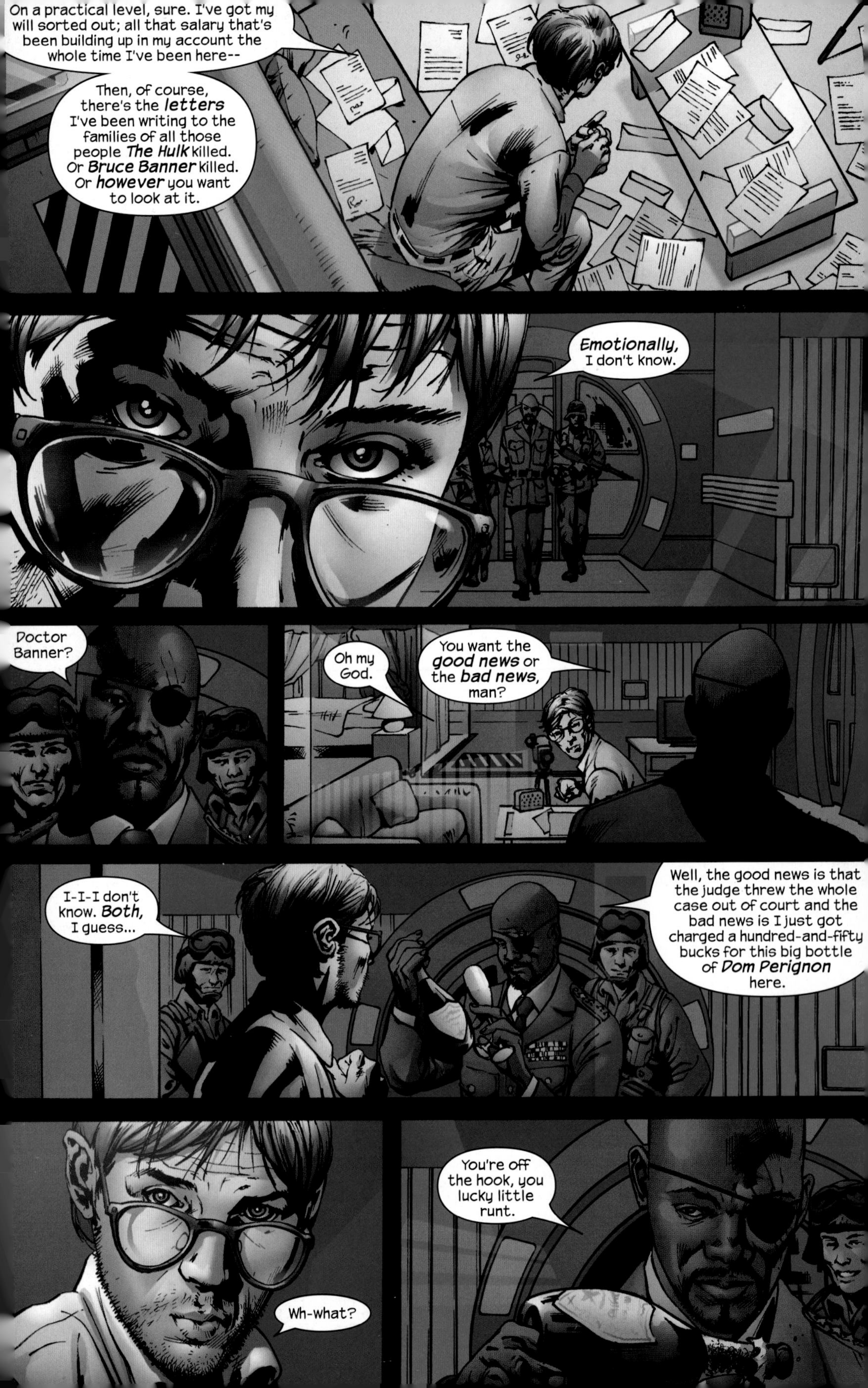
On a practical level, sure. I've got my will sorted out; all that salary that's been building up in my account the whole time I've been here--
Then, of course, there's the *letters* I've been writing to the families of all those people *The Hulk* killed. Or *Bruce Banner* killed. Or *however* you want to look at it.
Emotionally, I don't know.
Doctor Banner?
Oh my God.
You want the *good news* or the *bad news,* man?
I-I-I don't know. *Both,* I guess...
Well, the good news is that the judge threw the whole case out of court and the bad news is I just got charged a hundred-and-fifty bucks for this big bottle of *Dom Perignon* here.
You're off the hook, you lucky little runt.
Wh-what?

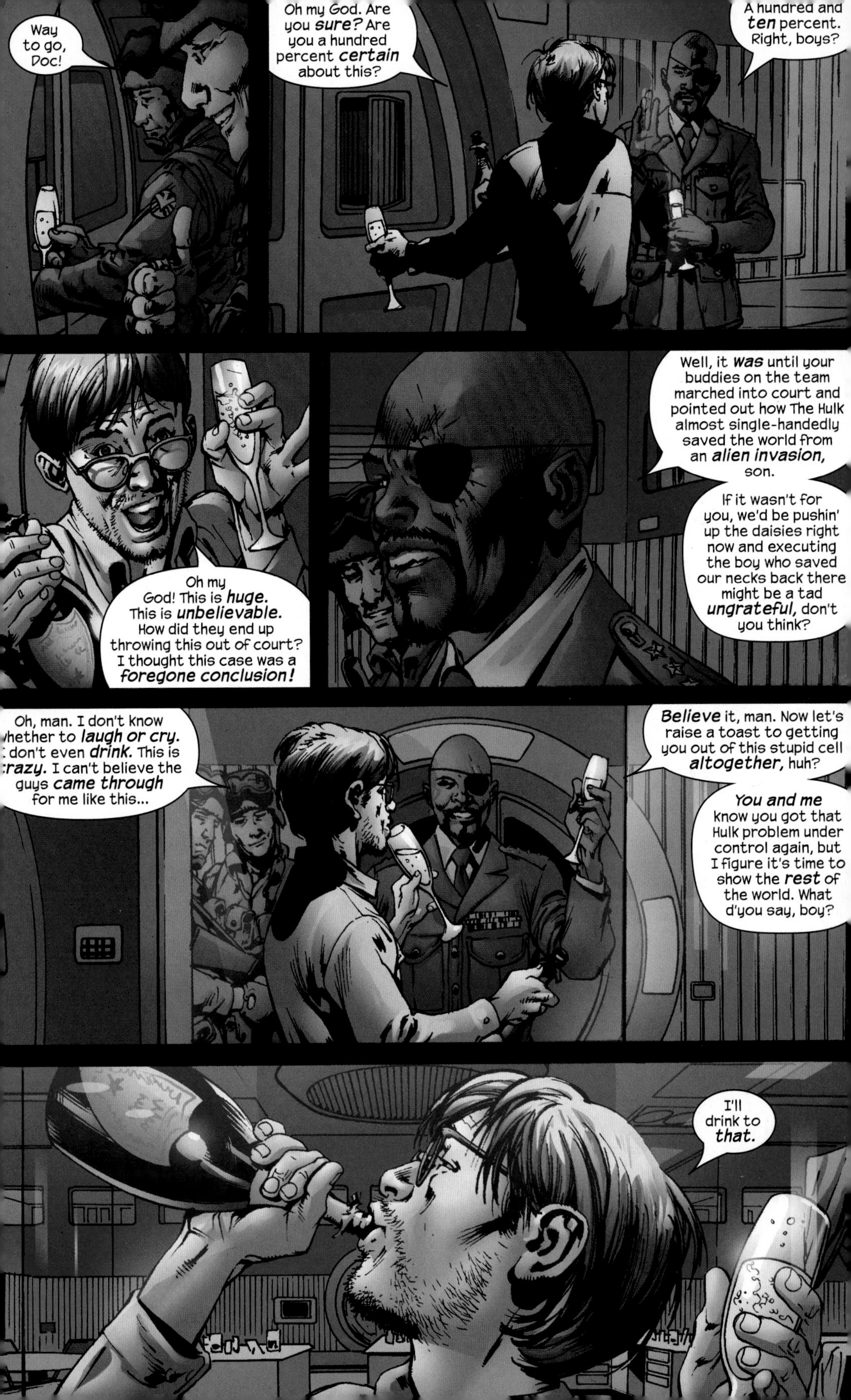
Way to go, Doc!
Oh my God. Are you *sure?* Are you a hundred percent *certain* about this?
A hundred and *ten* percent. Right, boys?
Oh my God! This is *huge.* This is *unbelievable.* How did they end up throwing this out of court? I thought this case was a *foregone conclusion!*
Well, it *was* until your buddies on the team marched into court and pointed out how The Hulk almost single-handedly saved the world from an *alien invasion,* son.
If it wasn't for you, we'd be pushin' up the daisies right now and executing the boy who saved our necks back there might be a tad *ungrateful,* don't you think?
Oh, man. I don't know whether to *laugh or cry.* I don't even *drink.* This is *crazy.* I can't believe the guys *came through* for me like this...
Believe it, man. Now let's raise a toast to getting you out of this stupid cell *altogether,* huh?
You and me know you got that Hulk problem under control again, but I figure it's time to show the *rest* of the world. What d'you say, boy?
I'll drink to *that.*

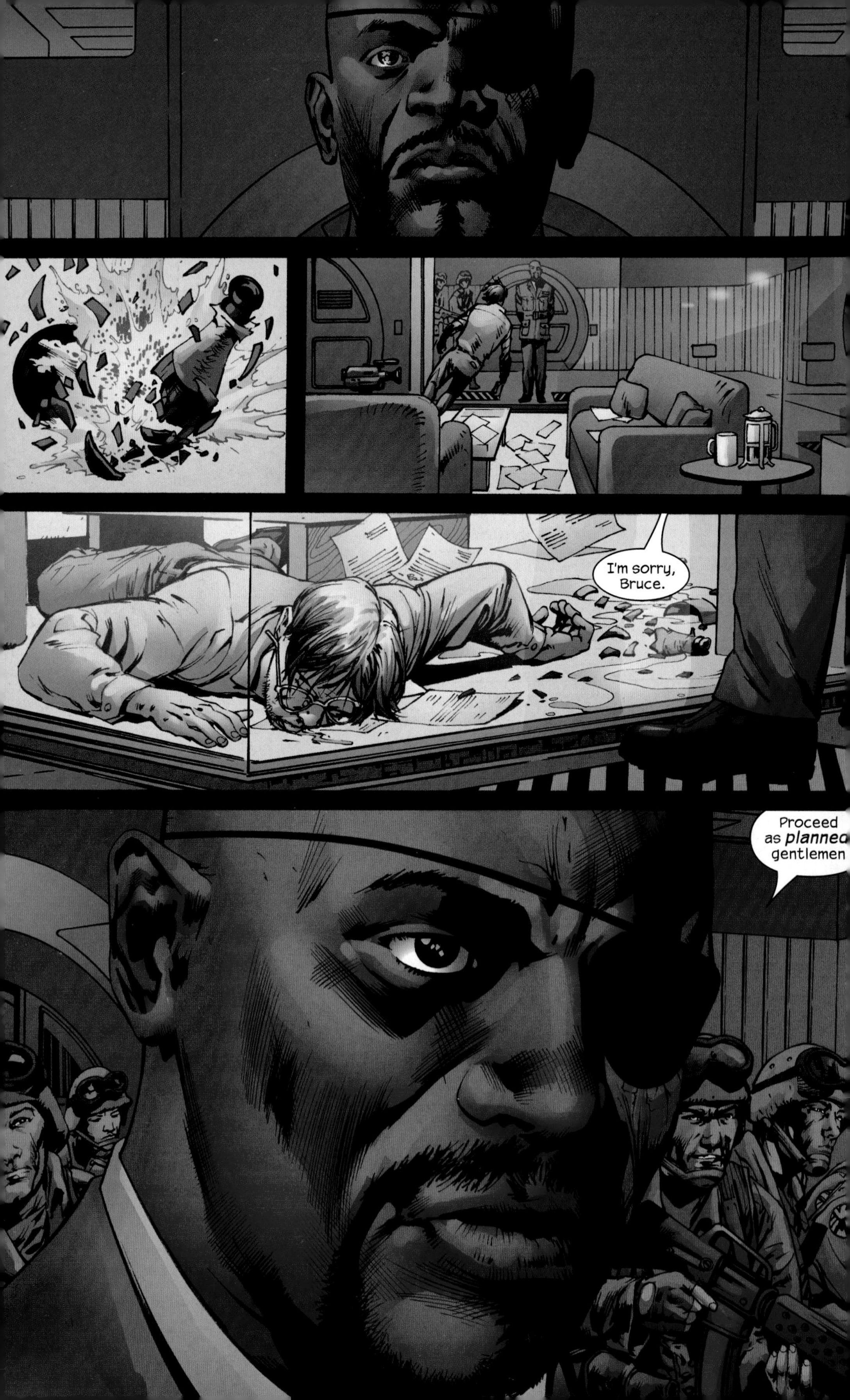
I'm sorry, Bruce.
Proceed as *planned* gentlemen

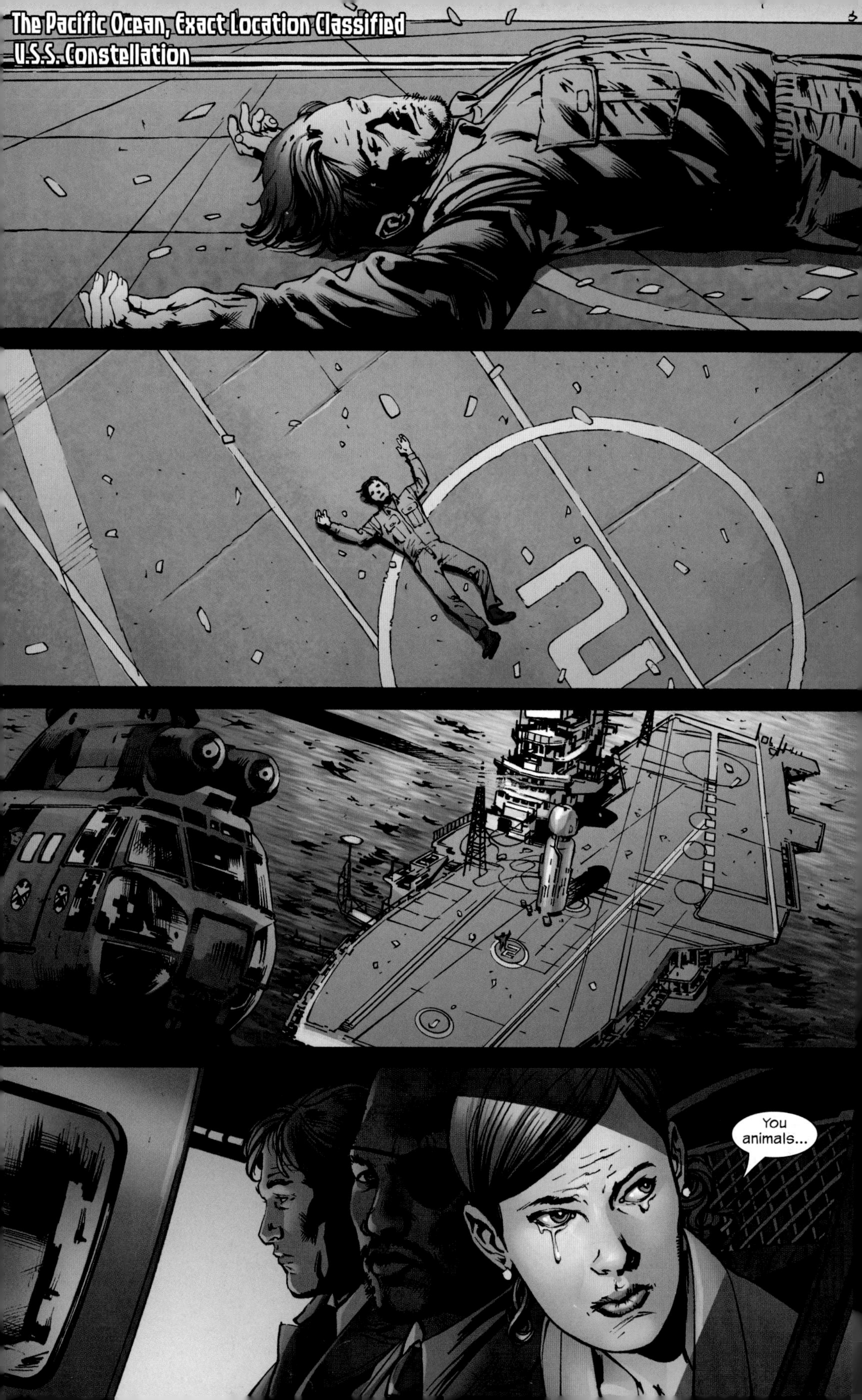

The Pacific Ocean, Exact Location Classified
U.S.S. Constellation
You animals...

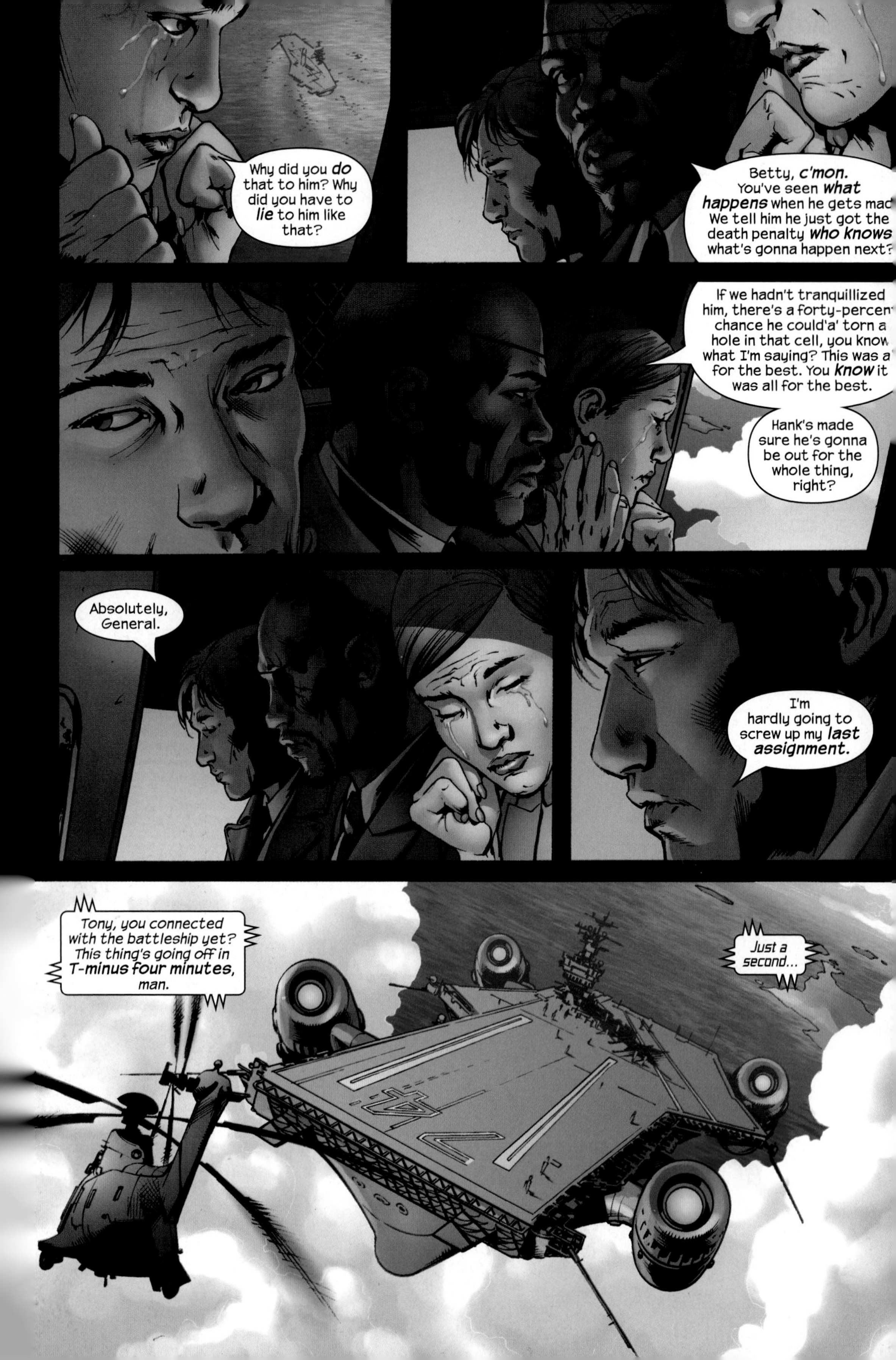
Why did you **do** that to him? Why did you have to **lie** to him like that?
Betty, **c'mon.** You've seen **what happens** when he gets mad We tell him he just got the death penalty **who knows** what's gonna happen next?
If we hadn't tranquillized him, there's a forty-percent chance he could'a' torn a hole in that cell, you know what I'm saying? This was a for the best. You **know** it was all for the best.
Hank's made sure he's gonna be out for the whole thing, right?
Absolutely, General.
I'm hardly going to screw up my **last assignment.**
*Tony, you connected with the battleship yet? This thing's going off in **T-minus four minutes**, man.*
Just a second...

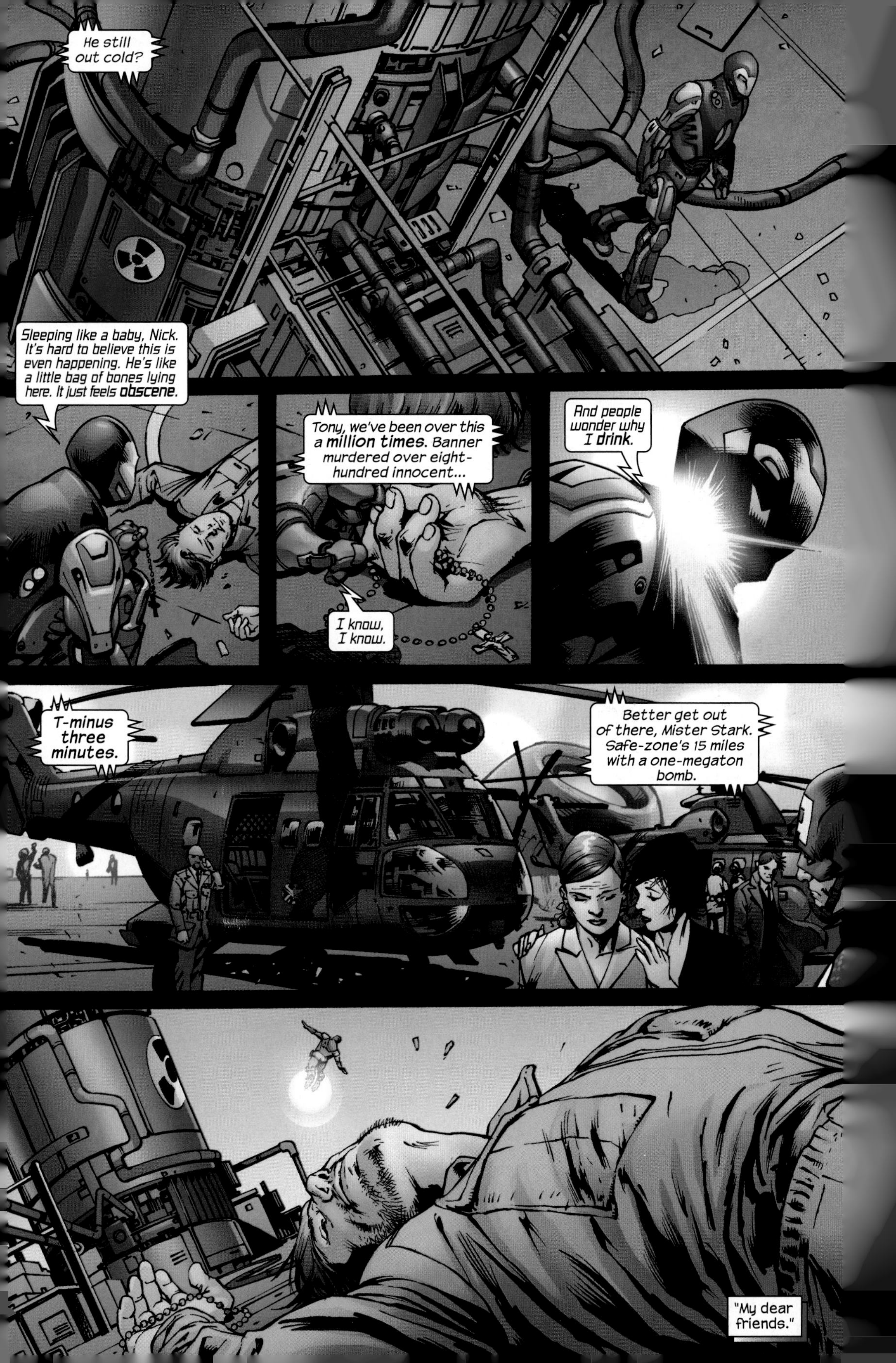
He still out cold?
Sleeping like a baby, Nick. It's hard to believe this is even happening. He's like a little bag of bones lying here. It just feels **obscene**.
Tony, we've been over this a **million times**. Banner murdered over eight-hundred innocent...
I know, I know.
And people wonder why I **drink**.
T-minus three minutes.
Better get out of there, Mister Stark. Safe-zone's 15 miles with a one-megaton bomb.
"My dear friends."

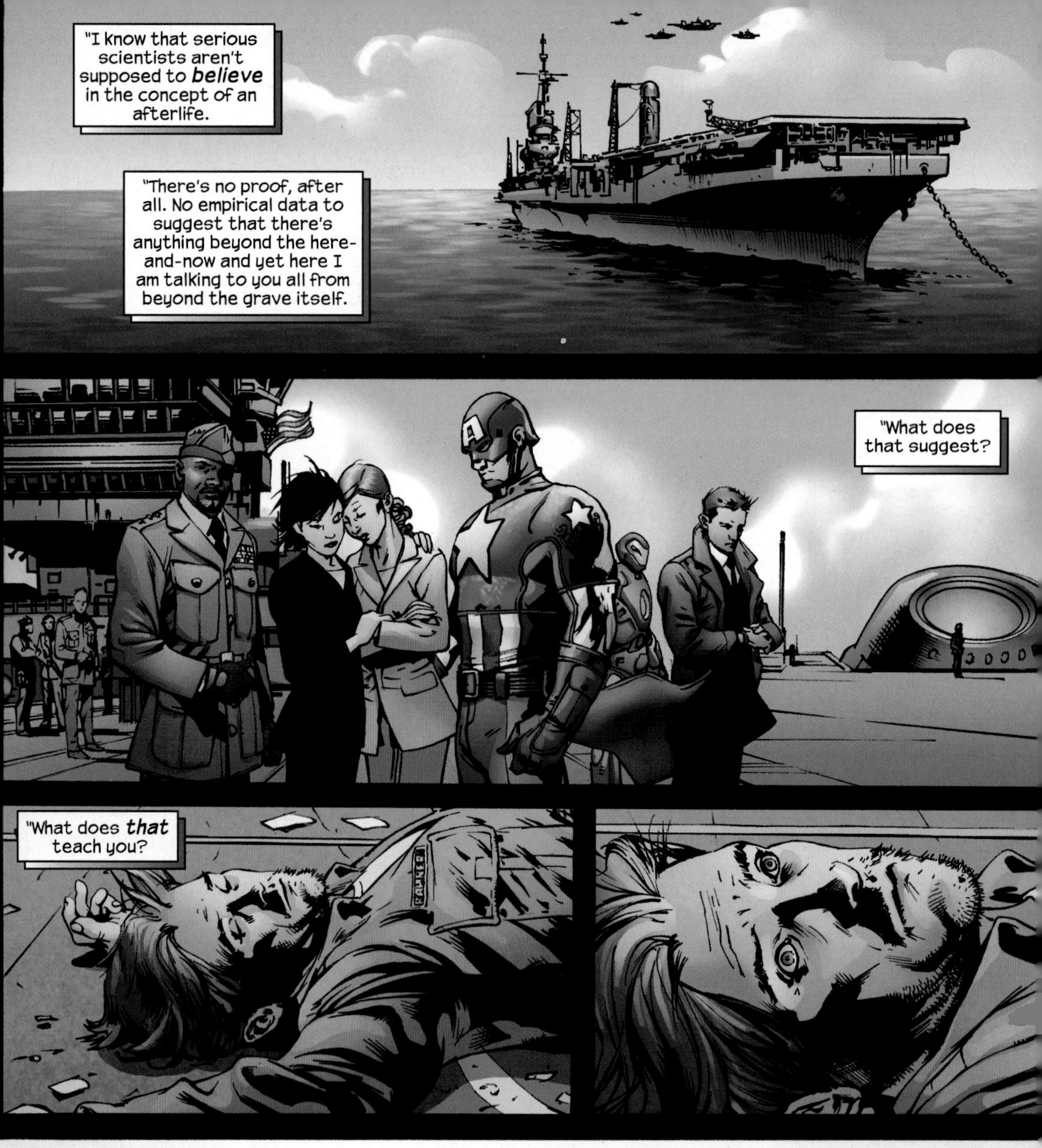
"I know that serious scientists aren't supposed to *believe* in the concept of an afterlife.
"There's no proof, after all. No empirical data to suggest that there's anything beyond the here-and-now and yet here I am talking to you all from beyond the grave itself.
"What does that suggest?
"What does *that* teach you?

"To me, it's a perfect illustration that the world is a far more complex place than even the brightest among us would dare to imagine.

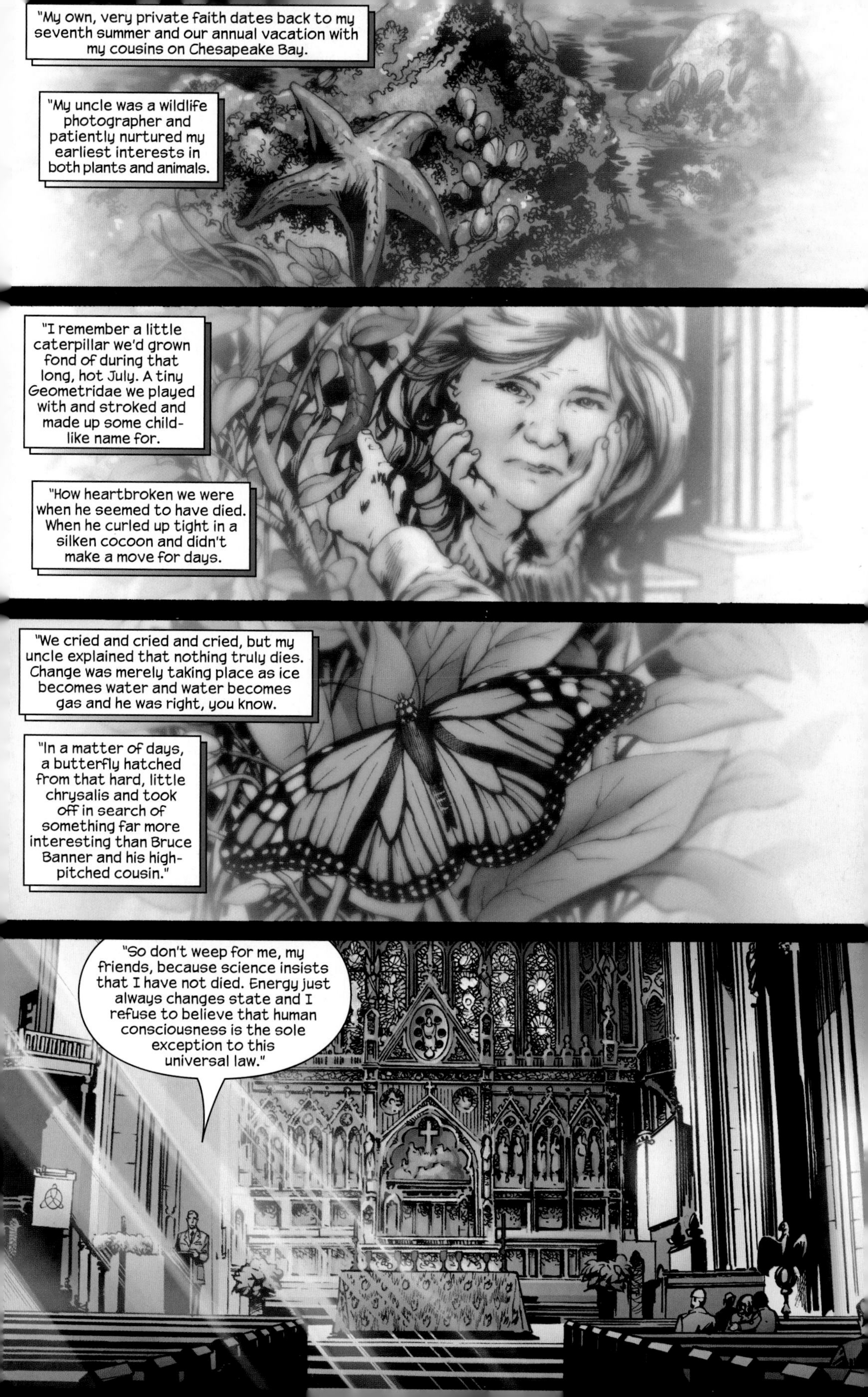
"My own, very private faith dates back to my seventh summer and our annual vacation with my cousins on Chesapeake Bay.
"My uncle was a wildlife photographer and patiently nurtured my earliest interests in both plants and animals.
"I remember a little caterpillar we'd grown fond of during that long, hot July. A tiny Geometridae we played with and stroked and made up some child-like name for.
"How heartbroken we were when he seemed to have died. When he curled up tight in a silken cocoon and didn't make a move for days.
"We cried and cried and cried, but my uncle explained that nothing truly dies. Change was merely taking place as ice becomes water and water becomes gas and he was right, you know.
"In a matter of days, a butterfly hatched from that hard, little chrysalis and took off in search of something far more interesting than Bruce Banner and his high-pitched cousin."
"So don't weep for me, my friends, because science insists that I have not died. Energy just always changes state and I refuse to believe that human consciousness is the sole exception to this universal law."

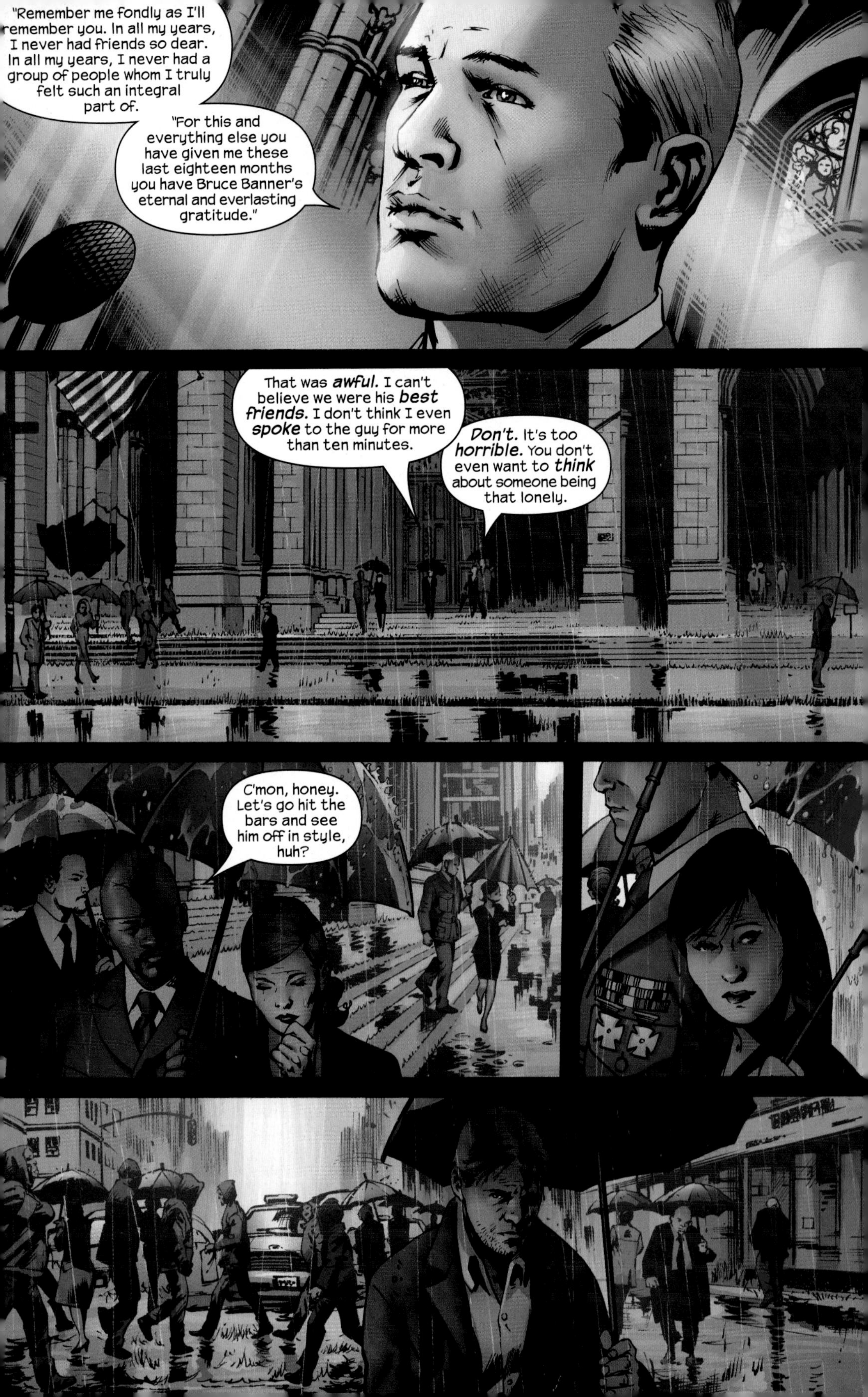
"Remember me fondly as I'll remember you. In all my years, I never had friends so dear. In all my years, I never had a group of people whom I truly felt such an integral part of.
"For this and everything else you have given me these last eighteen months you have Bruce Banner's eternal and everlasting gratitude."
That was awful. I can't believe we were his best friends. I don't think I even spoke to the guy for more than ten minutes.
Don't. It's too horrible. You don't even want to think about someone being that lonely.
C'mon, honey. Let's go hit the bars and see him off in style, huh?

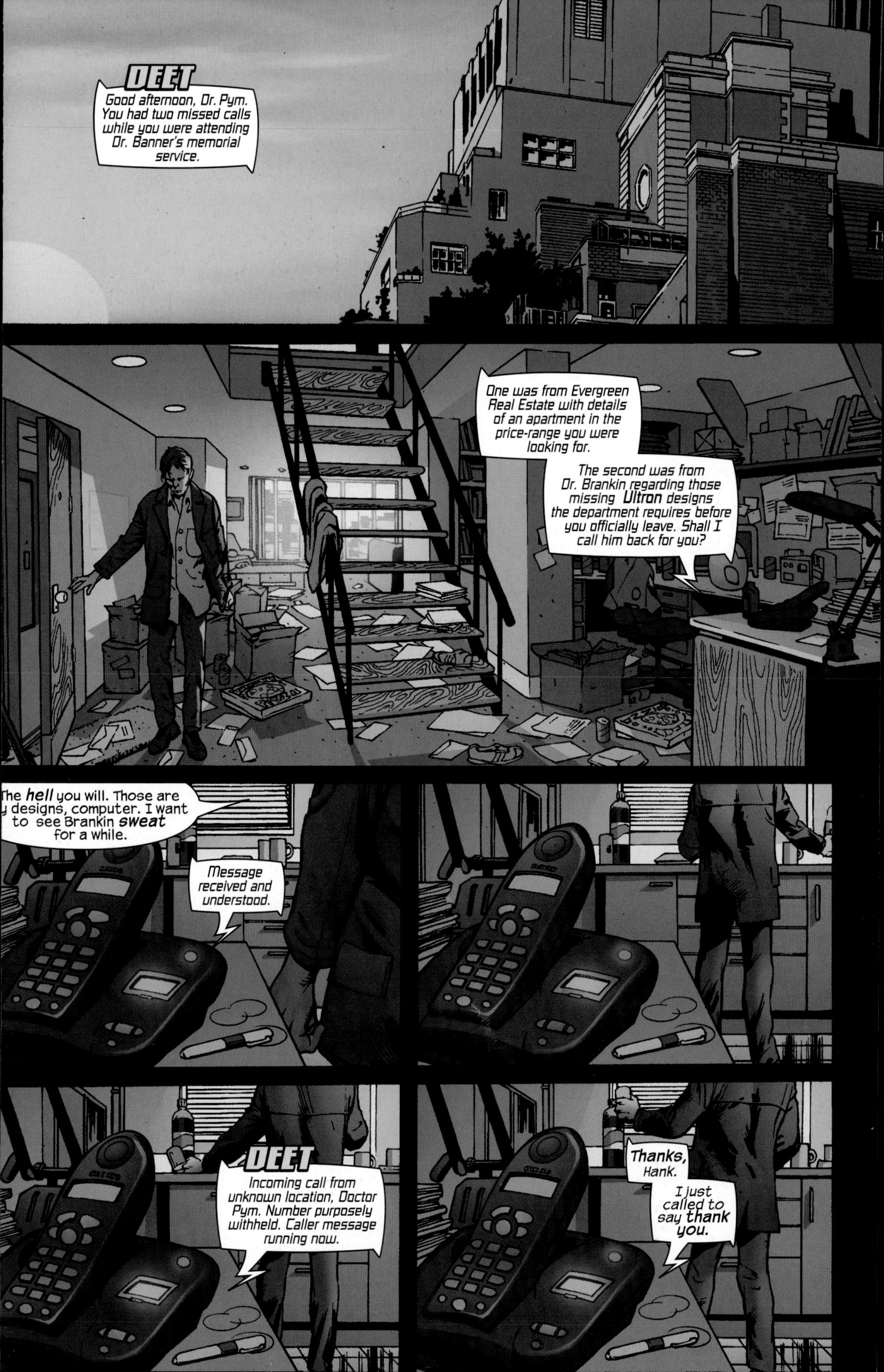
DEET
Good afternoon, Dr. Pym. You had two missed calls while you were attending Dr. Banner's memorial service.
One was from Evergreen Real Estate with details of an apartment in the price-range you were looking for.
The second was from Dr. Brankin regarding those missing Ultron designs the department requires before you officially leave. Shall I call him back for you?
The hell you will. Those are designs, computer. I want to see Brankin sweat for a while.
Message received and understood.
DEET
Incoming call from unknown location, Doctor Pym. Number purposely withheld. Caller message running now.
Thanks, Hank.
I just called to say thank you.

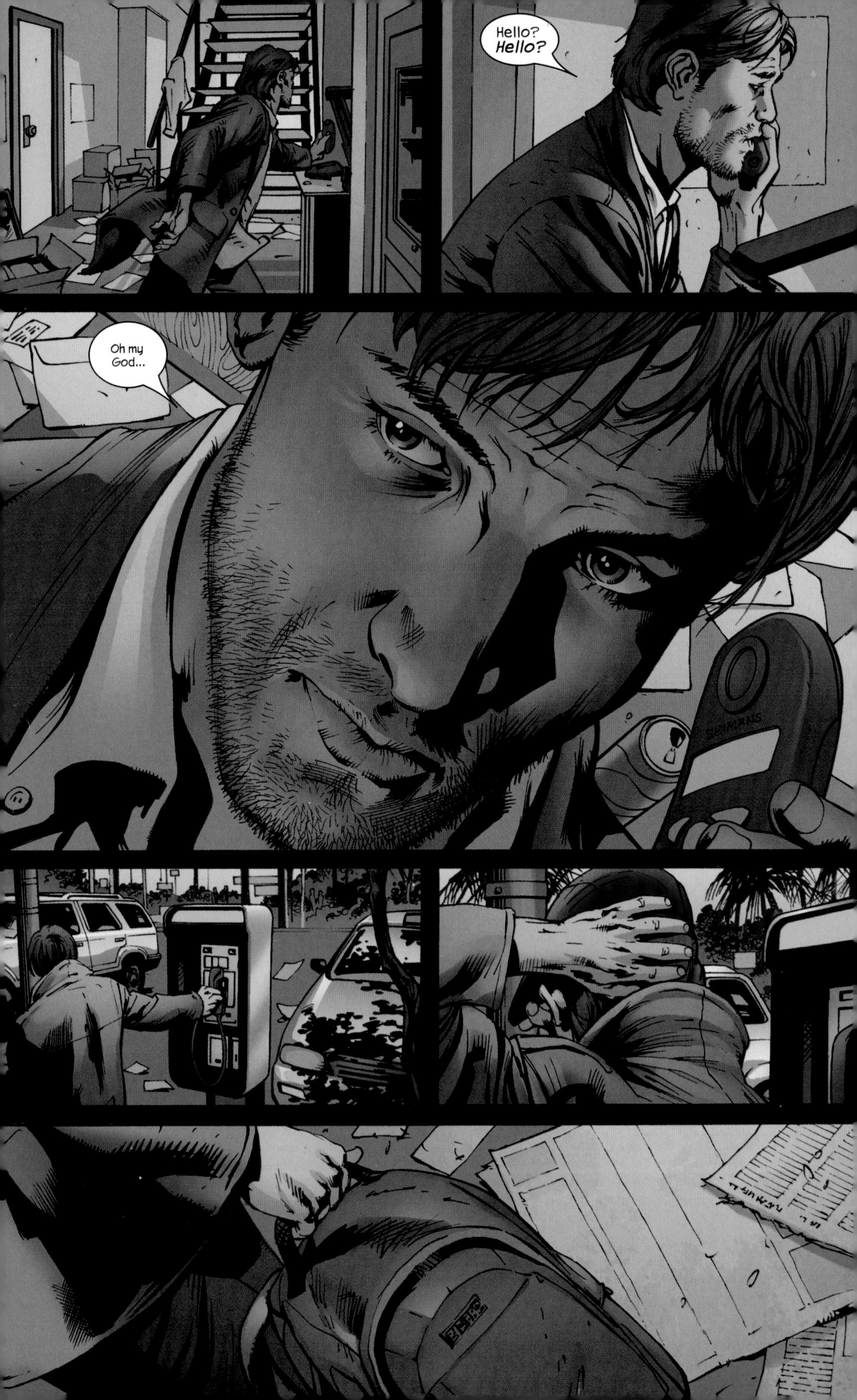
Hello? Hello?
Oh my God...

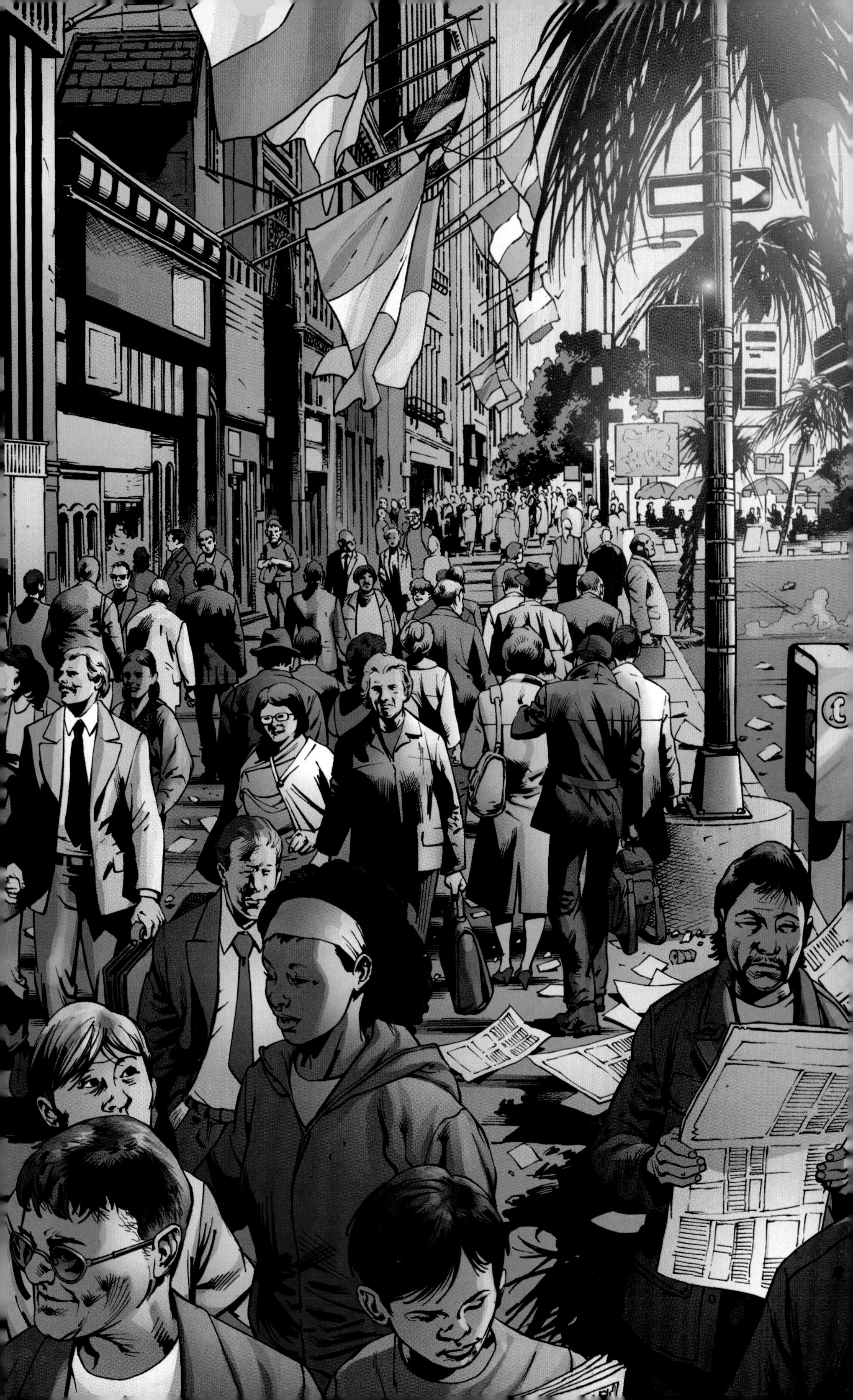

BROTHERS

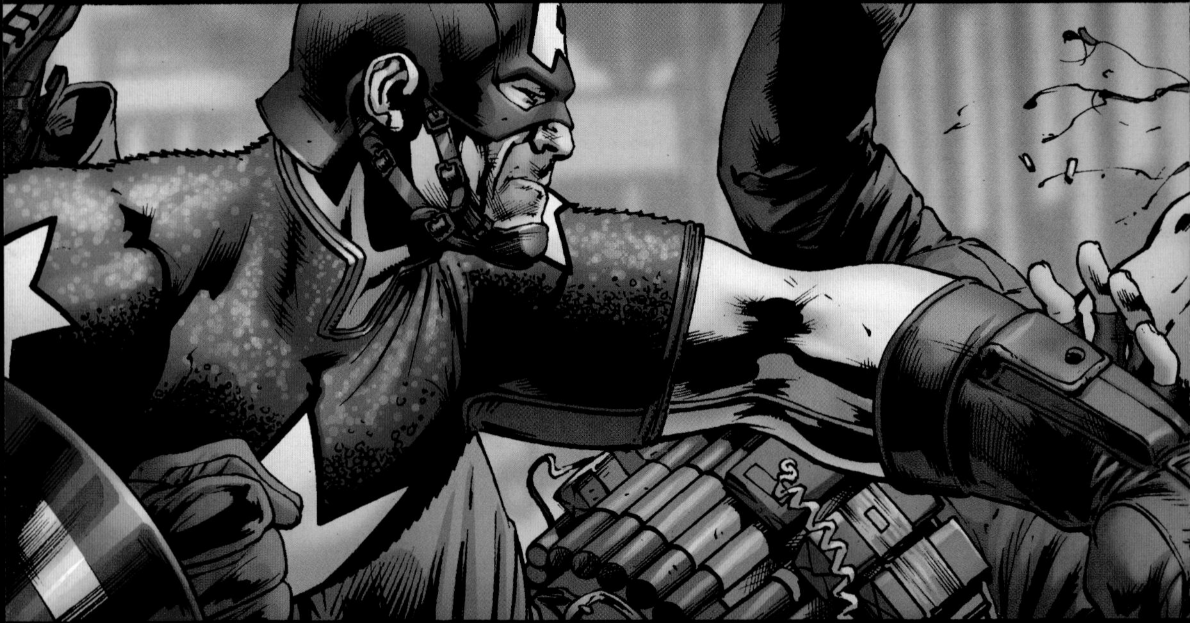

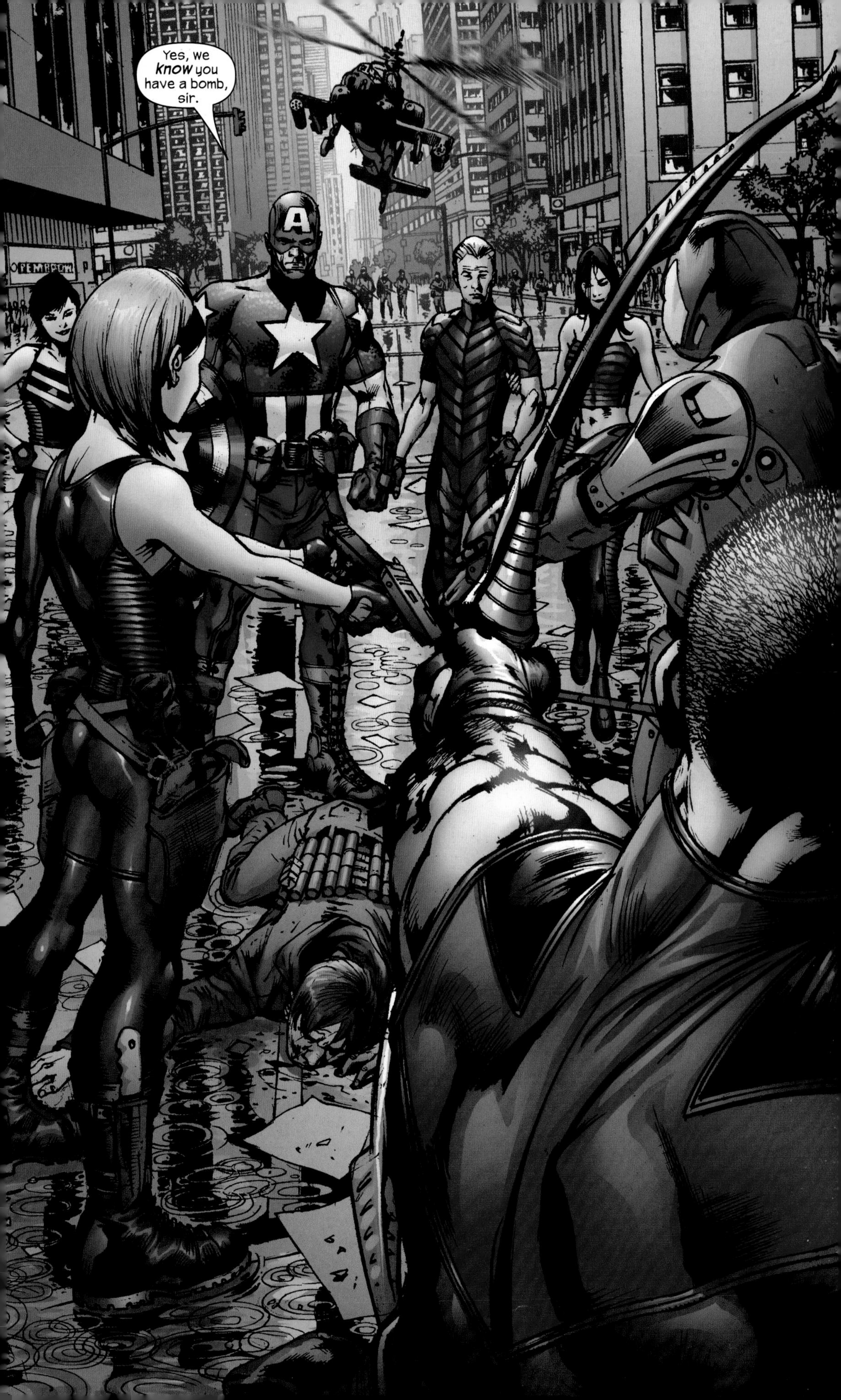
Yes, we KNOW you have a bomb, sir.

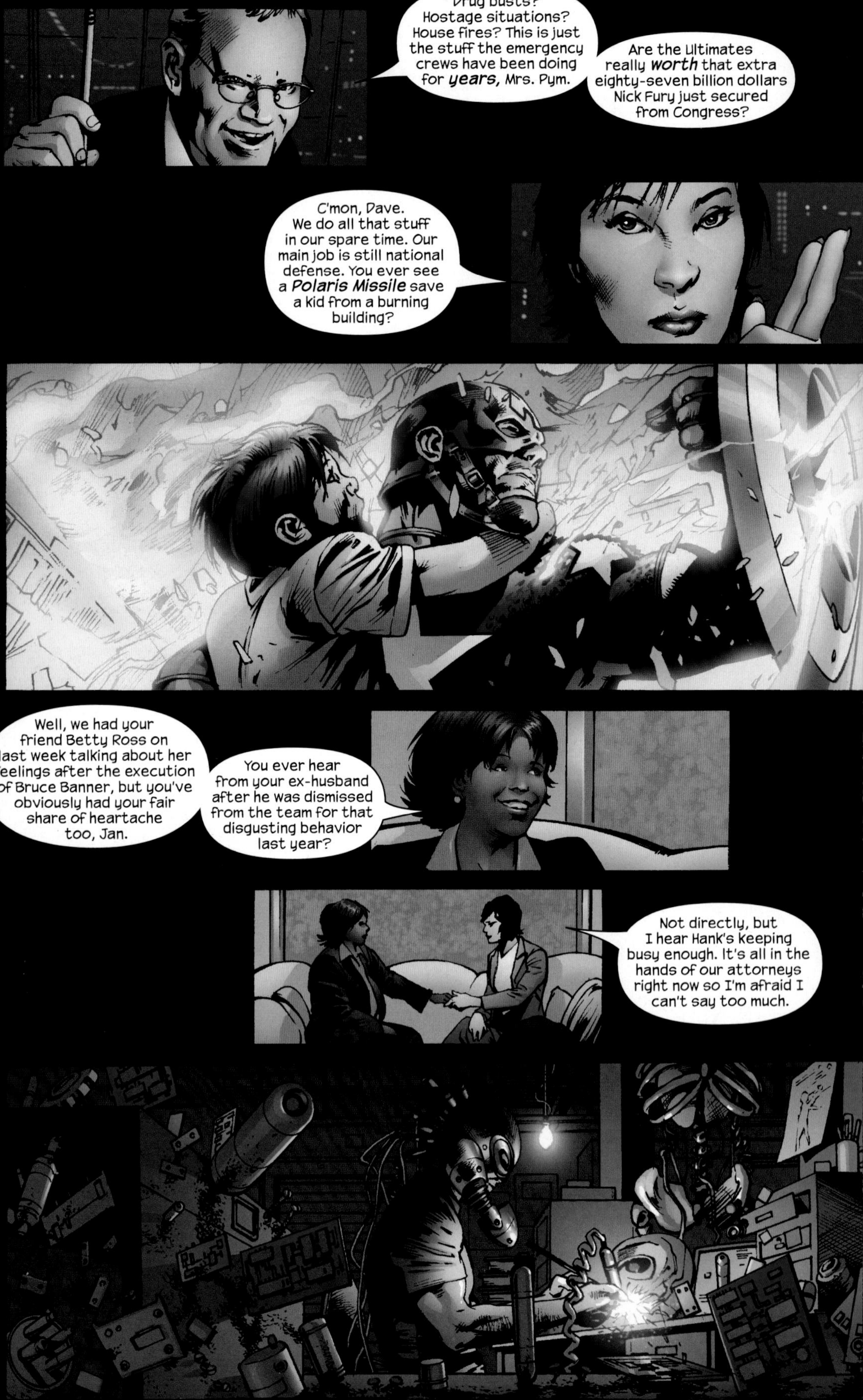

Drug busts? Hostage situations? House fires? This is just the stuff the emergency crews have been doing for *years,* Mrs. Pym.
Are the Ultimates really *worth* that extra eighty-seven billion dollars Nick Fury just secured from Congress?
C'mon, Dave. We do all that stuff in our spare time. Our main job is still national defense. You ever see a *Polaris Missile* save a kid from a burning building?
Well, we had your friend Betty Ross on last week talking about her feelings after the execution of Bruce Banner, but you've obviously had your fair share of heartache too, Jan.
You ever hear from your ex-husband after he was dismissed from the team for that disgusting behavior last year?
Not directly, but I hear Hank's keeping busy enough. It's all in the hands of our attorneys right now so I'm afraid I can't say too much.

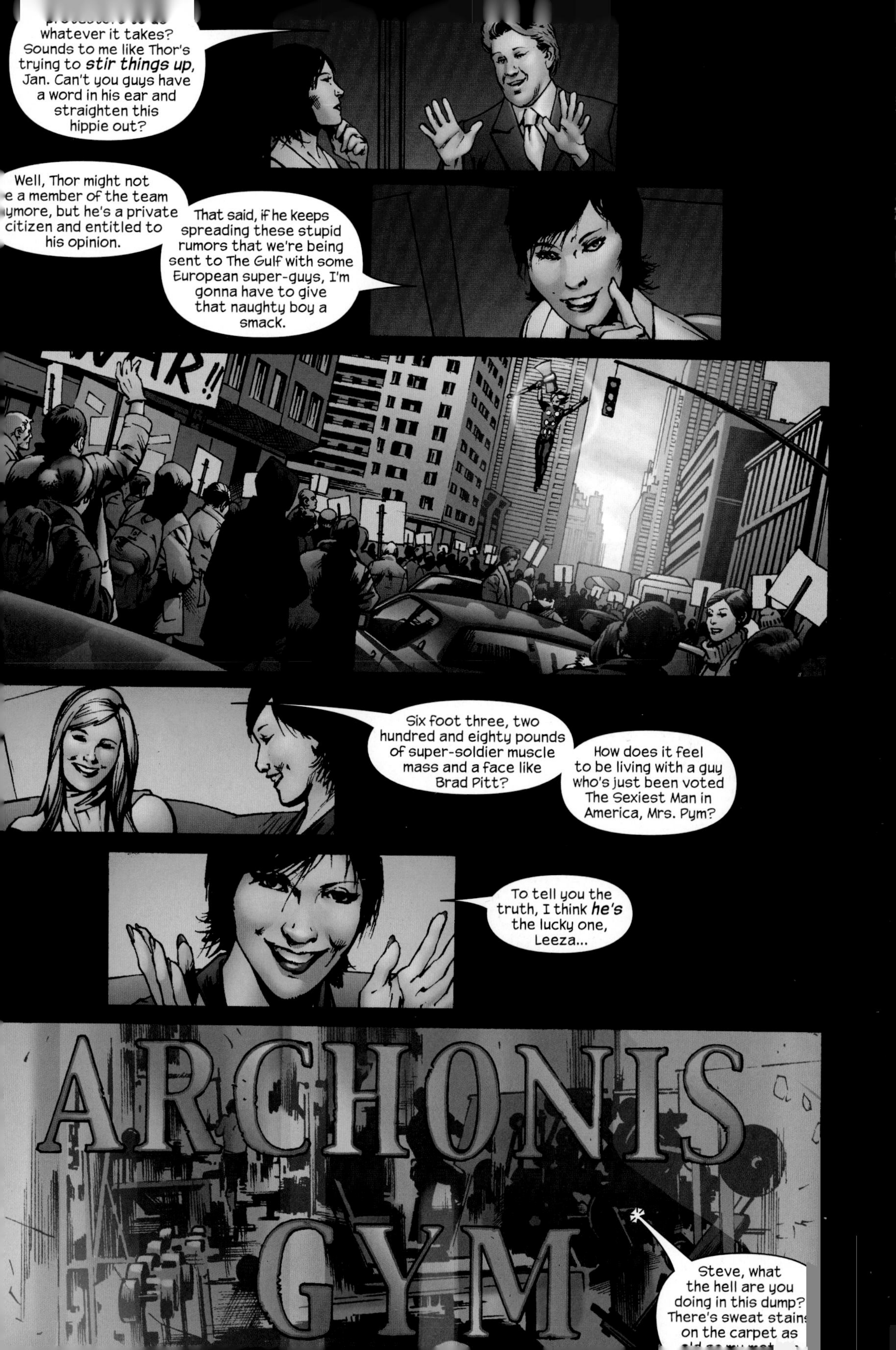
whatever it takes? Sounds to me like Thor's trying to *stir things up*, Jan. Can't you guys have a word in his ear and straighten this hippie out?
Well, Thor might not e a member of the team ymore, but he's a private citizen and entitled to his opinion.
That said, if he keeps spreading these stupid rumors that we're being sent to The Gulf with some European super-guys, I'm gonna have to give that naughty boy a smack.
R!!
Six foot three, two hundred and eighty pounds of super-soldier muscle mass and a face like Brad Pitt?
How does it feel to be living with a guy who's just been voted The Sexiest Man in America, Mrs. Pym?
To tell you the truth, I think *he's* the lucky one, Leeza...
ARCHONIS GYM
Steve, what the hell are you doing in this dump? There's sweat stain on the carpet as

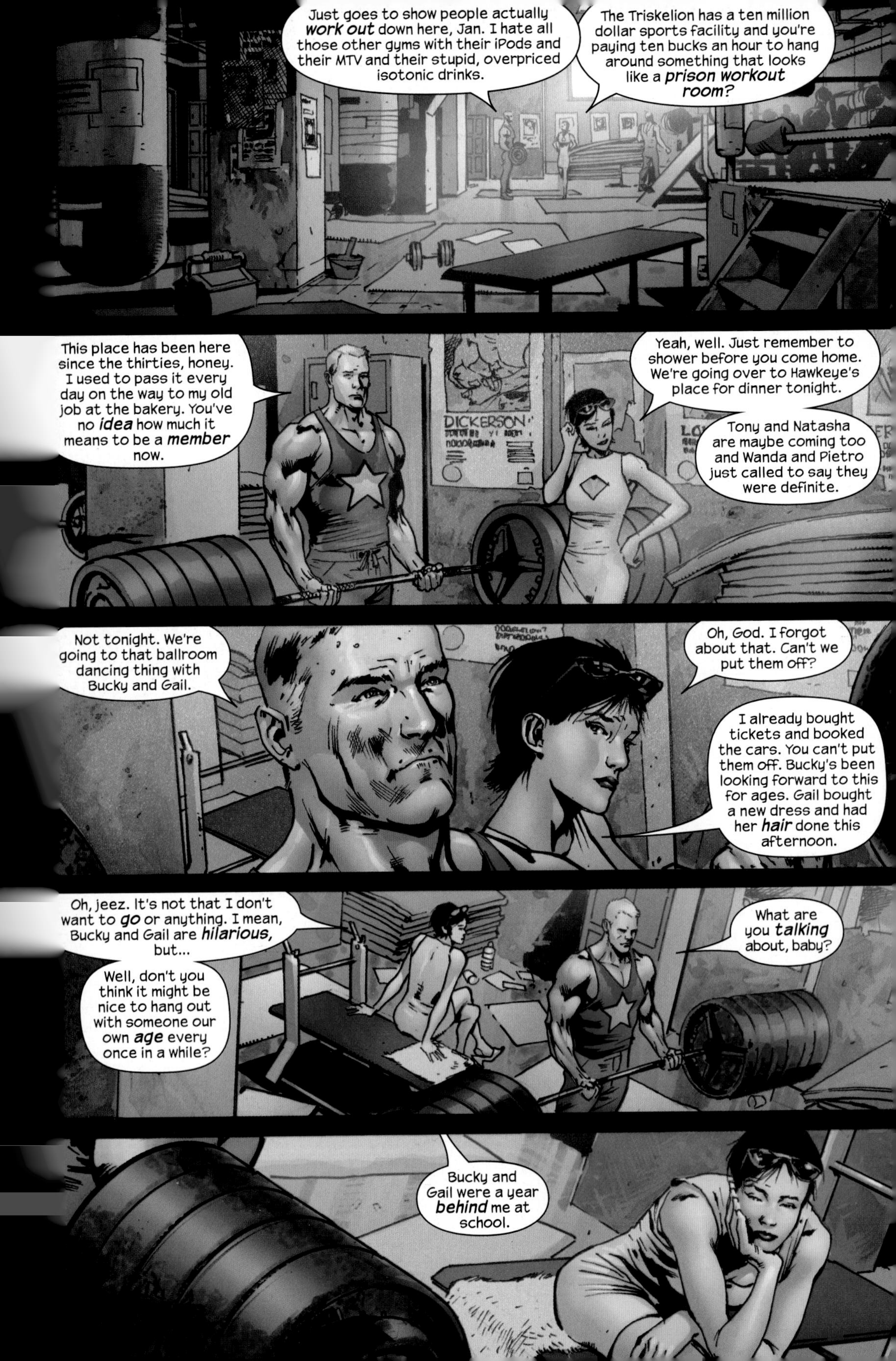
Just goes to show people actually work out down here, Jan. I hate all those other gyms with their iPods and their MTV and their stupid, overpriced isotonic drinks.
The Triskelion has a ten million dollar sports facility and you're paying ten bucks an hour to hang around something that looks like a prison workout room?
This place has been here since the thirties, honey. I used to pass it every day on the way to my old job at the bakery. You've no idea how much it means to be a member now.
Yeah, well. Just remember to shower before you come home. We're going over to Hawkeye's place for dinner tonight.
Tony and Natasha are maybe coming too and Wanda and Pietro just called to say they were definite.
DICKERSON
Not tonight. We're going to that ballroom dancing thing with Bucky and Gail.
Oh, God. I forgot about that. Can't we put them off?
I already bought tickets and booked the cars. You can't put them off. Bucky's been looking forward to this for ages. Gail bought a new dress and had her hair done this afternoon.
Oh, jeez. It's not that I don't want to go or anything. I mean, Bucky and Gail are hilarious, but...
Well, don't you think it might be nice to hang out with someone our own age every once in a while?
What are you talking about, baby?
Bucky and Gail were a year behind me at school.

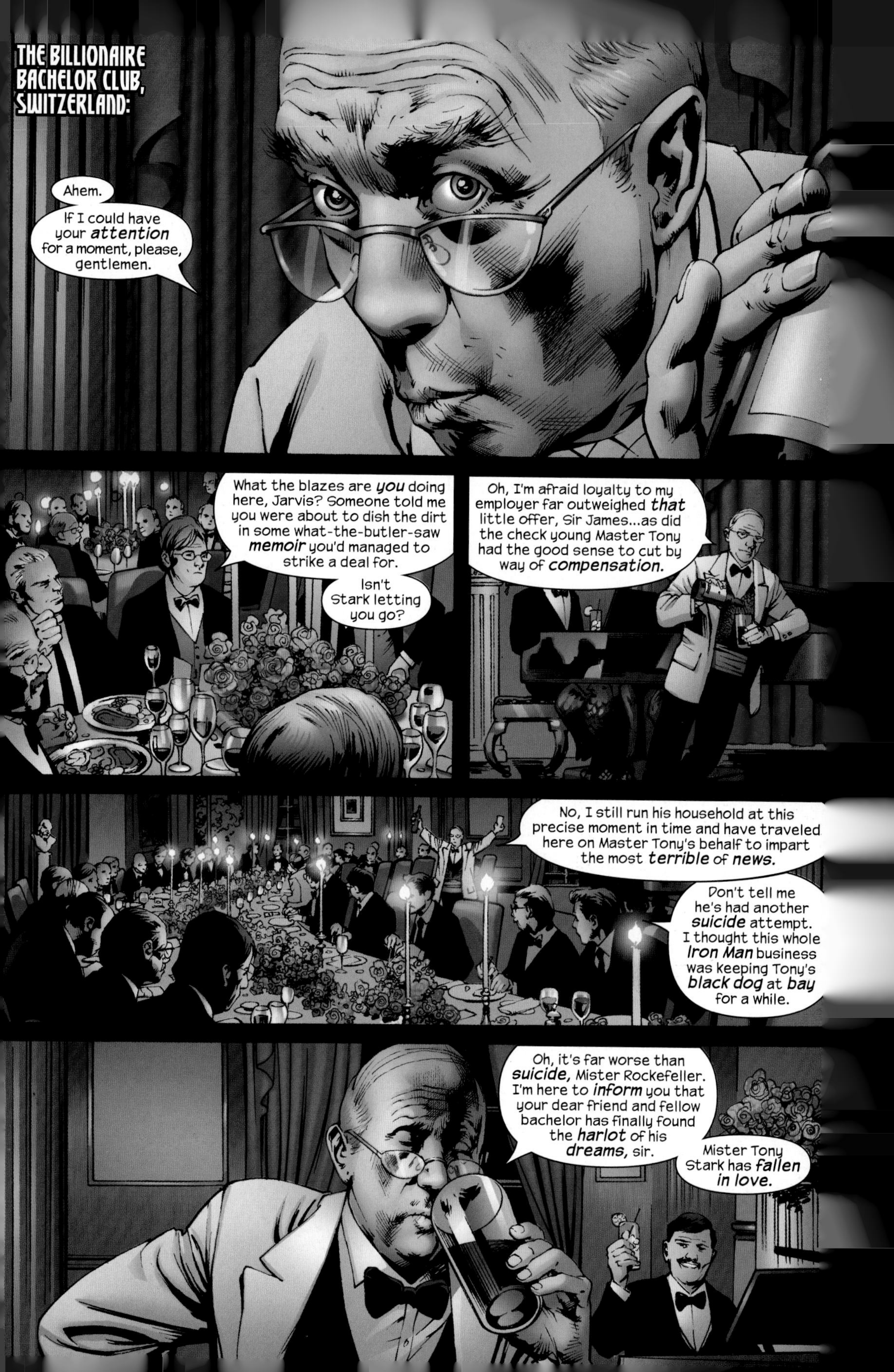
THE BILLIONAIRE BACHELOR CLUB, SWITZERLAND:
Ahem.
If I could have your attention for a moment, please, gentlemen.
What the blazes are you doing here, Jarvis? Someone told me you were about to dish the dirt in some what-the-butler-saw memoir you'd managed to strike a deal for.
Isn't Stark letting you go?
Oh, I'm afraid loyalty to my employer far outweighed that little offer, Sir James...as did the check young Master Tony had the good sense to cut by way of compensation.
No, I still run his household at this precise moment in time and have traveled here on Master Tony's behalf to impart the most terrible of news.
Don't tell me he's had another suicide attempt. I thought this whole Iron Man business was keeping Tony's black dog at bay for a while.
Oh, it's far worse than suicide, Mister Rockefeller. I'm here to inform you that your dear friend and fellow bachelor has finally found the harlot of his dreams, sir.
Mister Tony Stark has fallen in love.

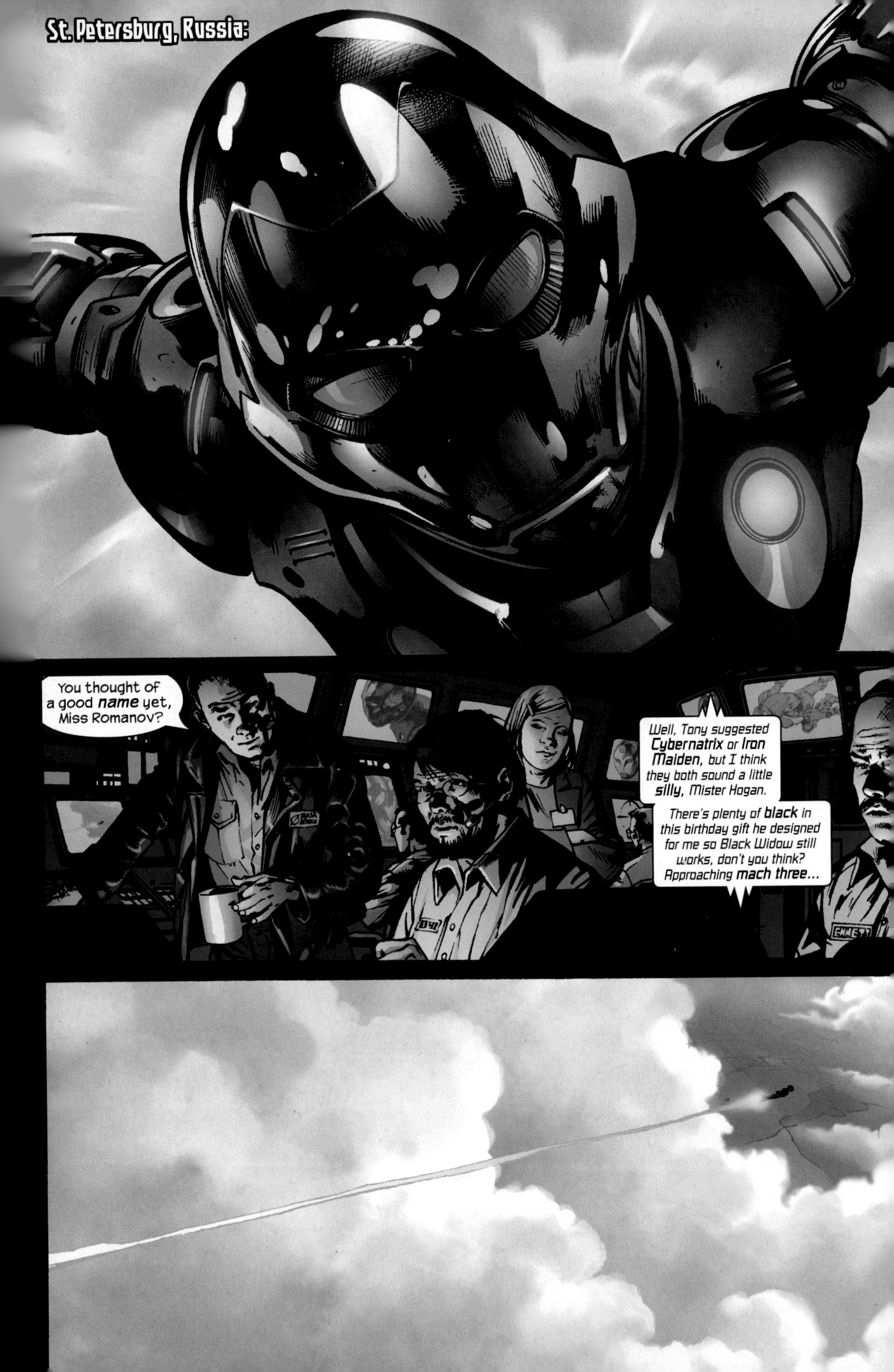
St. Petersburg, Russia:
You thought of a good name yet, Miss Romanov?
Well, Tony suggested Cybernatrix or Iron Maiden, but I think they both sound a little silly, Mister Hogan.
There's plenty of black in this birthday gift he designed for me so Black Widow still works, don't you think? Approaching mach three...

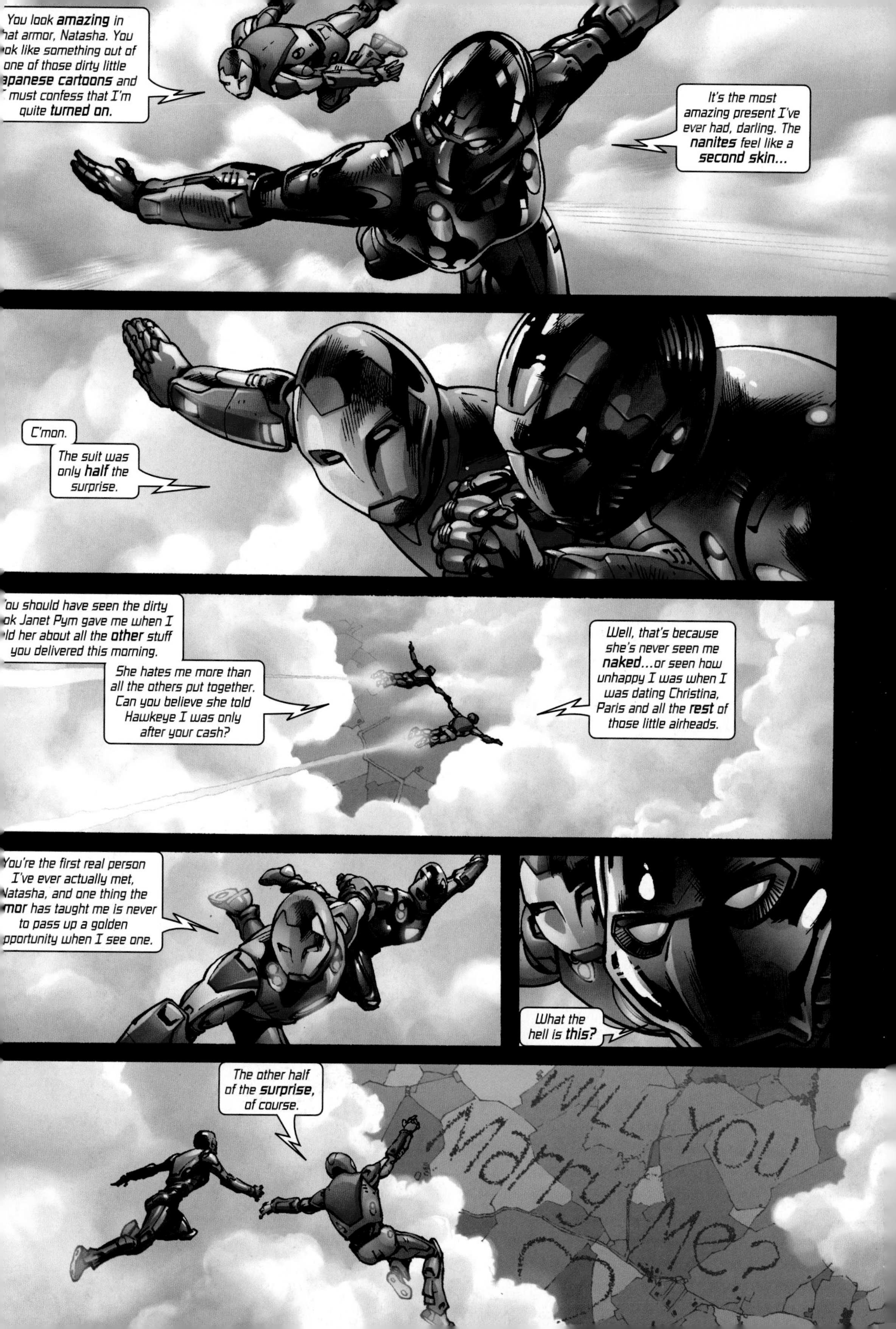

You look **amazing** in hat armor, Natasha. You ok like something out of one of those dirty little apanese cartoons and must confess that I'm quite **turned on.**
It's the most amazing present I've ever had, darling. The **nanites** feel like a **second skin...**
C'mon.
The suit was only **half** the surprise.
ou should have seen the dirty ok Janet Pym gave me when I ld her about all the **other** stuff you delivered this morning.
She hates me more than all the others put together. Can you believe she told Hawkeye I was only after your cash?
Well, that's because she's never seen me **naked**...or seen how unhappy I was when I was dating Christina, Paris and all the **rest** of those little airheads.
You're the first real person I've ever actually met, Natasha, and one thing the mor has taught me is never to pass up a golden pportunity when I see one.
What the hell is **this?**
The other half of the **surprise,** of course.
WILL YOU Marry Me?

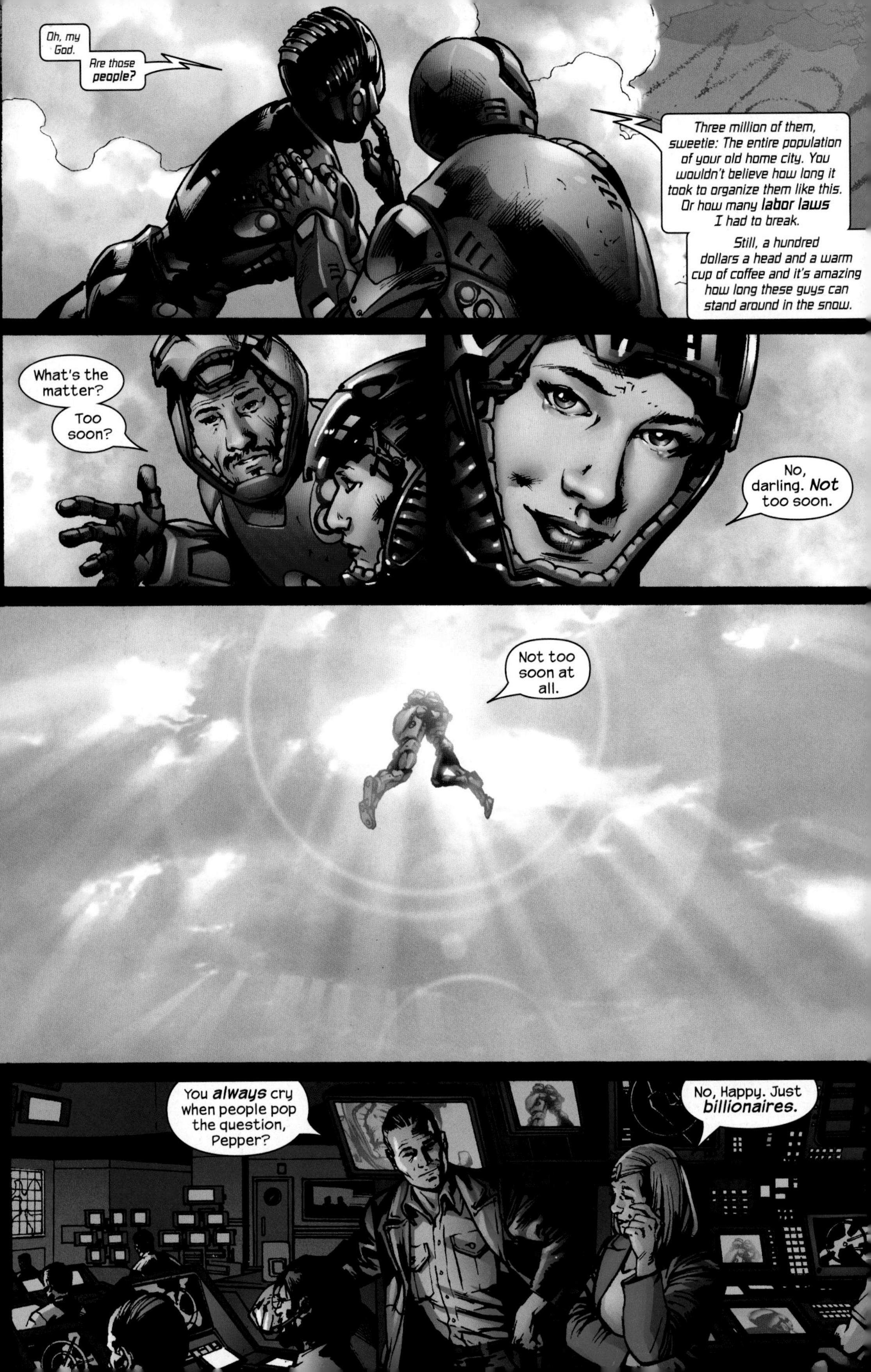
Oh, my God.
Are those people?
Three million of them, sweetie: The entire population of your old home city. You wouldn't believe how long it took to organize them like this. Or how many labor laws I had to break.
Still, a hundred dollars a head and a warm cup of coffee and it's amazing how long these guys can stand around in the snow.
What's the matter?
Too soon?
No, darling. Not too soon.
Not too soon at all.
You always cry when people pop the question, Pepper?
No, Happy. Just billionaires.

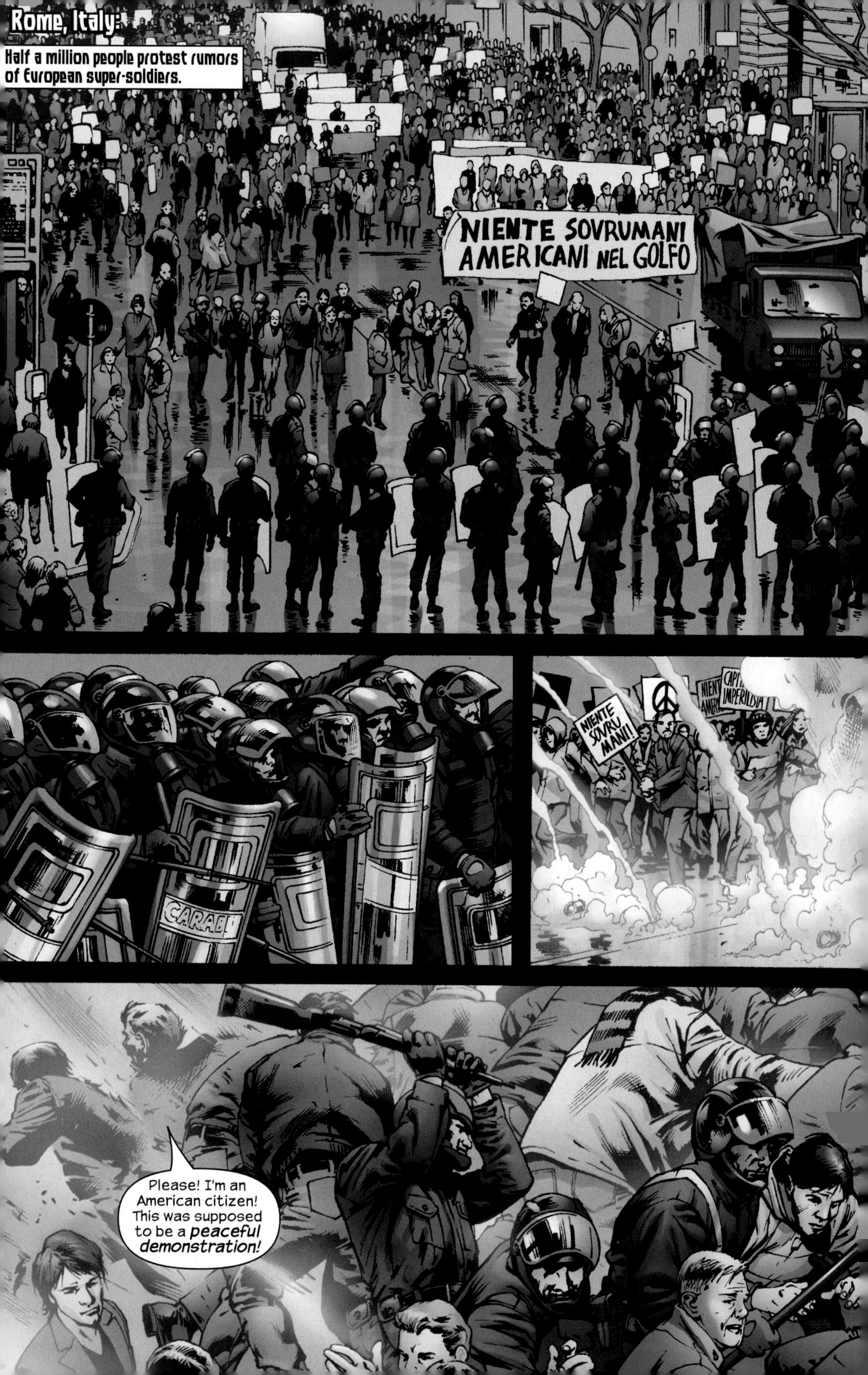

Rome, Italy:
Half a million people protest rumors of European super-soldiers.
NIENTE SOVRUMANI AMERICANI NEL GOLFO
NIENTE SOVRUMANI!
Please! I'm an American citizen! This was supposed to be a *peaceful demonstration!*

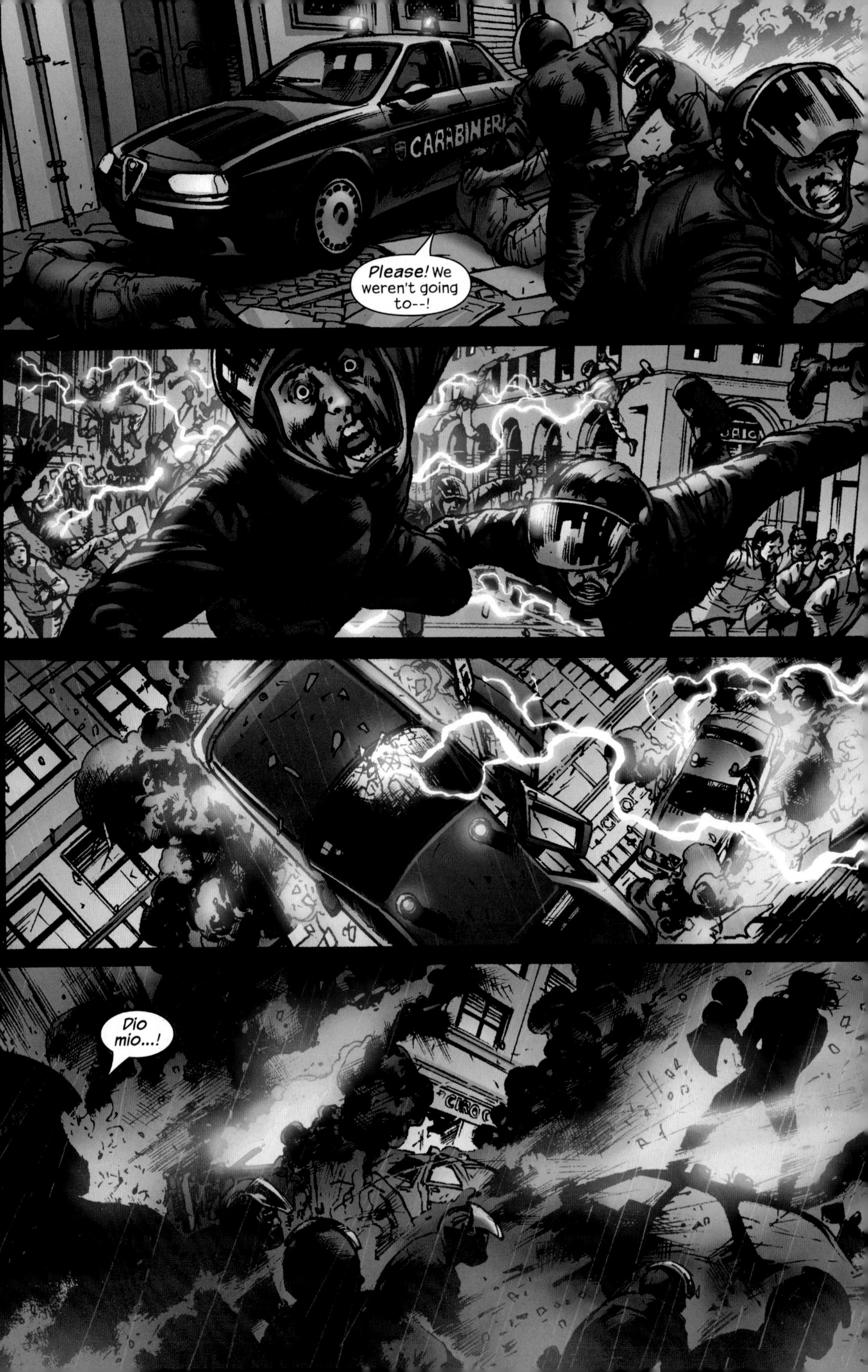
CARABINIERI
Please! We weren't going to--!
Dio mio...!

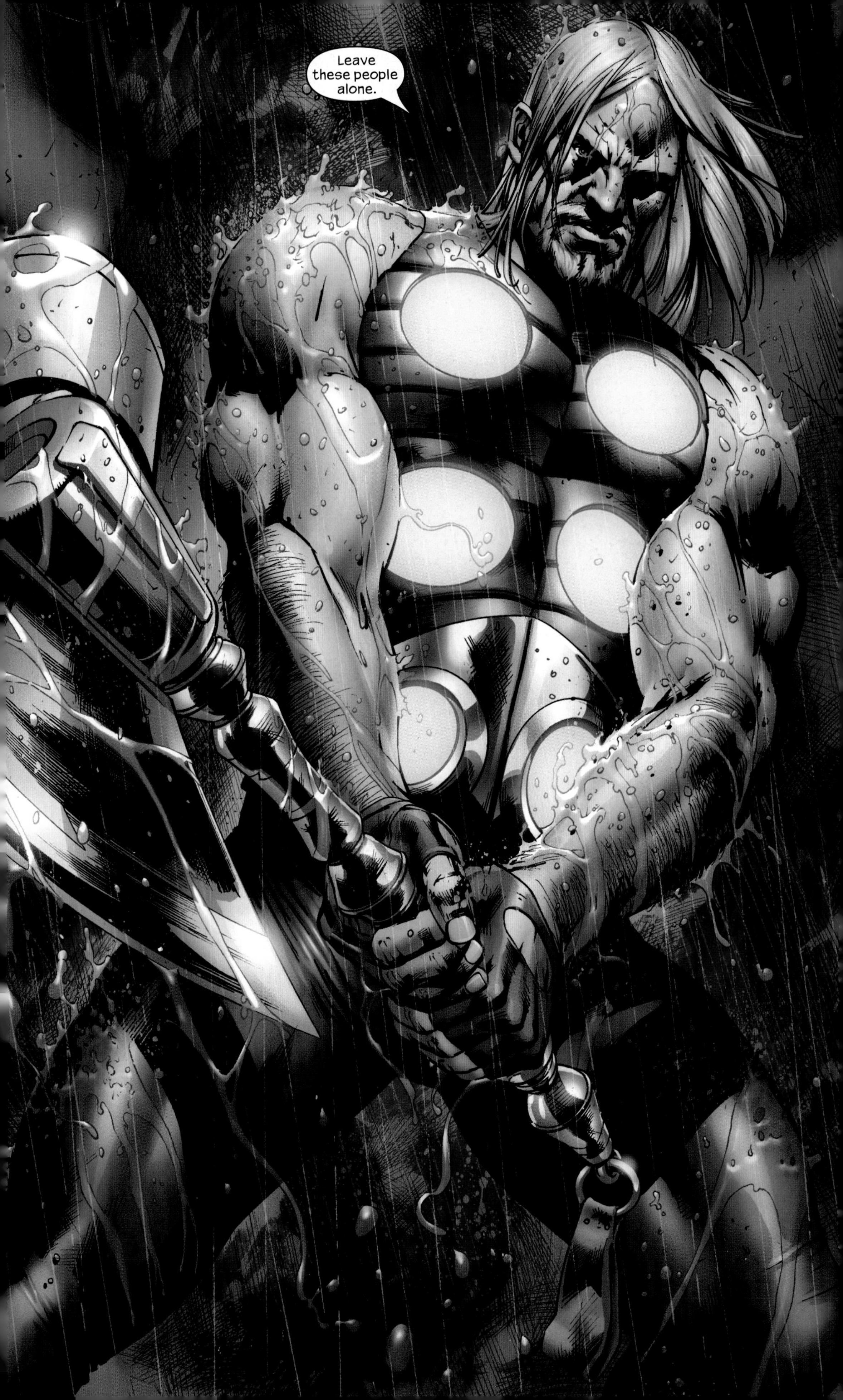
Leave these people alone.

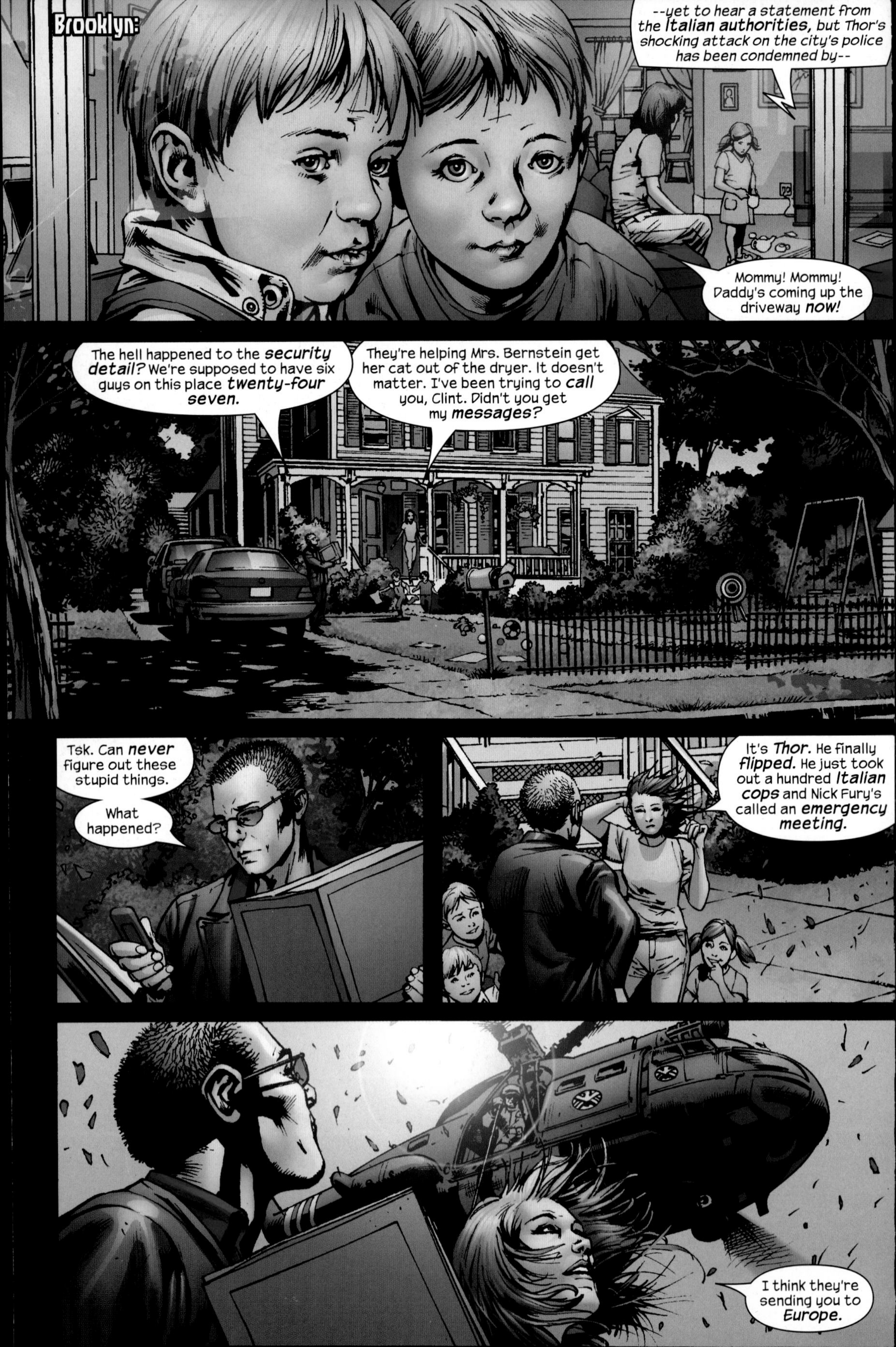
Brooklyn:
--yet to hear a statement from the Italian authorities, but Thor's shocking attack on the city's police has been condemned by--
Mommy! Mommy! Daddy's coming up the driveway now!
The hell happened to the security detail? We're supposed to have six guys on this place twenty-four seven.
They're helping Mrs. Bernstein get her cat out of the dryer. It doesn't matter. I've been trying to call you, Clint. Didn't you get my messages?
Tsk. Can never figure out these stupid things.
What happened?
It's Thor. He finally flipped. He just took out a hundred Italian cops and Nick Fury's called an emergency meeting.
I think they're sending you to Europe.

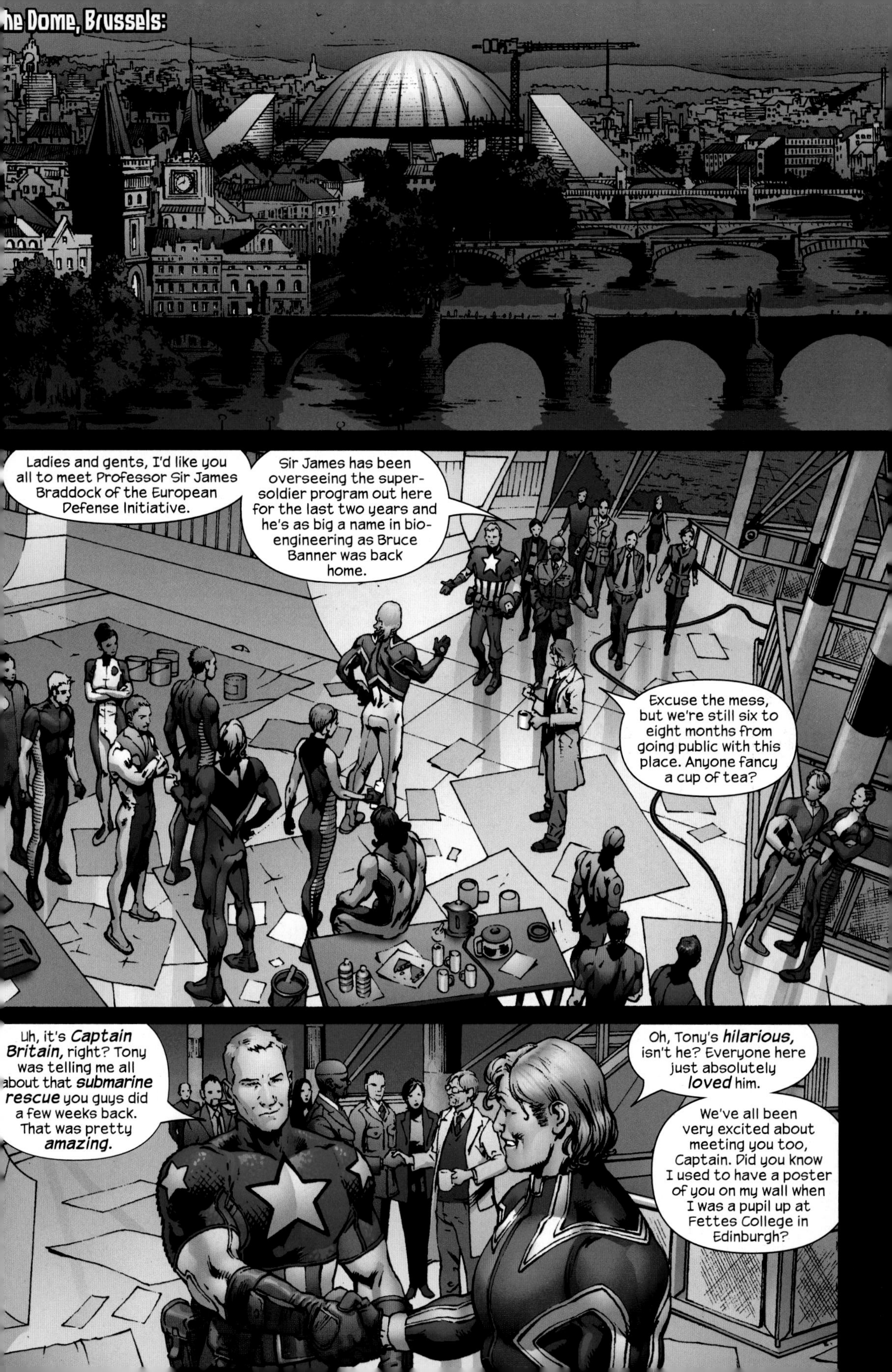
he Dome, Brussels:
Ladies and gents, I'd like you all to meet Professor Sir James Braddock of the European Defense Initiative.
Sir James has been overseeing the super-soldier program out here for the last two years and he's as big a name in bio-engineering as Bruce Banner was back home.
Excuse the mess, but we're still six to eight months from going public with this place. Anyone fancy a cup of tea?
Uh, it's *Captain Britain,* right? Tony was telling me all about that *submarine rescue* you guys did a few weeks back. That was pretty *amazing.*
Oh, Tony's *hilarious,* isn't he? Everyone here just absolutely *loved* him.
We've all been very excited about meeting you too, Captain. Did you know I used to have a poster of you on my wall when I was a pupil up at Fettes College in Edinburgh?

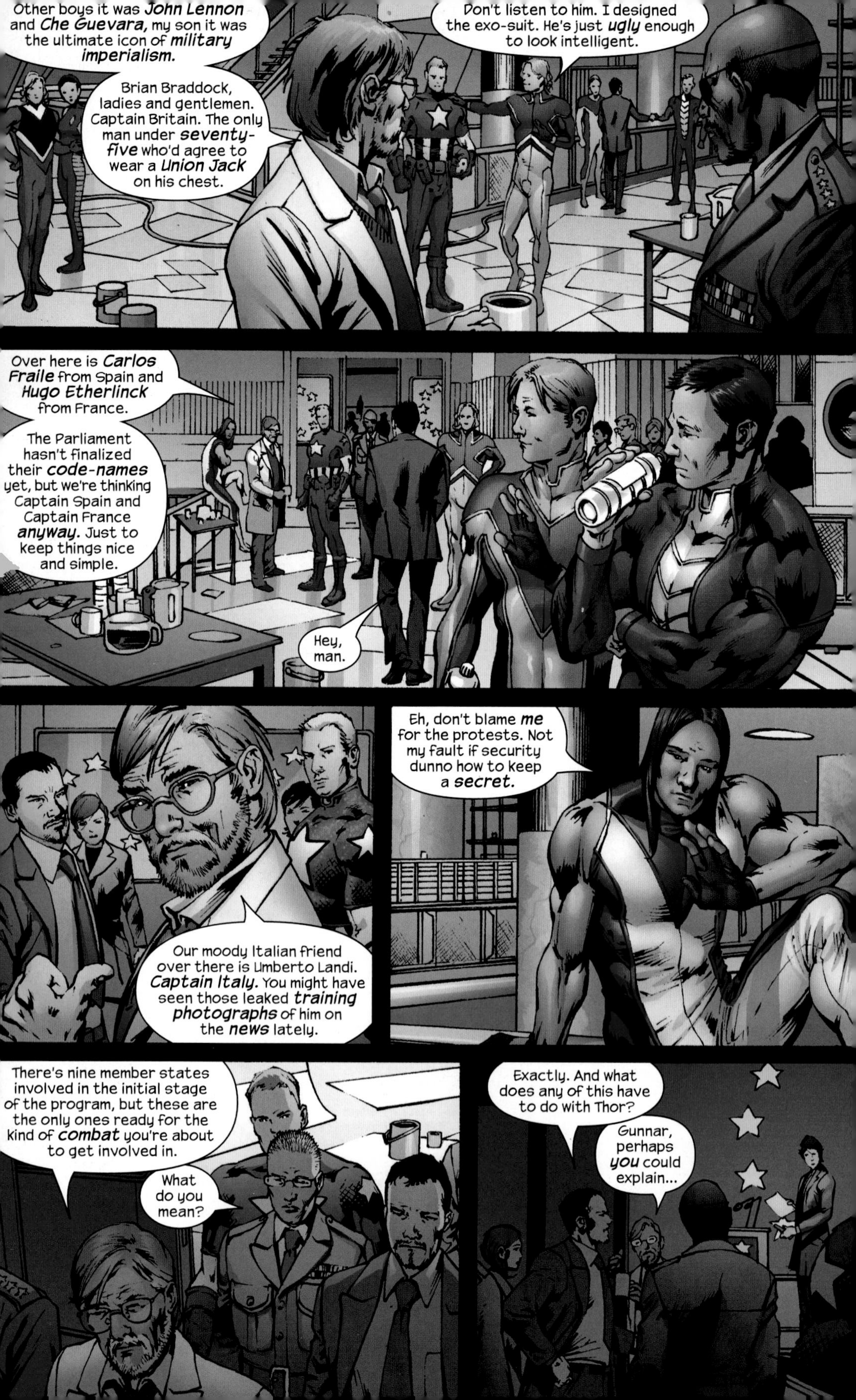
Other boys it was John Lennon and Che Guevara, my son it was the ultimate icon of military imperialism.
Don't listen to him. I designed the exo-suit. He's just ugly enough to look intelligent.
Brian Braddock, ladies and gentlemen. Captain Britain. The only man under seventy-five who'd agree to wear a Union Jack on his chest.
Over here is Carlos Fraile from Spain and Hugo Etherlinck from France.
The Parliament hasn't finalized their code-names yet, but we're thinking Captain Spain and Captain France anyway. Just to keep things nice and simple.
Hey, man.
Our moody Italian friend over there is Umberto Landi. Captain Italy. You might have seen those leaked training photographs of him on the news lately.
Eh, don't blame me for the protests. Not my fault if security dunno how to keep a secret.
There's nine member states involved in the initial stage of the program, but these are the only ones ready for the kind of combat you're about to get involved in.
What do you mean?
Exactly. And what does any of this have to do with Thor?
Gunnar, perhaps you could explain...

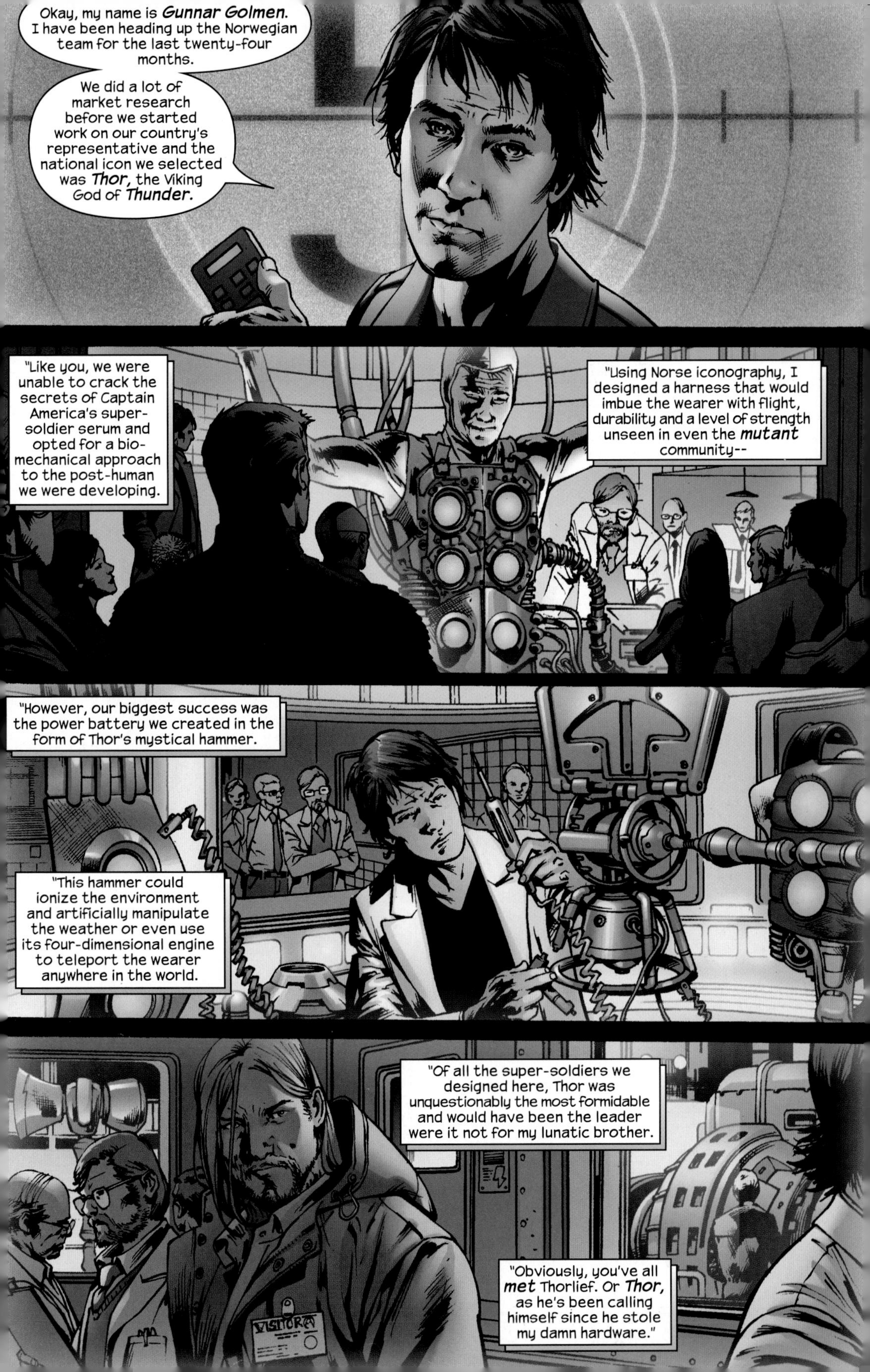
Okay, my name is *Gunnar Golmen.* I have been heading up the Norwegian team for the last twenty-four months.
We did a lot of market research before we started work on our country's representative and the national icon we selected was *Thor,* the Viking God of *Thunder.*
"Like you, we were unable to crack the secrets of Captain America's super-soldier serum and opted for a bio-mechanical approach to the post-human we were developing.
"Using Norse iconography, I designed a harness that would imbue the wearer with flight, durability and a level of strength unseen in even the *mutant* community--
"However, our biggest success was the power battery we created in the form of Thor's mystical hammer.
"This hammer could ionize the environment and artificially manipulate the weather or even use its four-dimensional engine to teleport the wearer anywhere in the world.
VISITOR
"Of all the super-soldiers we designed here, Thor was unquestionably the most formidable and would have been the leader were it not for my lunatic brother.
"Obviously, you've all *met* Thorlief. Or *Thor,* as he's been calling himself since he stole my damn hardware."

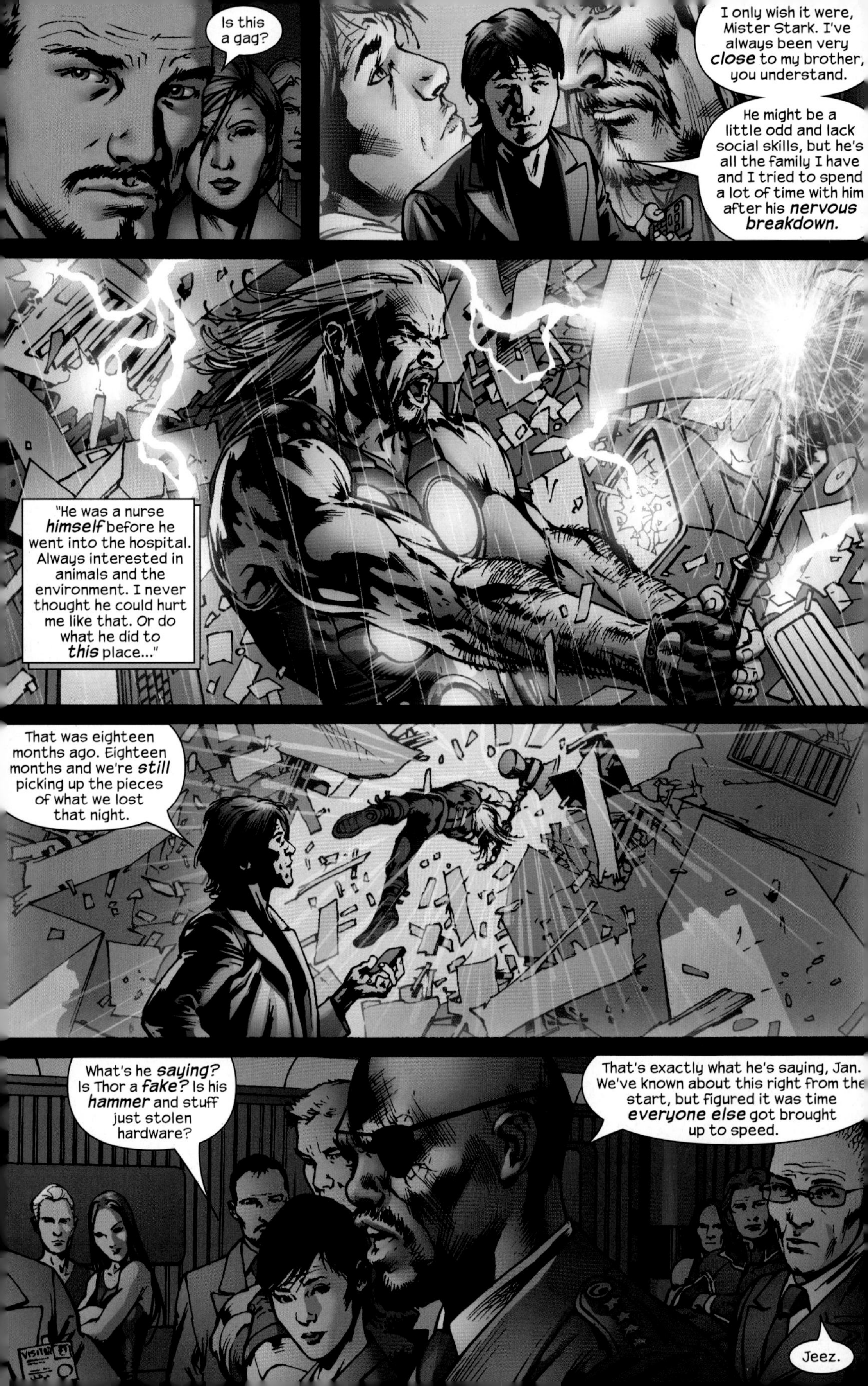
Is this a gag?
I only wish it were, Mister Stark. I've always been very close to my brother, you understand.
He might be a little odd and lack social skills, but he's all the family I have and I tried to spend a lot of time with him after his nervous breakdown.
"He was a nurse himself before he went into the hospital. Always interested in animals and the environment. I never thought he could hurt me like that. Or do what he did to this place..."
That was eighteen months ago. Eighteen months and we're still picking up the pieces of what we lost that night.
What's he saying? Is Thor a fake? Is his hammer and stuff just stolen hardware?
That's exactly what he's saying, Jan. We've known about this right from the start, but figured it was time everyone else got brought up to speed.
Jeez.

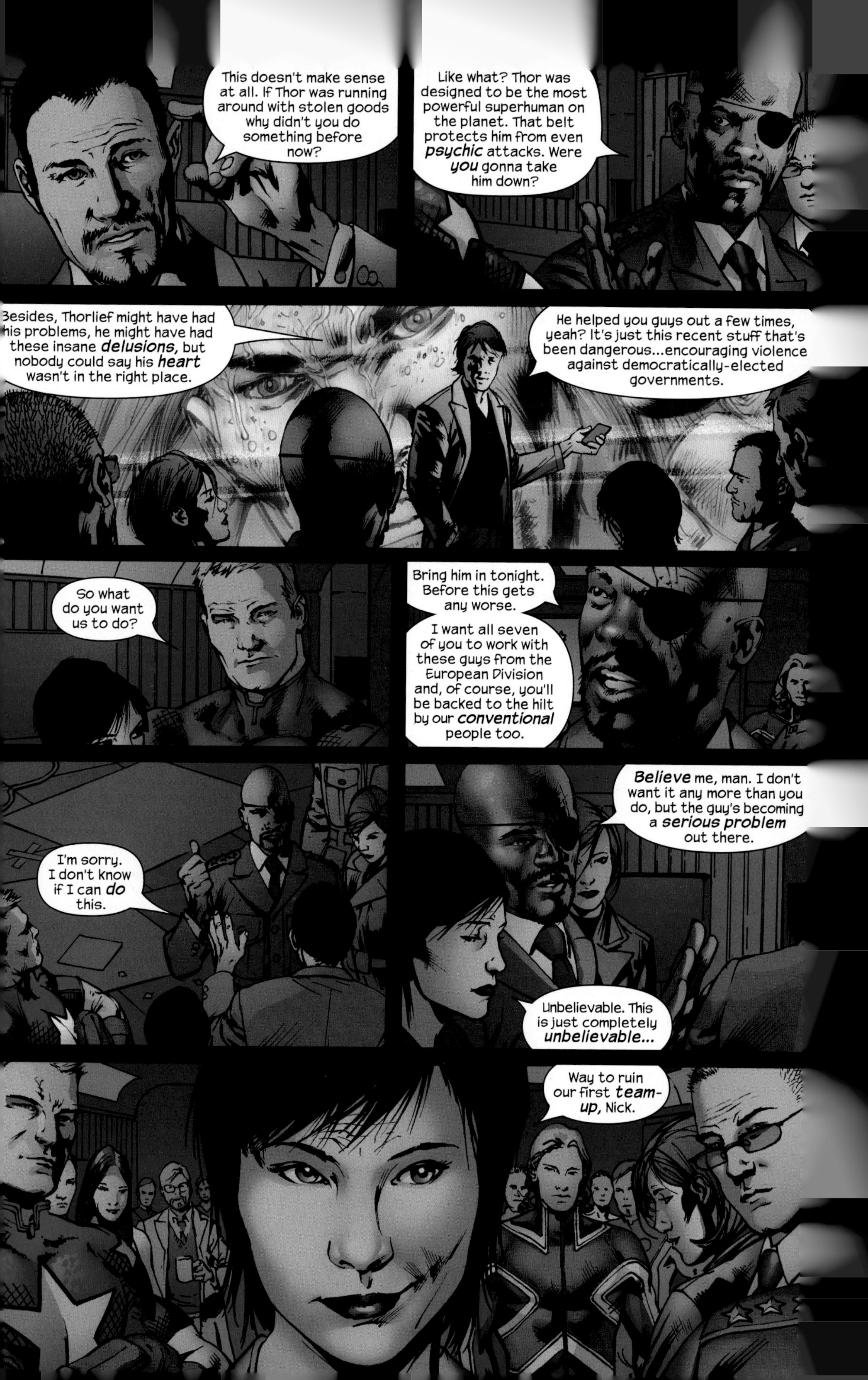
This doesn't make sense at all. If Thor was running around with stolen goods why didn't you do something before now?
Like what? Thor was designed to be the most powerful superhuman on the planet. That belt protects him from even psychic attacks. Were you gonna take him down?
Besides, Thorlief might have had his problems, he might have had these insane delusions, but nobody could say his heart wasn't in the right place.
He helped you guys out a few times, yeah? It's just this recent stuff that's been dangerous...encouraging violence against democratically-elected governments.
So what do you want us to do?
Bring him in tonight. Before this gets any worse.
I want all seven of you to work with these guys from the European Division and, of course, you'll be backed to the hilt by our conventional people too.
I'm sorry. I don't know if I can do this.
Believe me, man. I don't want it any more than you do, but the guy's becoming a serious problem out there.
Unbelievable. This is just completely unbelievable...
Way to ruin our first team-up, Nick.

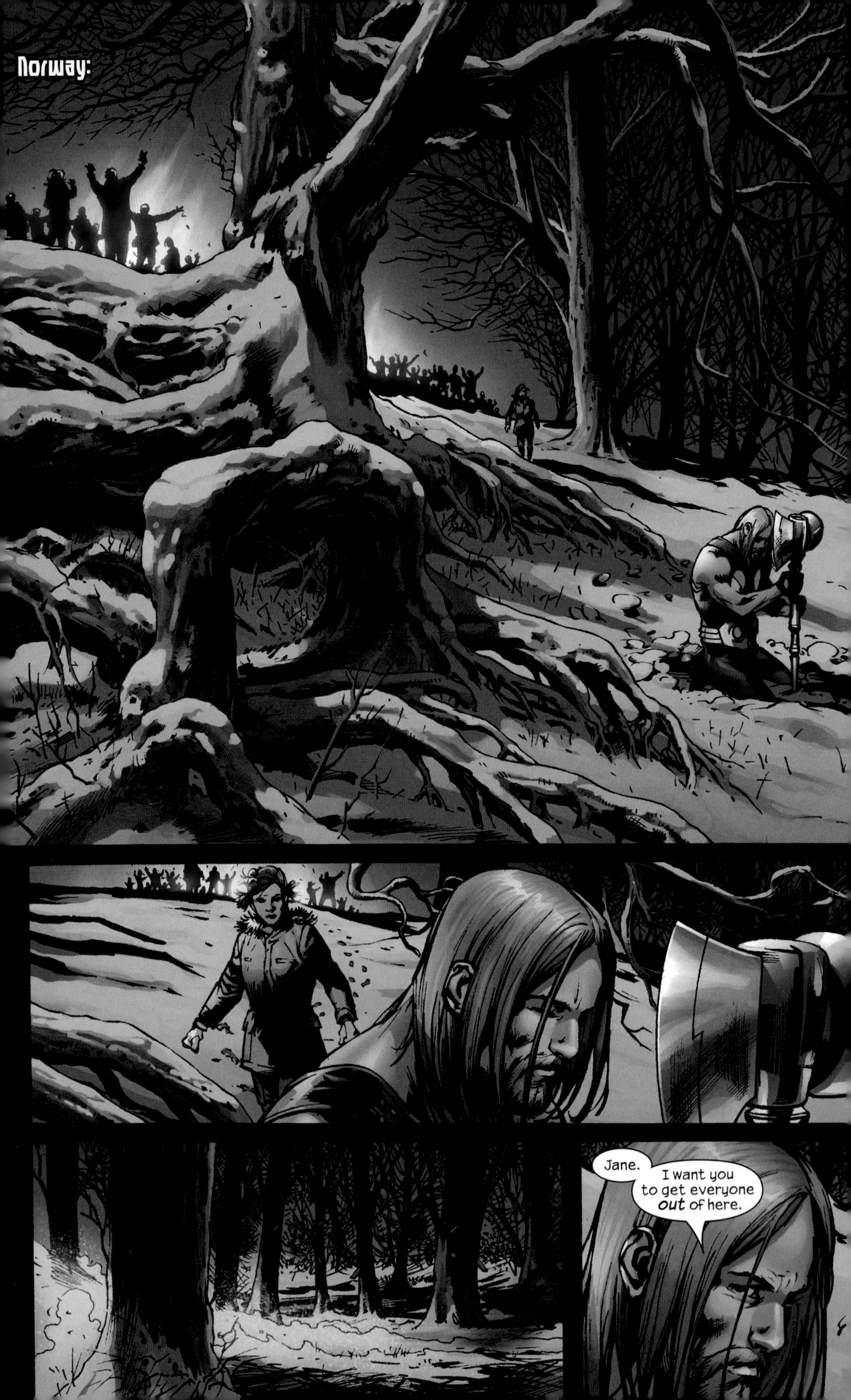
Norway:
Jane.
I want you to get everyone out of here.

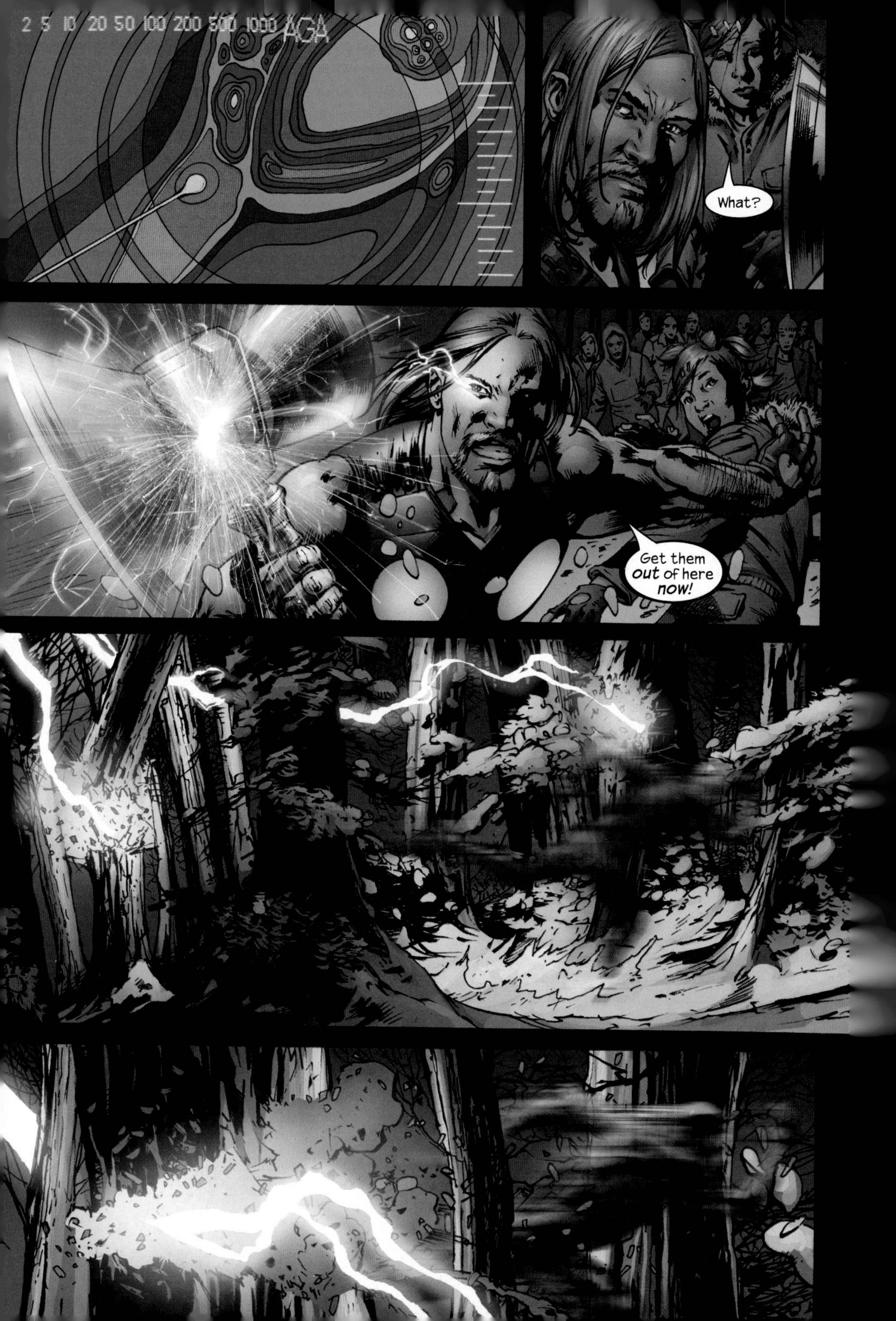
2 5 10 20 50 100 200 500 1000 AGA
What?
Get them out of here now!

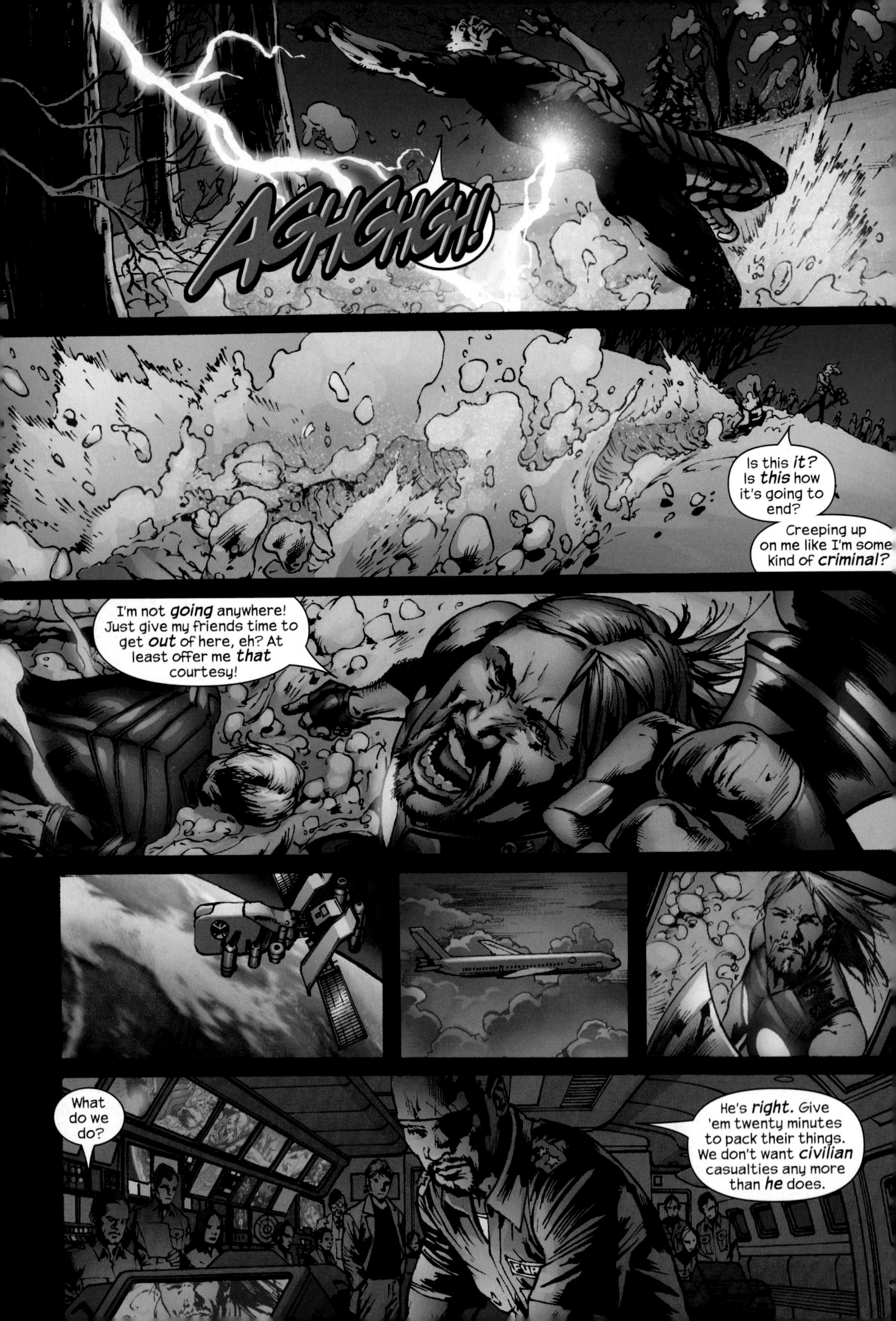
AGHGHGH!
Is this it? Is this how it's going to end?
Creeping up on me like I'm some kind of criminal?
I'm not going anywhere! Just give my friends time to get out of here, eh? At least offer me that courtesy!
What do we do?
He's right. Give 'em twenty minutes to pack their things. We don't want civilian casualties any more than he does.

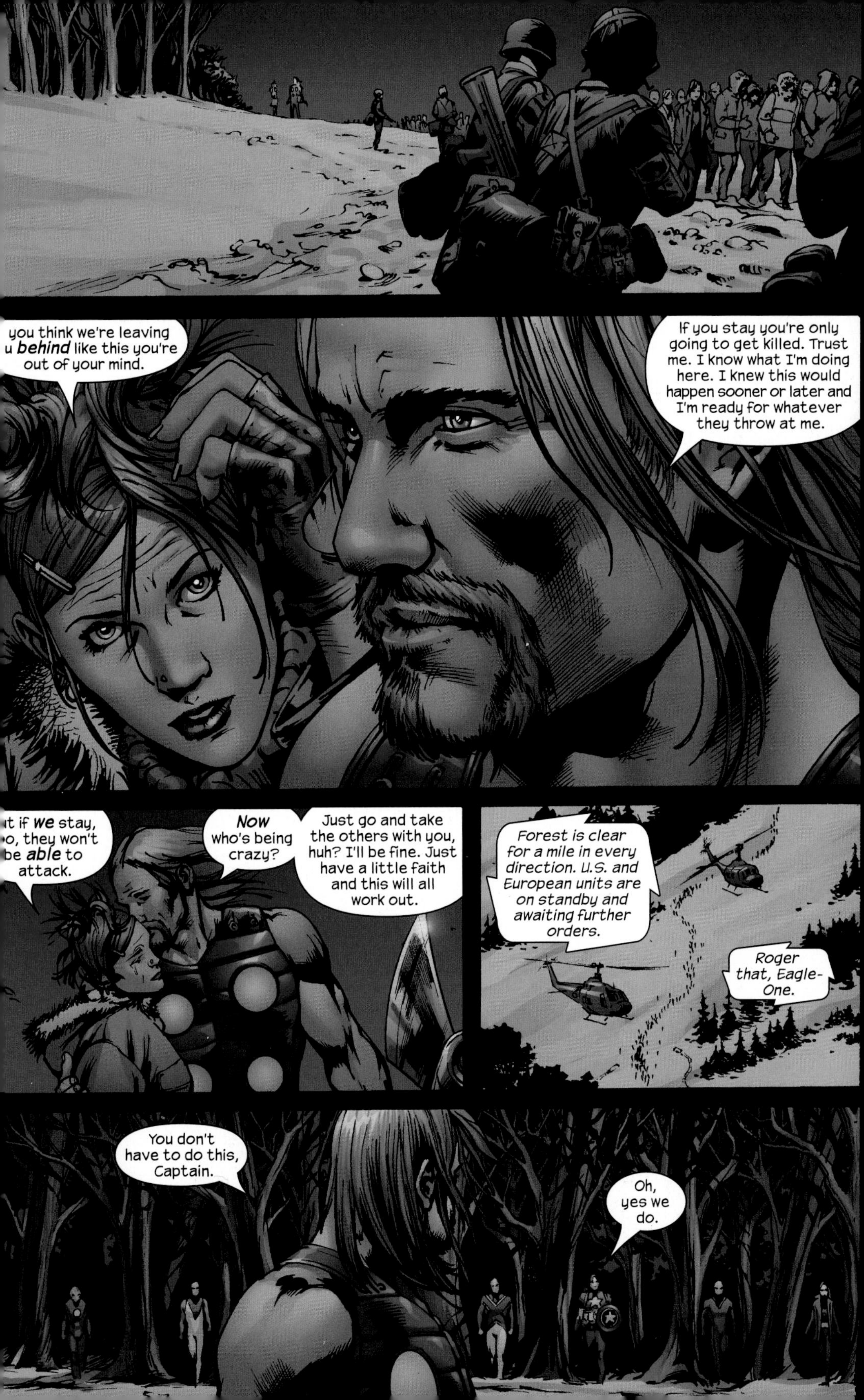
you think we're leaving u behind like this you're out of your mind.
If you stay you're only going to get killed. Trust me. I know what I'm doing here. I knew this would happen sooner or later and I'm ready for whatever they throw at me.
it if we stay, o, they won't be able to attack.
Now who's being crazy?
Just go and take the others with you, huh? I'll be fine. Just have a little faith and this will all work out.
Forest is clear for a mile in every direction. U.S. and European units are on standby and awaiting further orders.
Roger that, Eagle-One.
You don't have to do this, Captain.
Oh, yes we do.

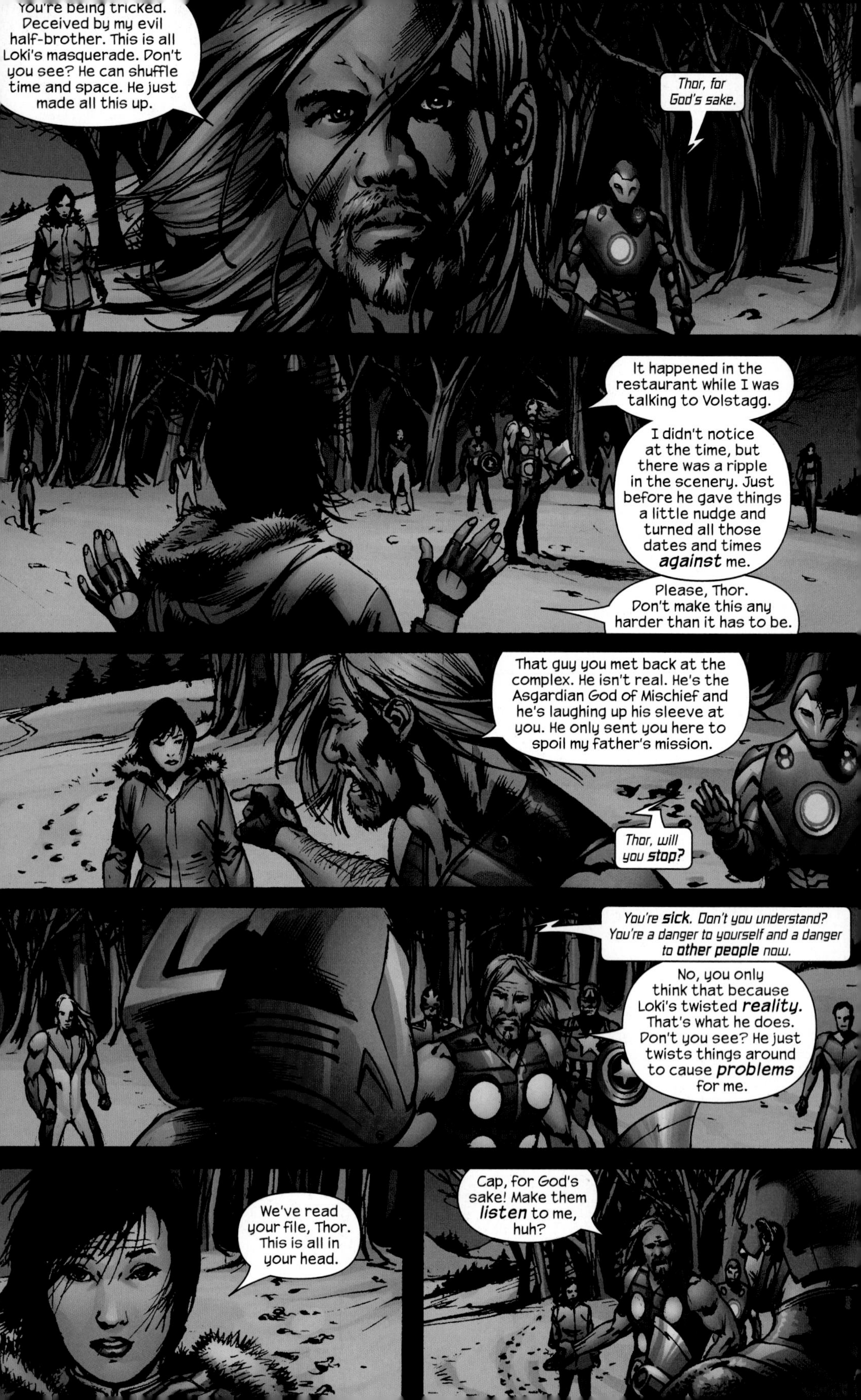
You're being tricked. Deceived by my evil half-brother. This is all Loki's masquerade. Don't you see? He can shuffle time and space. He just made all this up.
Thor, for God's sake.
It happened in the restaurant while I was talking to Volstagg.
I didn't notice at the time, but there was a ripple in the scenery. Just before he gave things a little nudge and turned all those dates and times against me.
Please, Thor. Don't make this any harder than it has to be.
That guy you met back at the complex. He isn't real. He's the Asgardian God of Mischief and he's laughing up his sleeve at you. He only sent you here to spoil my father's mission.
Thor, will you stop?
You're sick. Don't you understand? You're a danger to yourself and a danger to other people now.
No, you only think that because Loki's twisted reality. That's what he does. Don't you see? He just twists things around to cause problems for me.
We've read your file, Thor. This is all in your head.
Cap, for God's sake! Make them listen to me, huh?

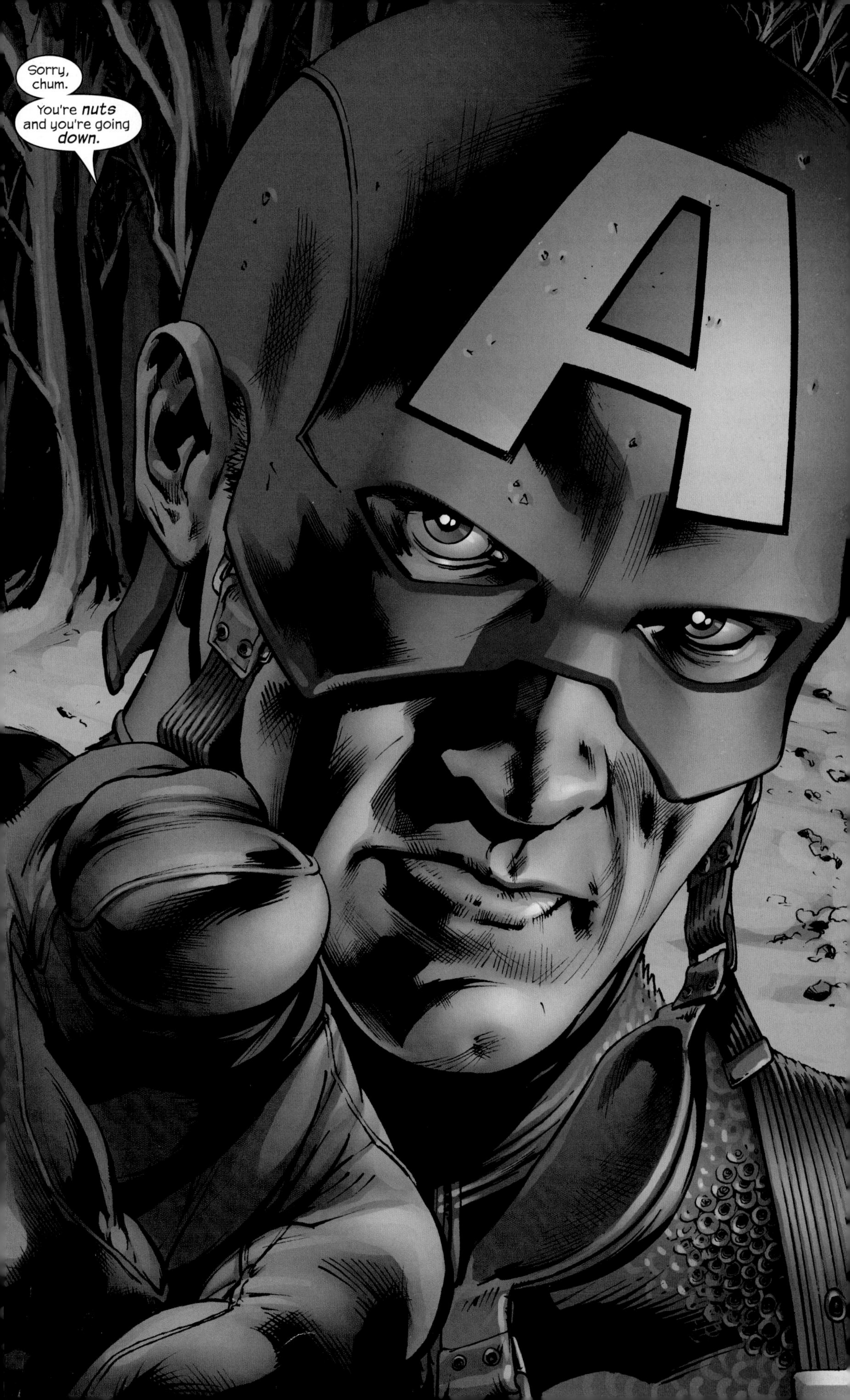
Sorry, chum.
You're **nuts** and you're going **down**.

THE PASSION

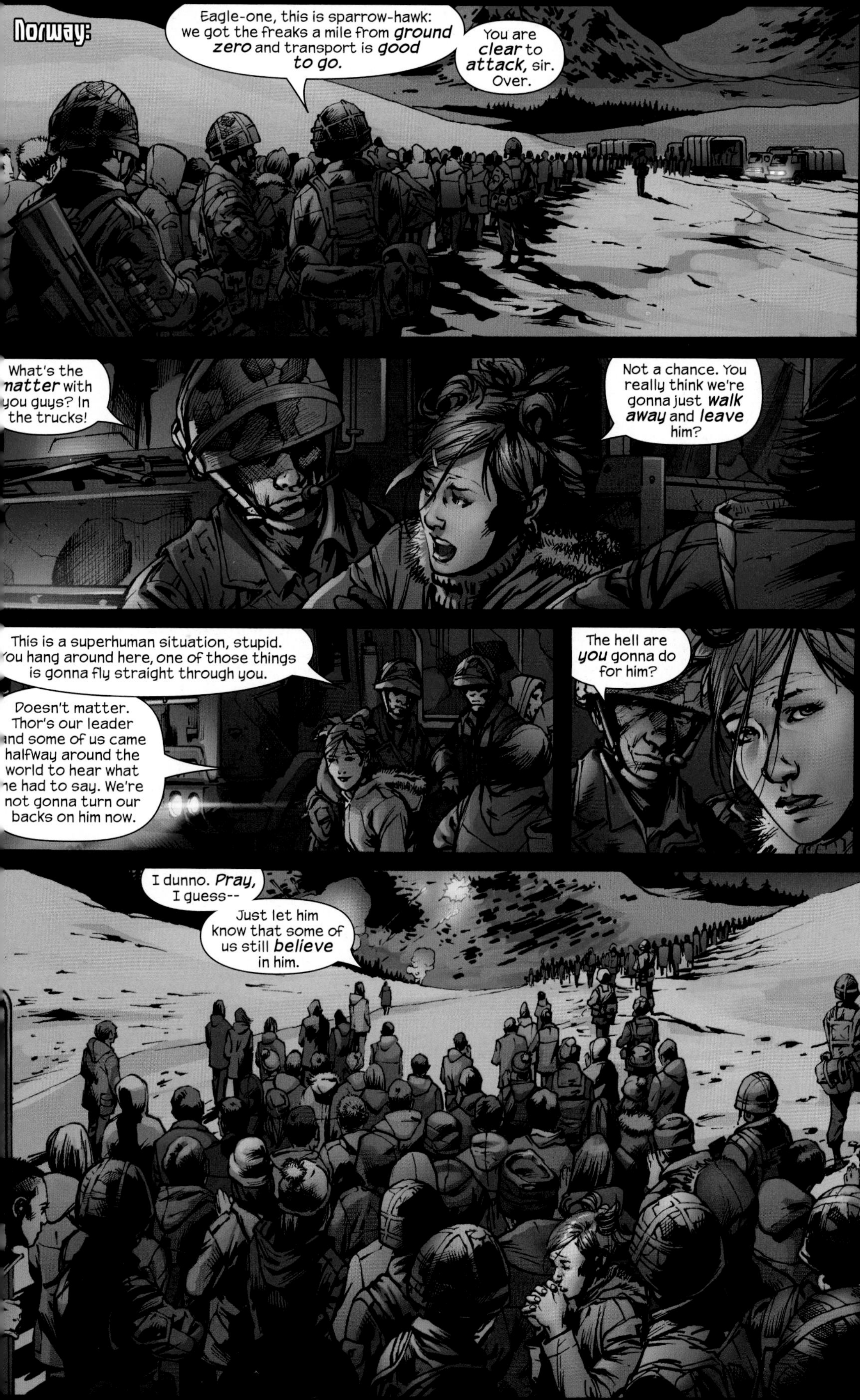
Norway:
Eagle-one, this is sparrow-hawk: we got the freaks a mile from ground zero and transport is good to go.
You are clear to attack, sir. Over.
What's the matter with you guys? In the trucks!
Not a chance. You really think we're gonna just walk away and leave him?
This is a superhuman situation, stupid. You hang around here, one of those things is gonna fly straight through you.
Doesn't matter. Thor's our leader and some of us came halfway around the world to hear what he had to say. We're not gonna turn our backs on him now.
The hell are you gonna do for him?
I dunno. Pray, I guess--
Just let him know that some of us still believe in him.

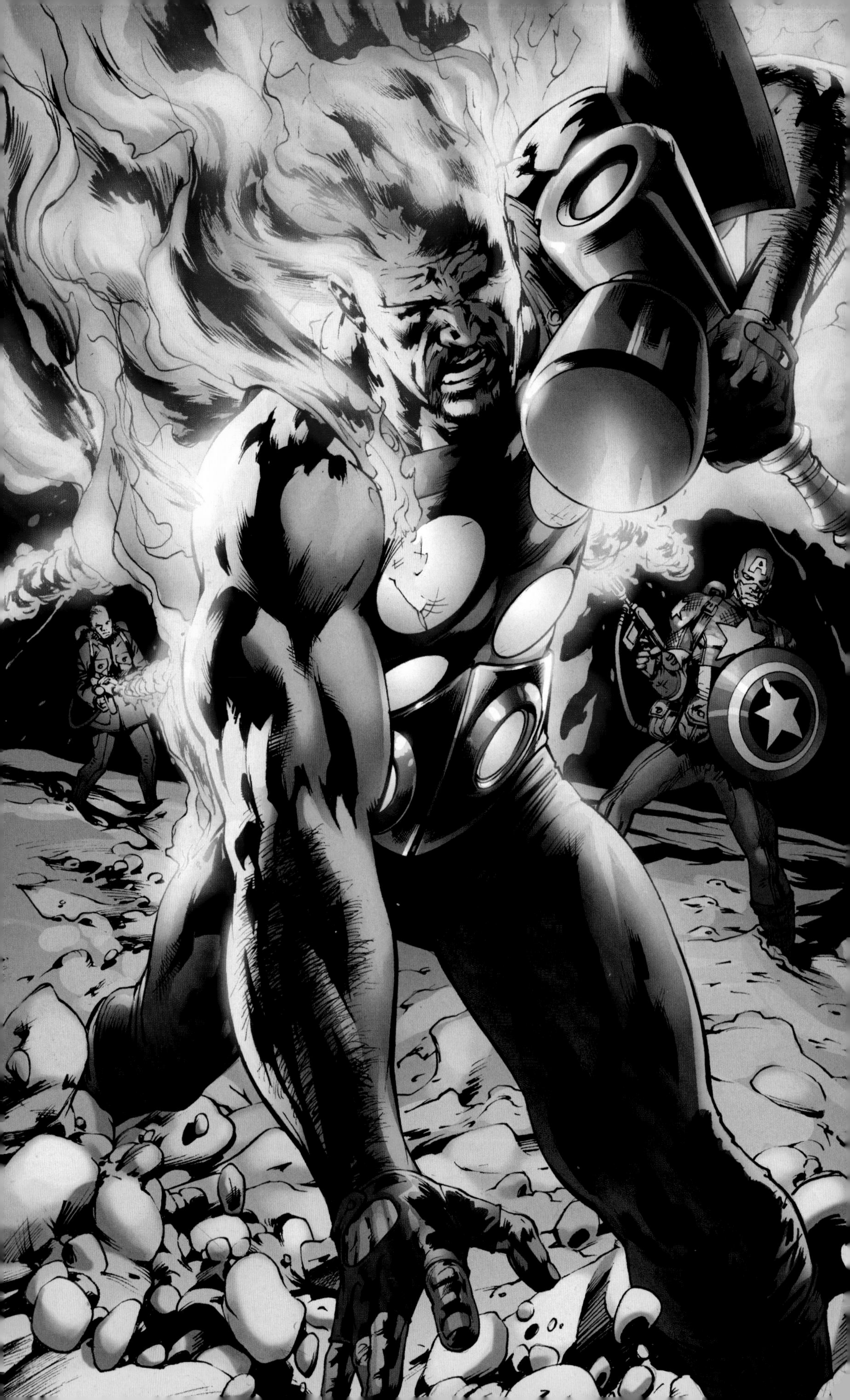

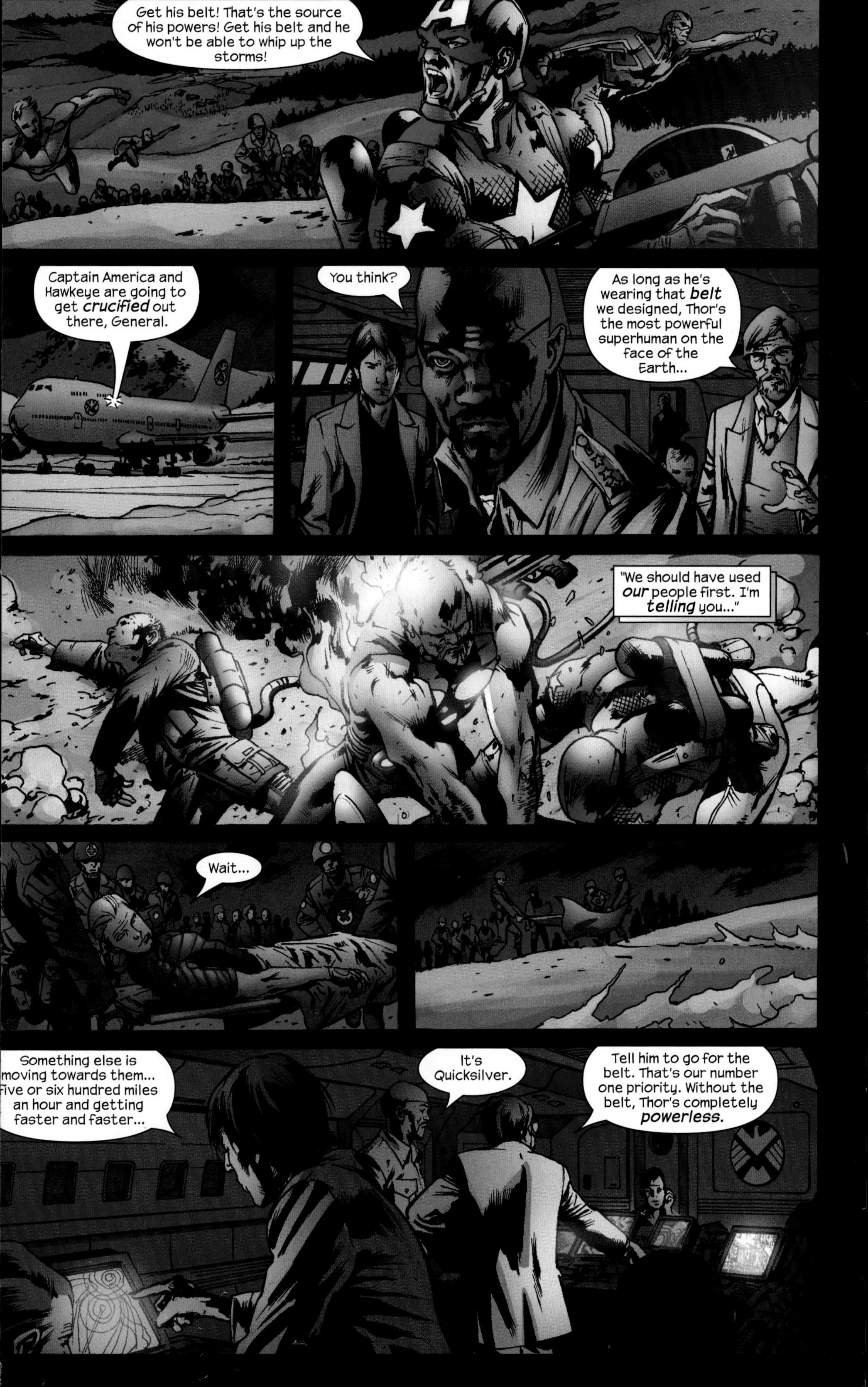
Get his belt! That's the source of his powers! Get his belt and he won't be able to whip up the storms!
Captain America and Hawkeye are going to get crucified out there, General.
You think?
As long as he's wearing that belt we designed, Thor's the most powerful superhuman on the face of the Earth...
"We should have used our people first. I'm telling you..."
Wait...
Something else is moving towards them... Five or six hundred miles an hour and getting faster and faster...
It's Quicksilver.
Tell him to go for the belt. That's our number one priority. Without the belt, Thor's completely powerless.

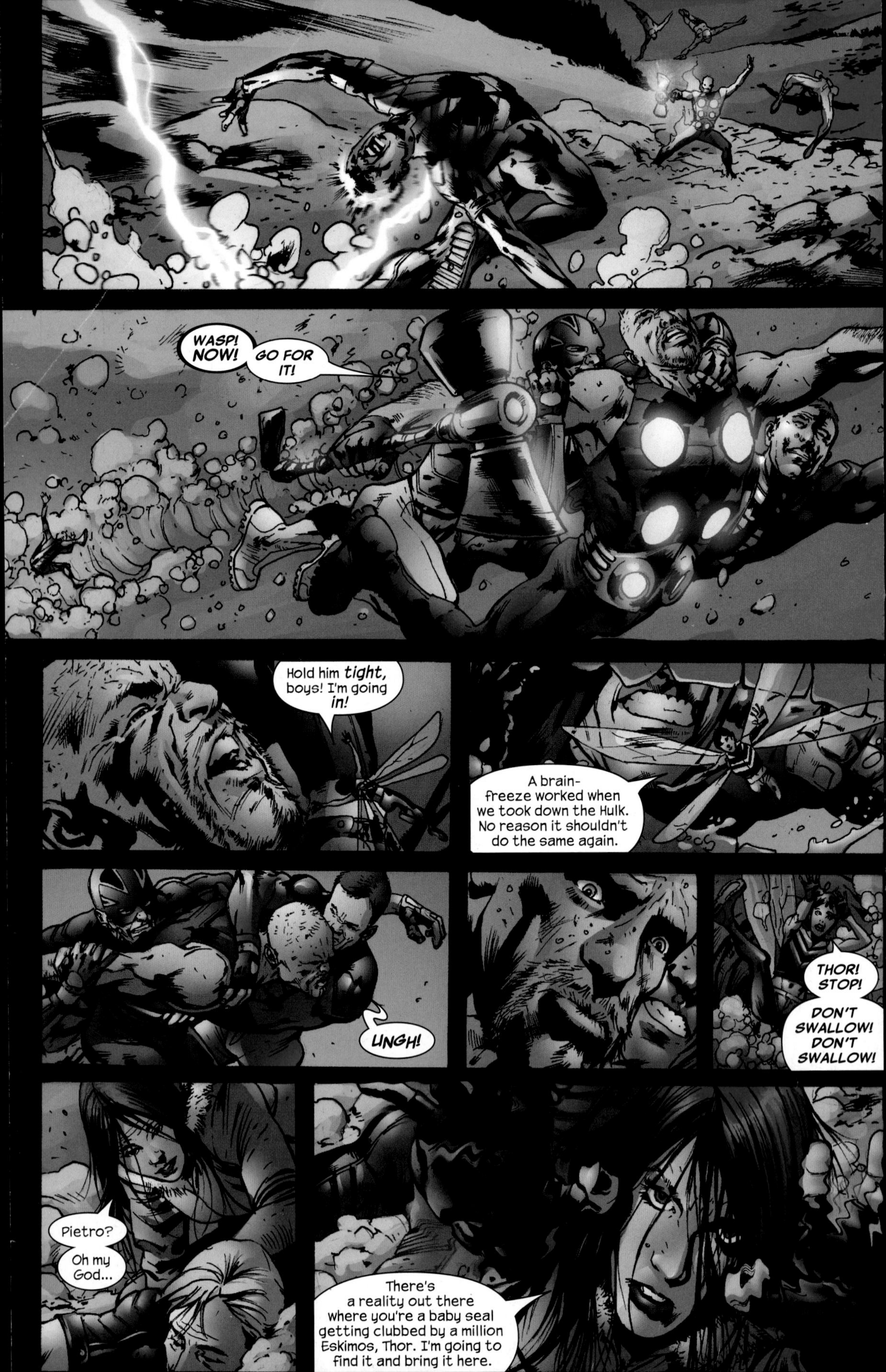
WASP! NOW!
GO FOR IT!
Hold him tight, boys! I'm going in!
A brain-freeze worked when we took down the Hulk. No reason it shouldn't do the same again.
UNGH!
THOR! STOP!
DON'T SWALLOW! DON'T SWALLOW!
Pietro?
Oh my God...
There's a reality out there where you're a baby seal getting clubbed by a million Eskimos, Thor. I'm going to find it and bring it here.

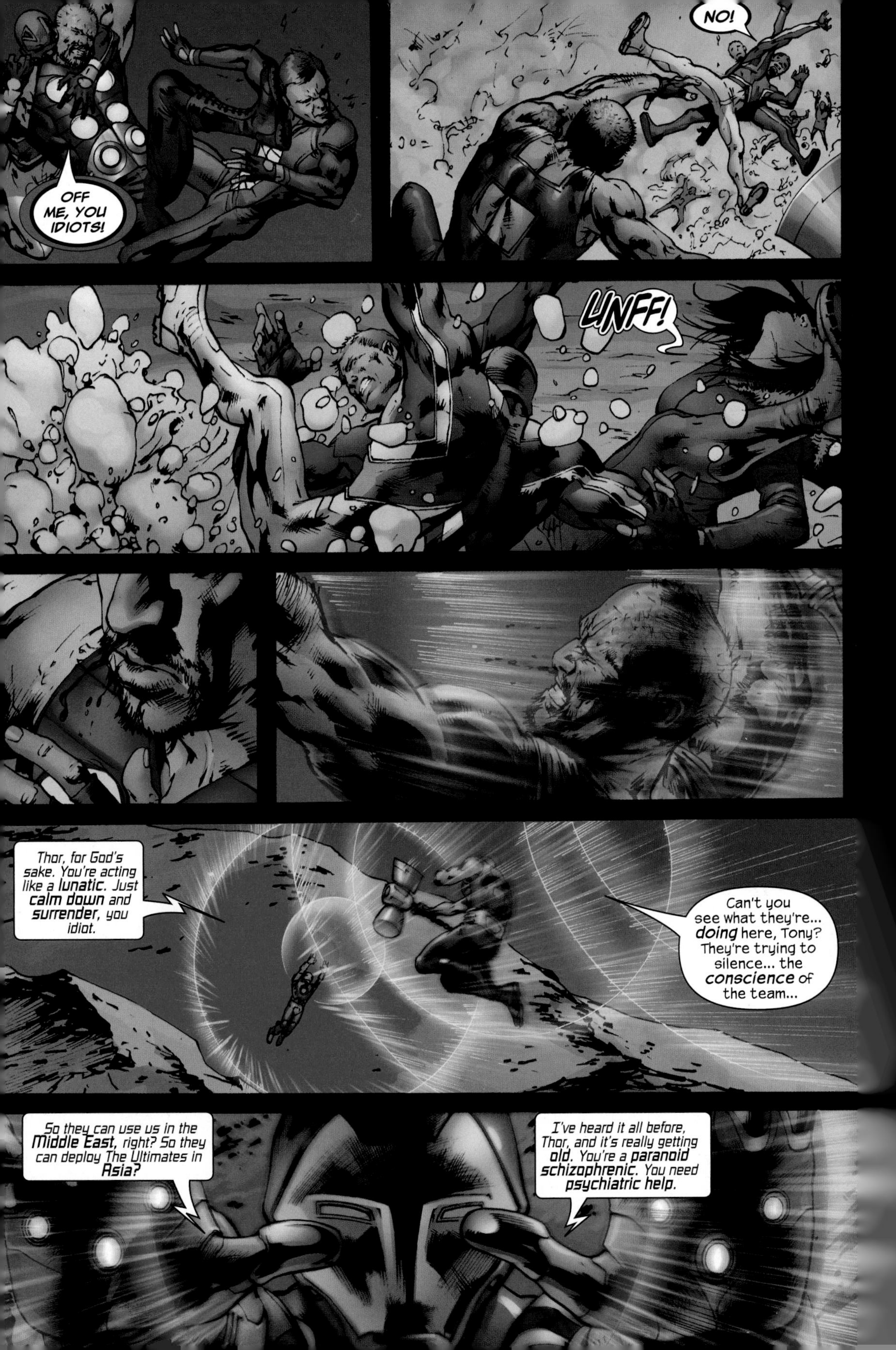
OFF ME, YOU IDIOTS!
NO!
UNFF!
Thor, for God's sake. You're acting like a lunatic. Just calm down and surrender, you idiot.
Can't you see what they're... doing here, Tony? They're trying to silence... the conscience of the team...
So they can use us in the Middle East, right? So they can deploy The Ultimates in Asia?
I've heard it all before, Thor, and it's really getting old. You're a paranoid schizophrenic. You need psychiatric help.

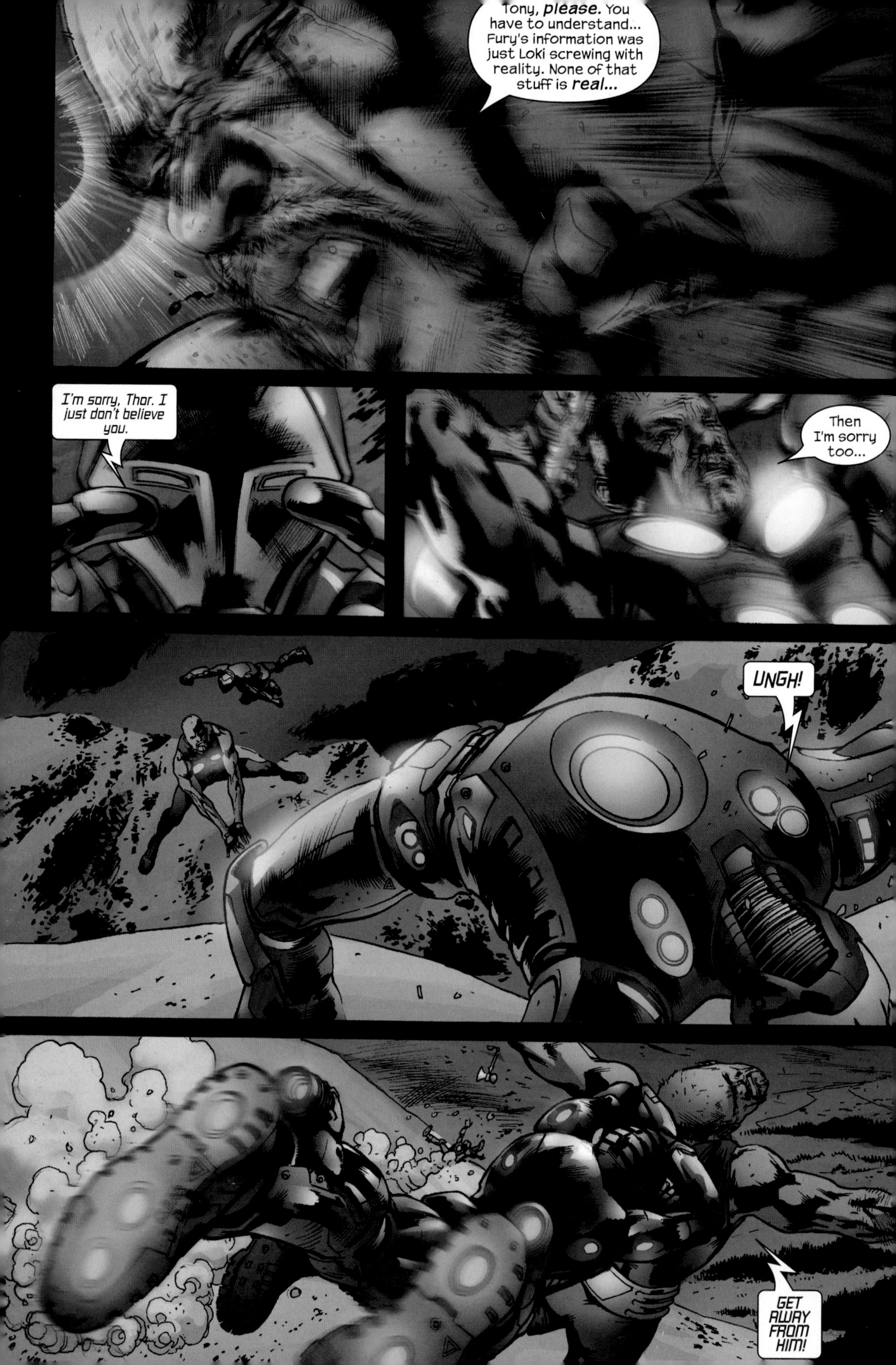
Tony, **please.** You have to understand... Fury's information was just Loki screwing with reality. None of that stuff is ***real...***
I'm sorry, Thor. I just don't believe you.
Then I'm sorry too...
UNGH!
GET AWAY FROM HIM!

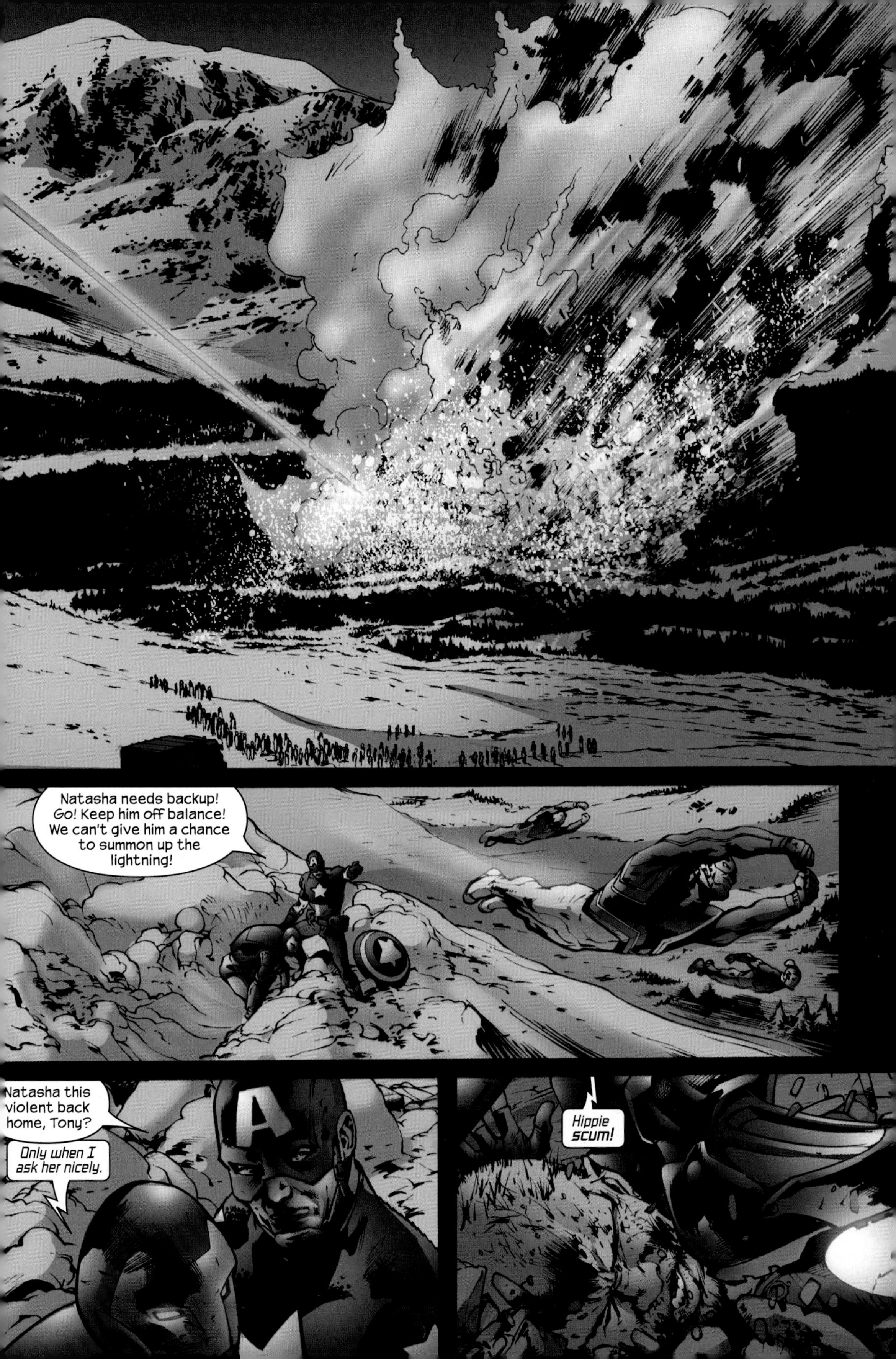
Natasha needs backup! Go! Keep him off balance! We can't give him a chance to summon up the lightning!
Natasha this violent back home, Tony?
Only when I ask her nicely.
Hippie scum!

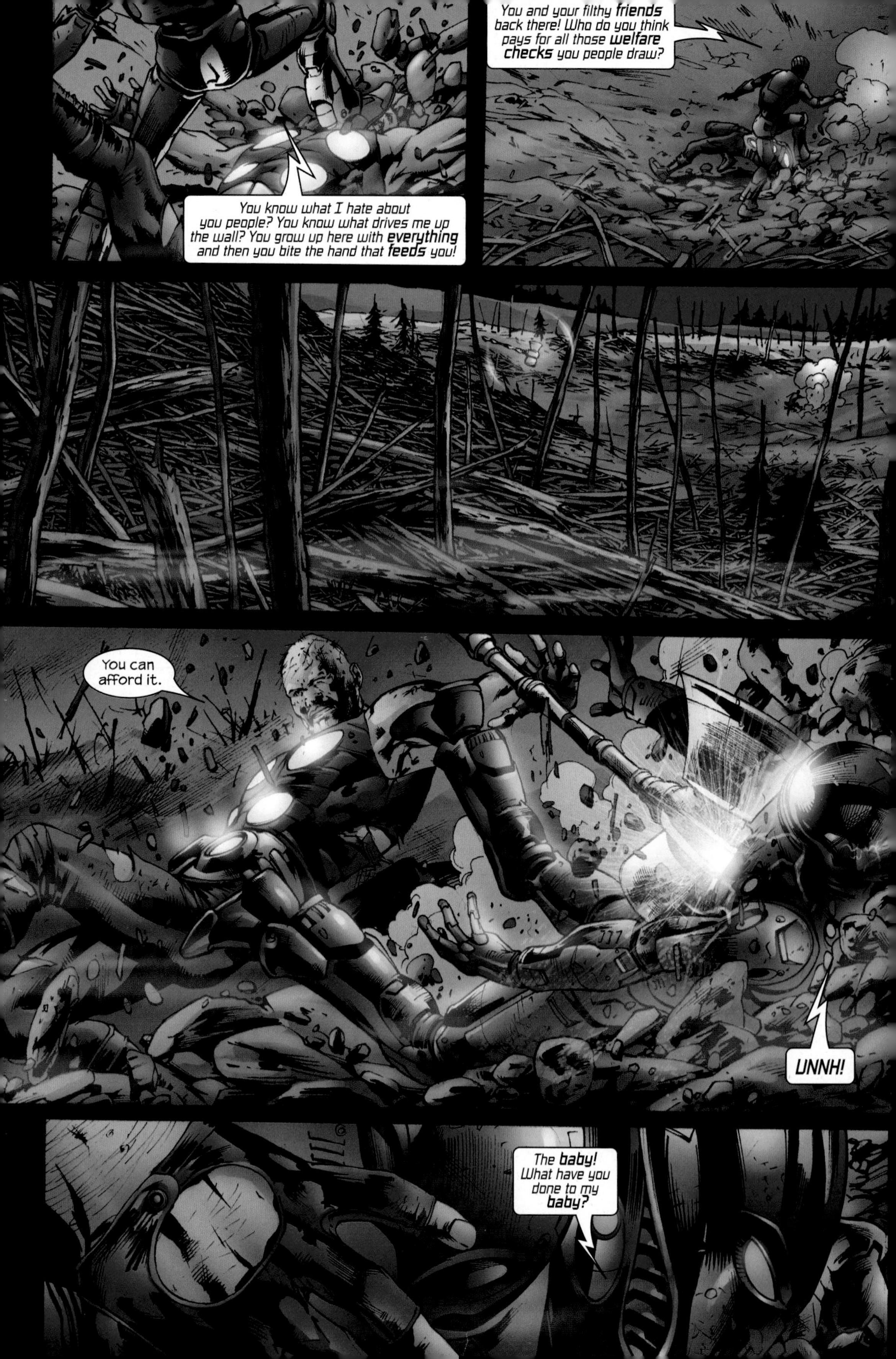
You know what I hate about you people? You know what drives me up the wall? You grow up here with everything and then you bite the hand that feeds you!
You and your filthy friends back there! Who do you think pays for all those welfare checks you people draw?
You can afford it.
UNNH!
The baby! What have you done to my baby?

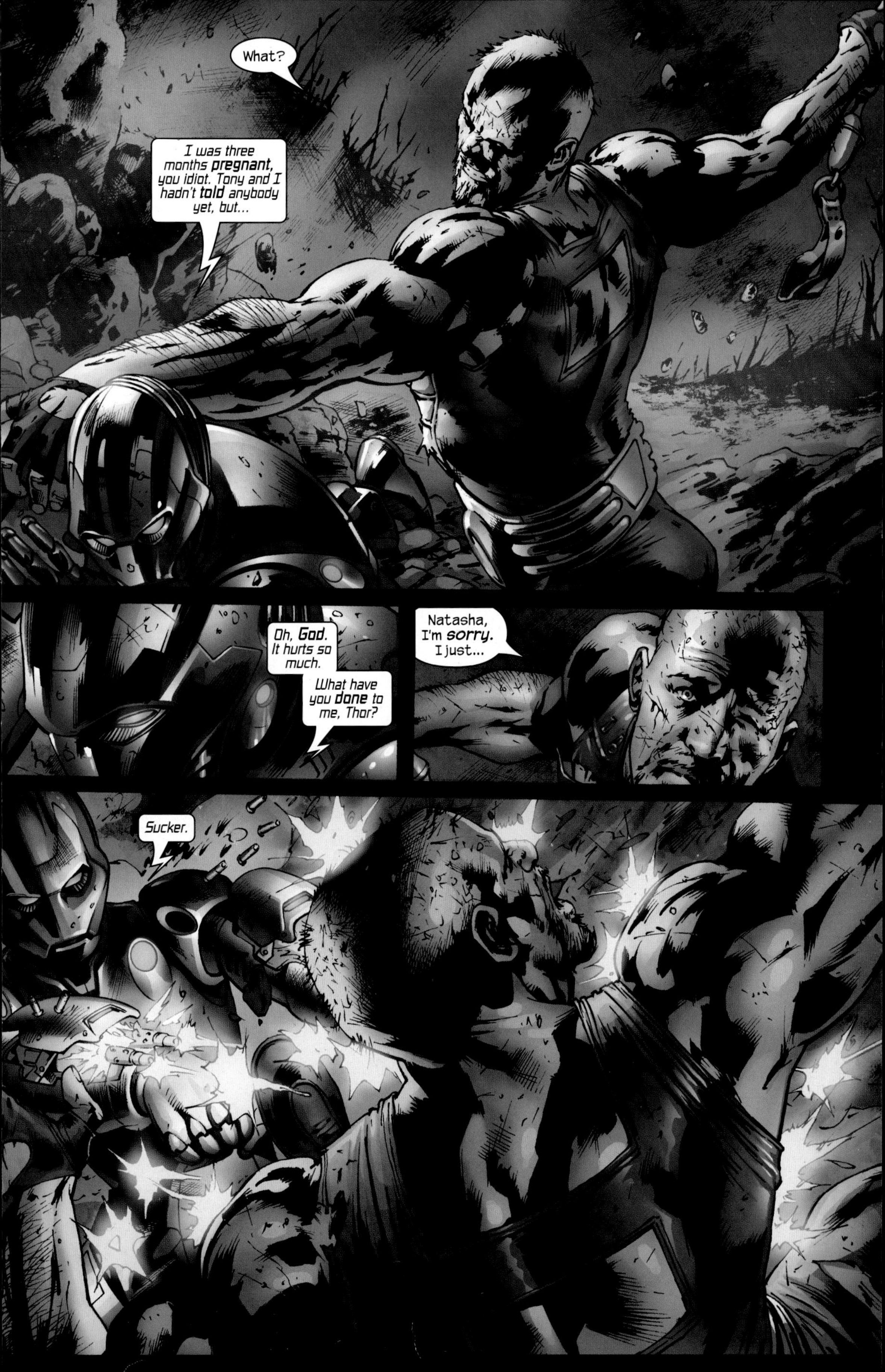
What?
I was three months **pregnant**, you idiot. Tony and I hadn't **told** anybody yet, but...
Oh, **God**. It hurts so much.
What have you **done** to me, Thor?
Natasha, I'm **sorry**. I just...
Sucker.

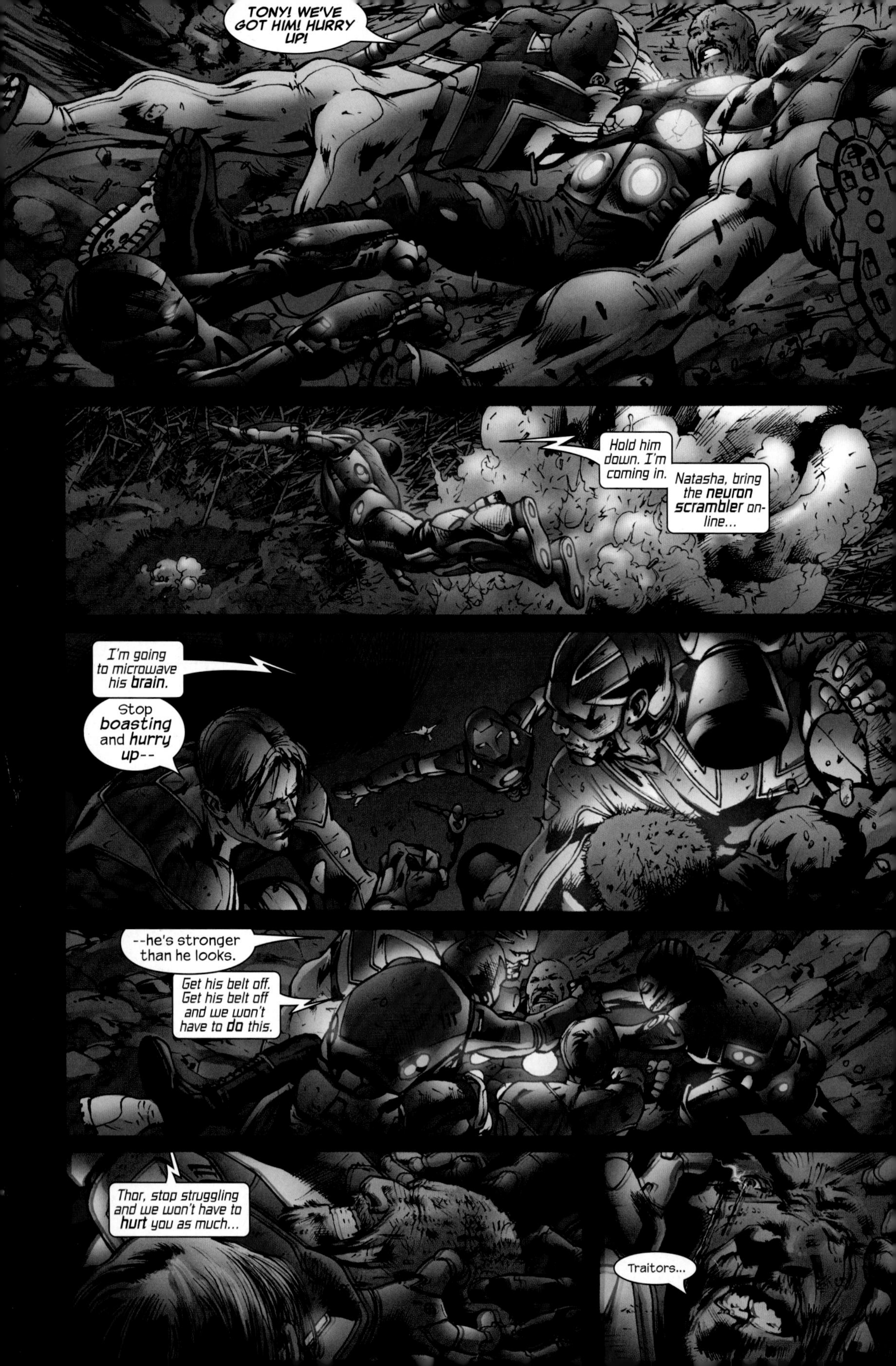
TONY! WE'VE GOT HIM! HURRY UP!
Hold him down. I'm coming in.
Natasha, bring the neuron scrambler on-line...
I'm going to microwave his brain.
Stop boasting and hurry up--
--he's stronger than he looks.
Get his belt off. Get his belt off and we won't have to do this.
Thor, stop struggling and we won't have to hurt you as much...
Traitors...

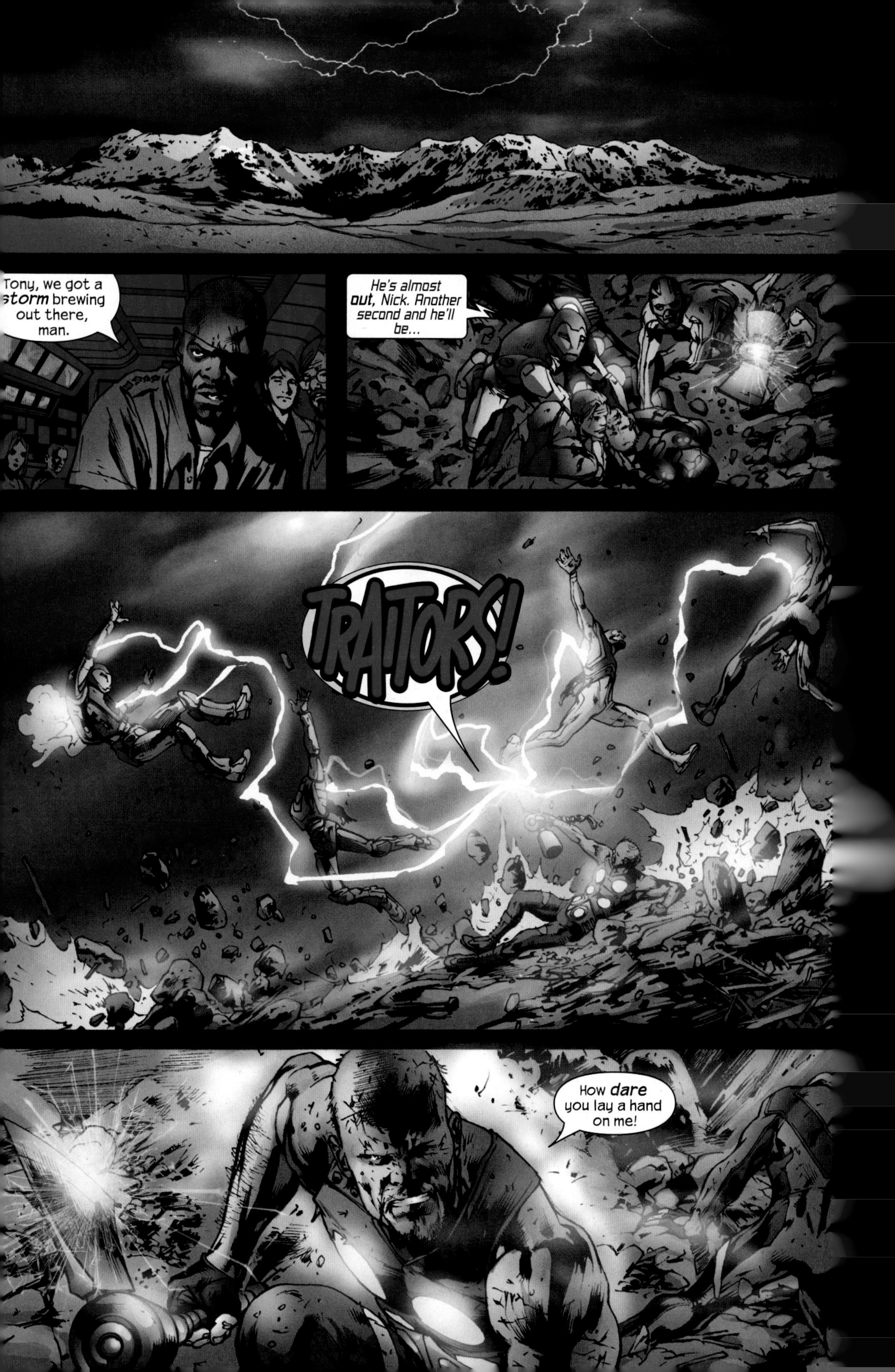
Tony, we got a storm brewing out there, man.
He's almost out, Nick. Another second and he'll be...
TRAITORS!
How dare you lay a hand on me!

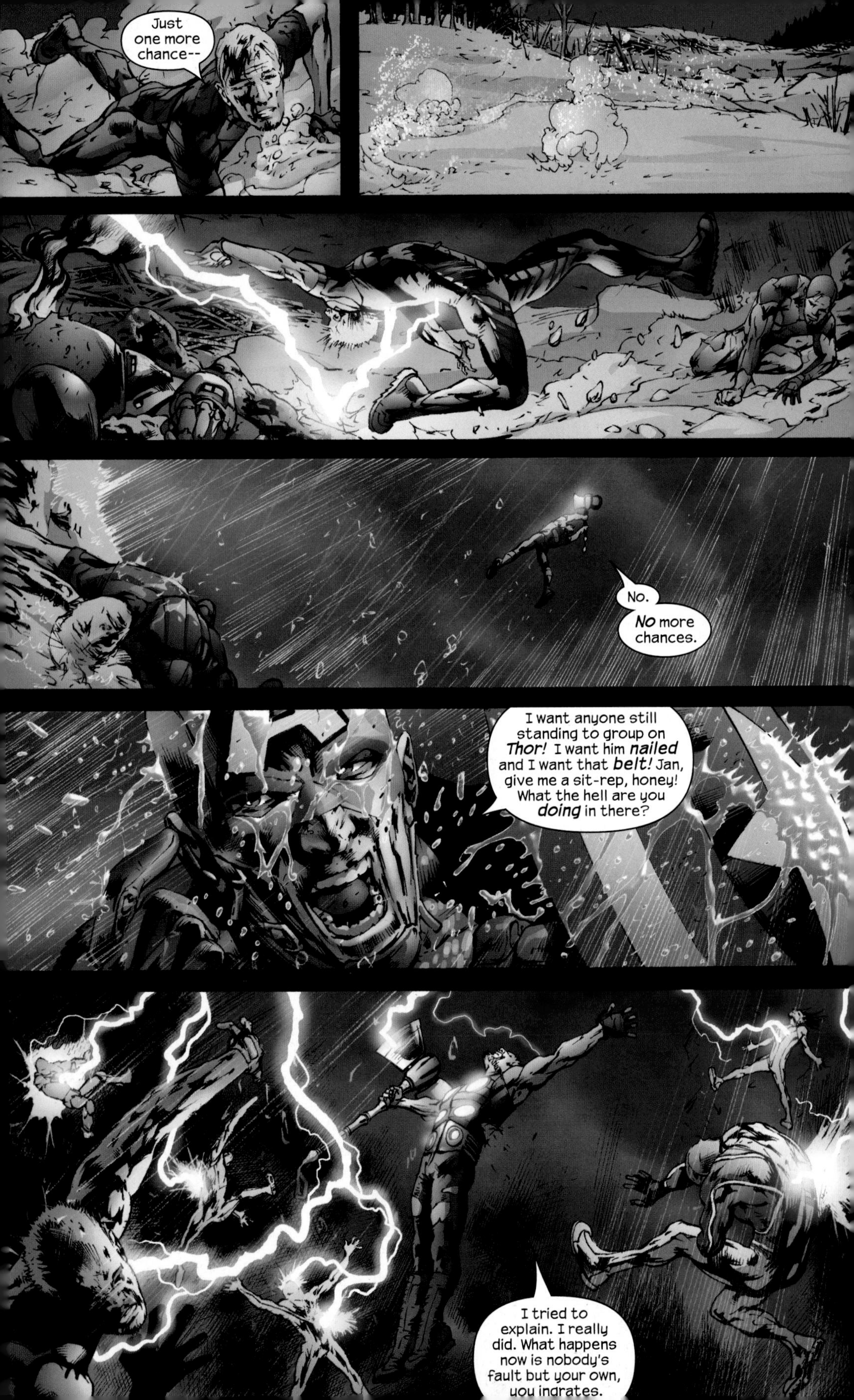
Just one more chance--
No.
NO more chances.
I want anyone still standing to group on Thor! I want him nailed and I want that belt! Jan, give me a sit-rep, honey! What the hell are you doing in there?
I tried to explain. I really did. What happens now is nobody's fault but your own, you ingrates.

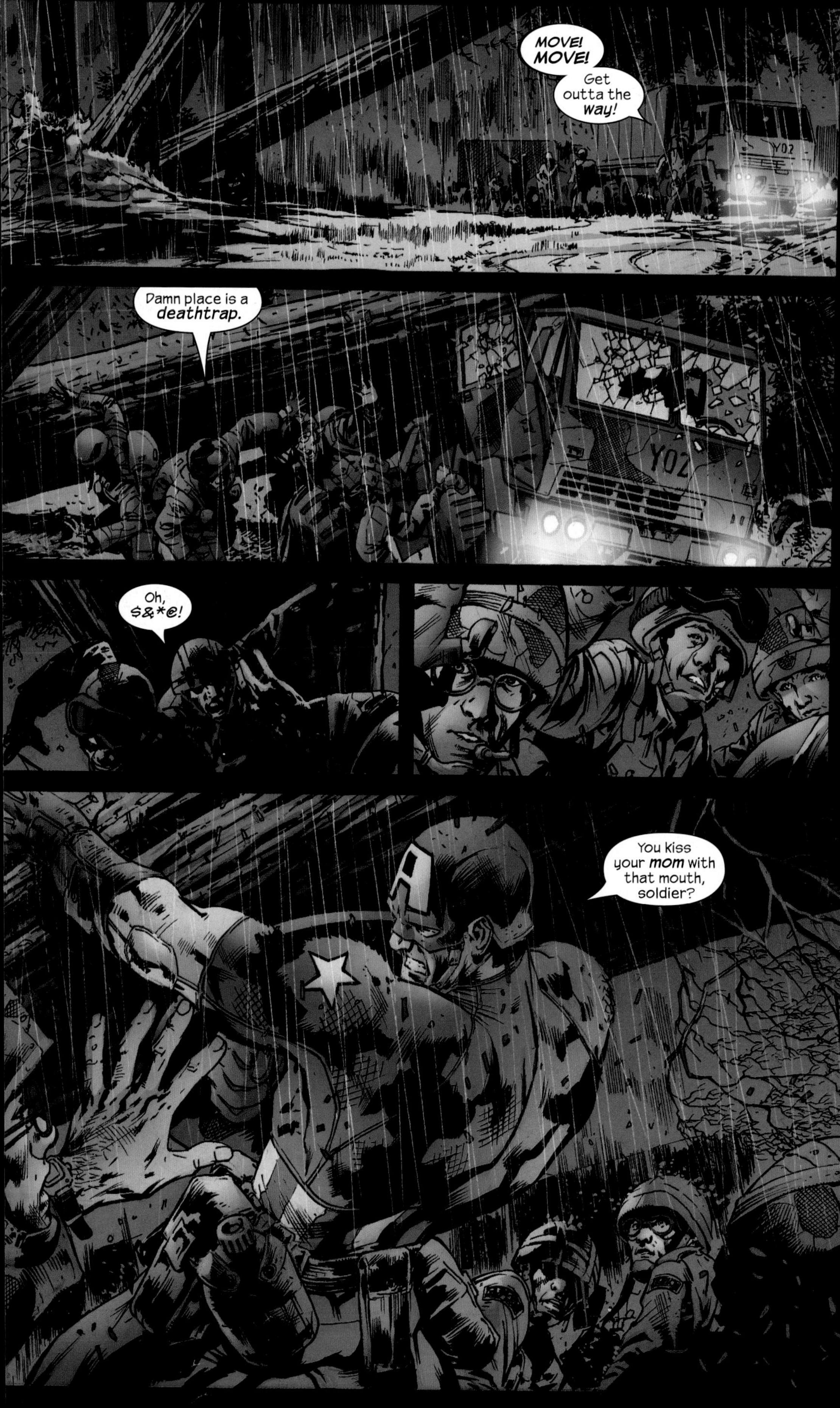
MOVE! MOVE!
Get outta the way!
Damn place is a deathtrap.
Oh, $&*@!
You kiss your mom with that mouth, soldier?

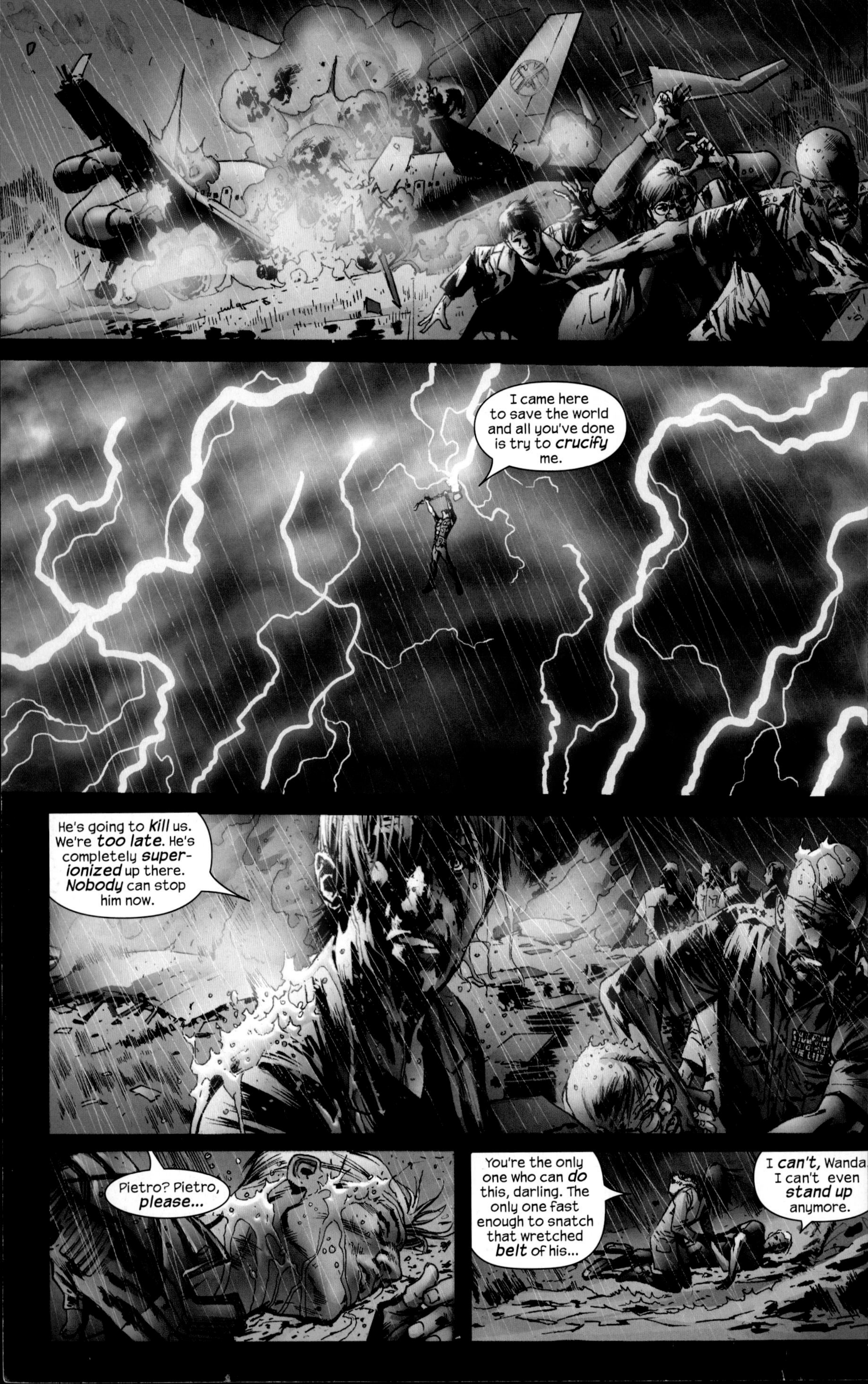

I came here to save the world and all you've done is try to *crucify* me.
He's going to *kill* us. We're *too late*. He's completely *super-ionized* up there. *Nobody* can stop him now.
Pietro? Pietro, *please...*
You're the only one who can *do* this, darling. The only one fast enough to snatch that wretched *belt* of his...
I *can't,* Wanda. I can't even *stand up* anymore.

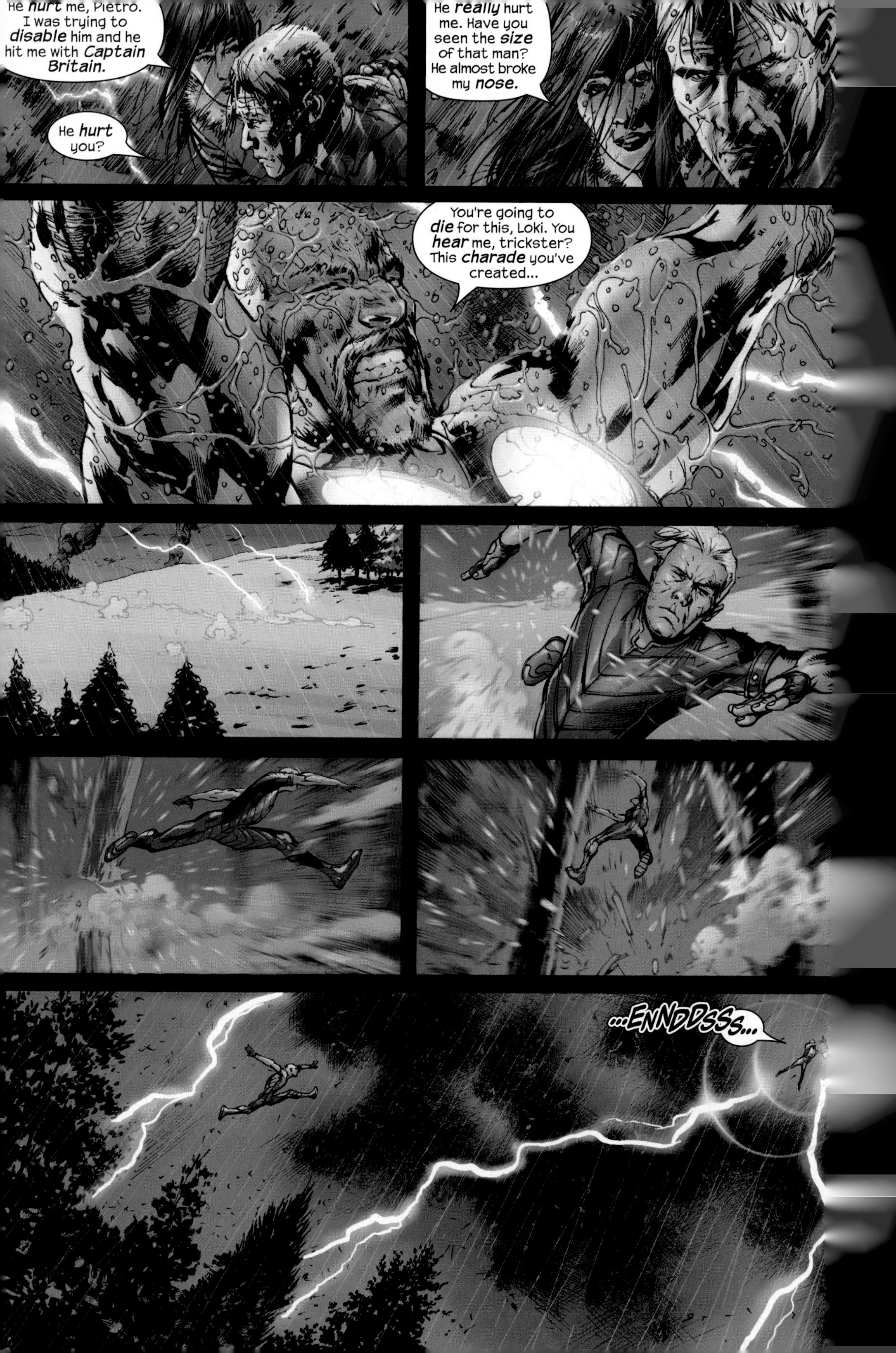
He hurt me, Pietro. I was trying to disable him and he hit me with Captain Britain.
He hurt you?
He really hurt me. Have you seen the size of that man? He almost broke my nose.
You're going to die for this, Loki. You hear me, trickster? This charade you've created...
...ENNDDSSS...

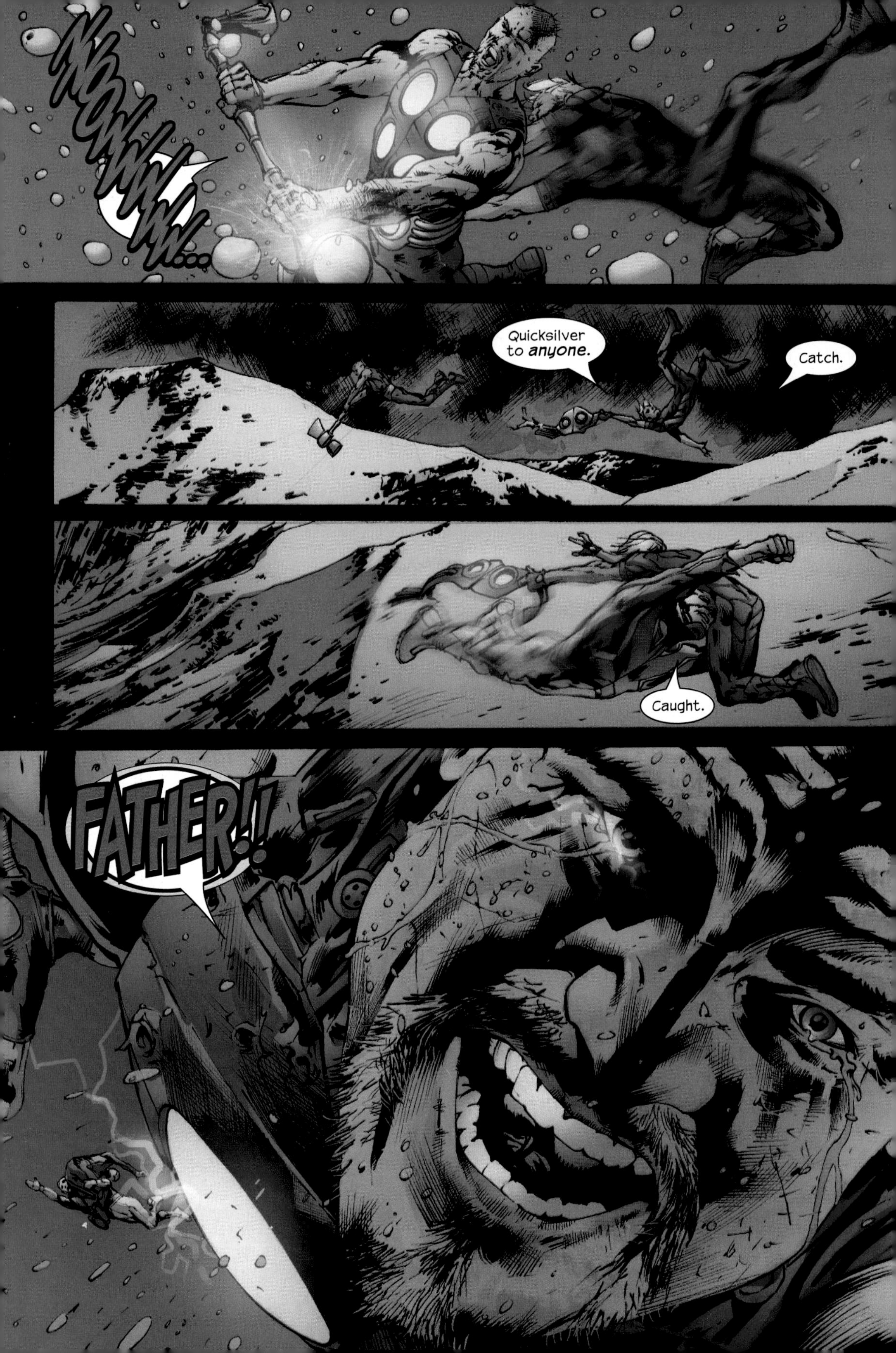
NOOOWWWWW...
Quicksilver to *anyone*.
Catch.
Caught.
FATHER!!

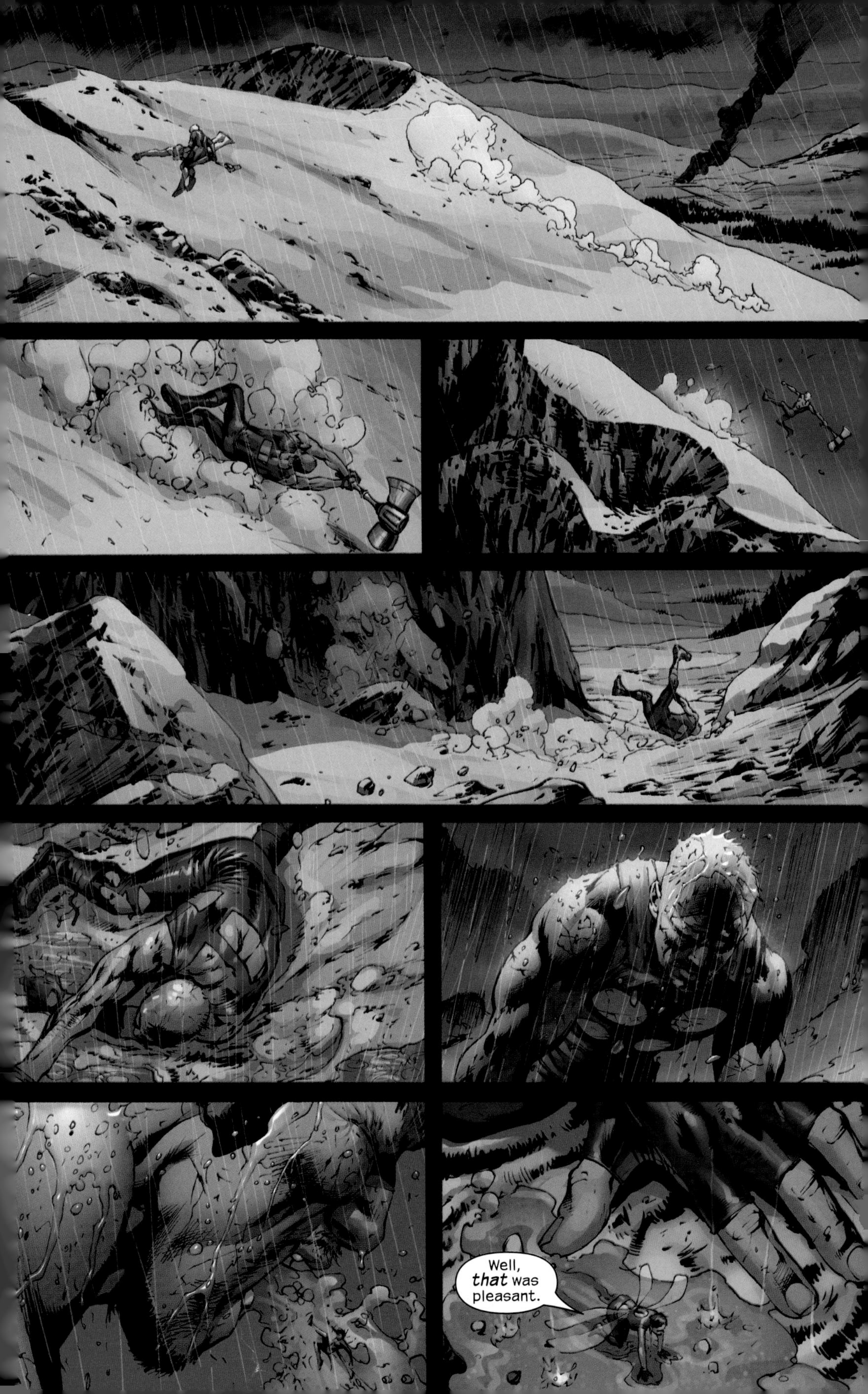
Well, *that* was pleasant.

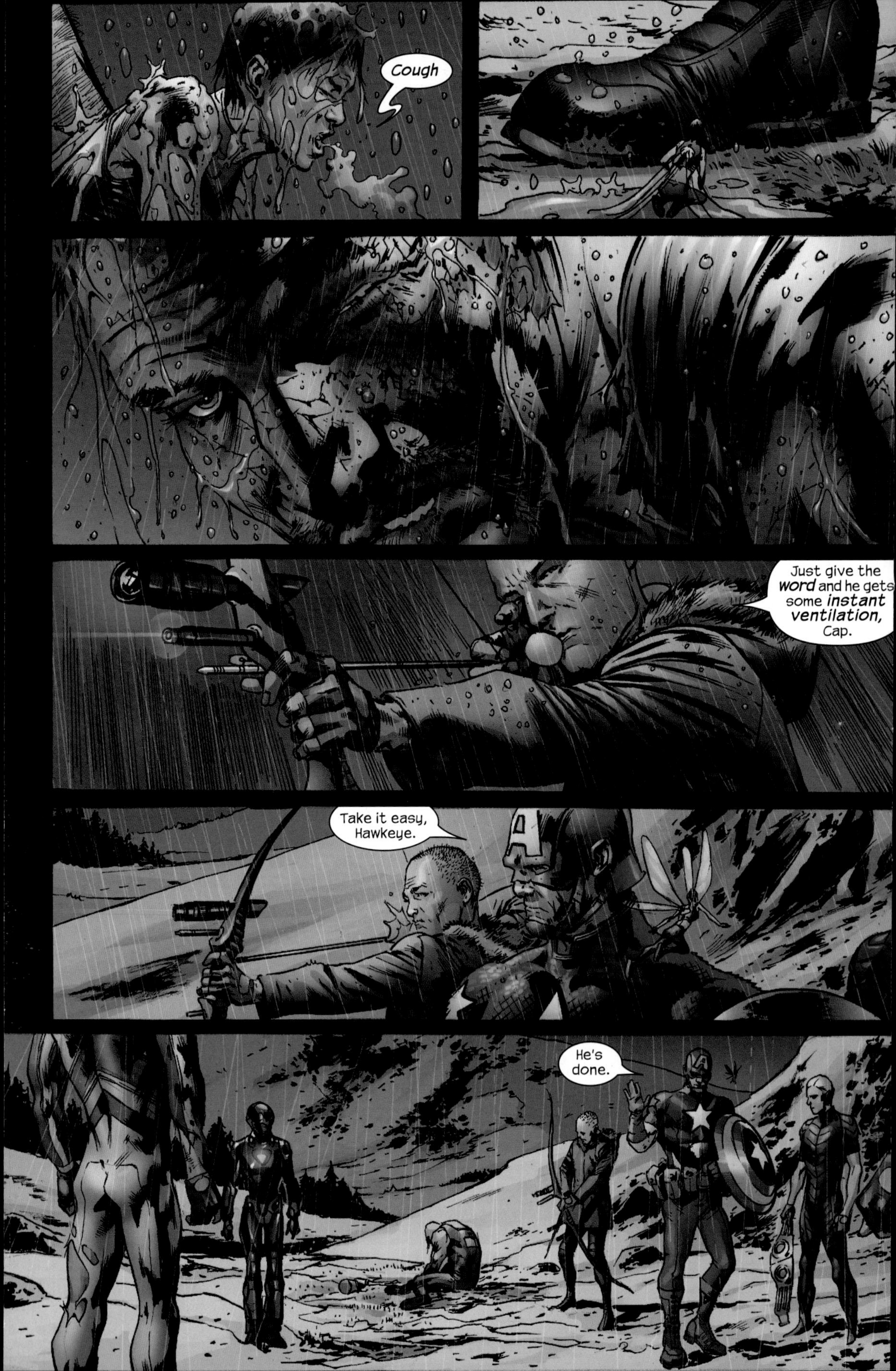
Cough
Just give the word and he gets some instant ventilation, Cap.
Take it easy, Hawkeye.
He's done.

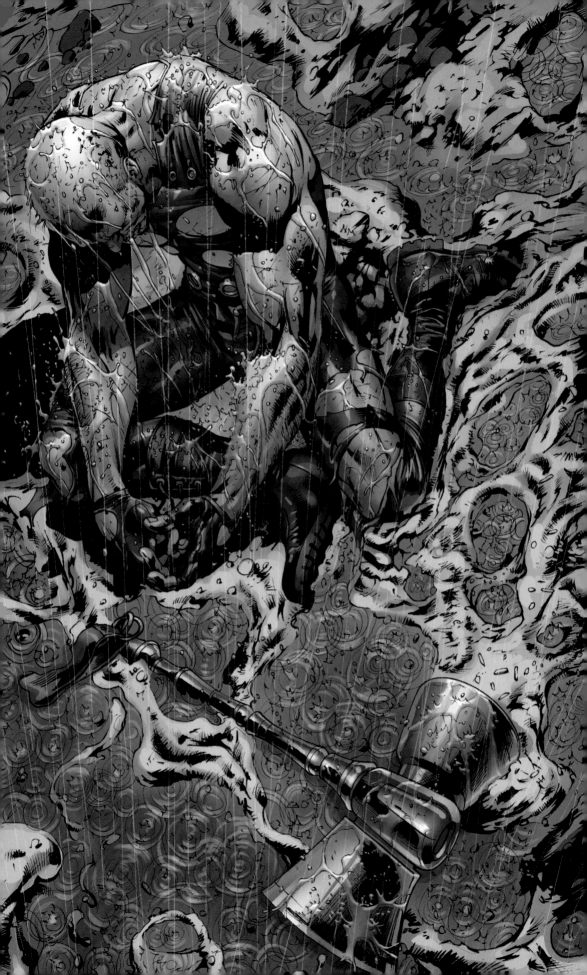

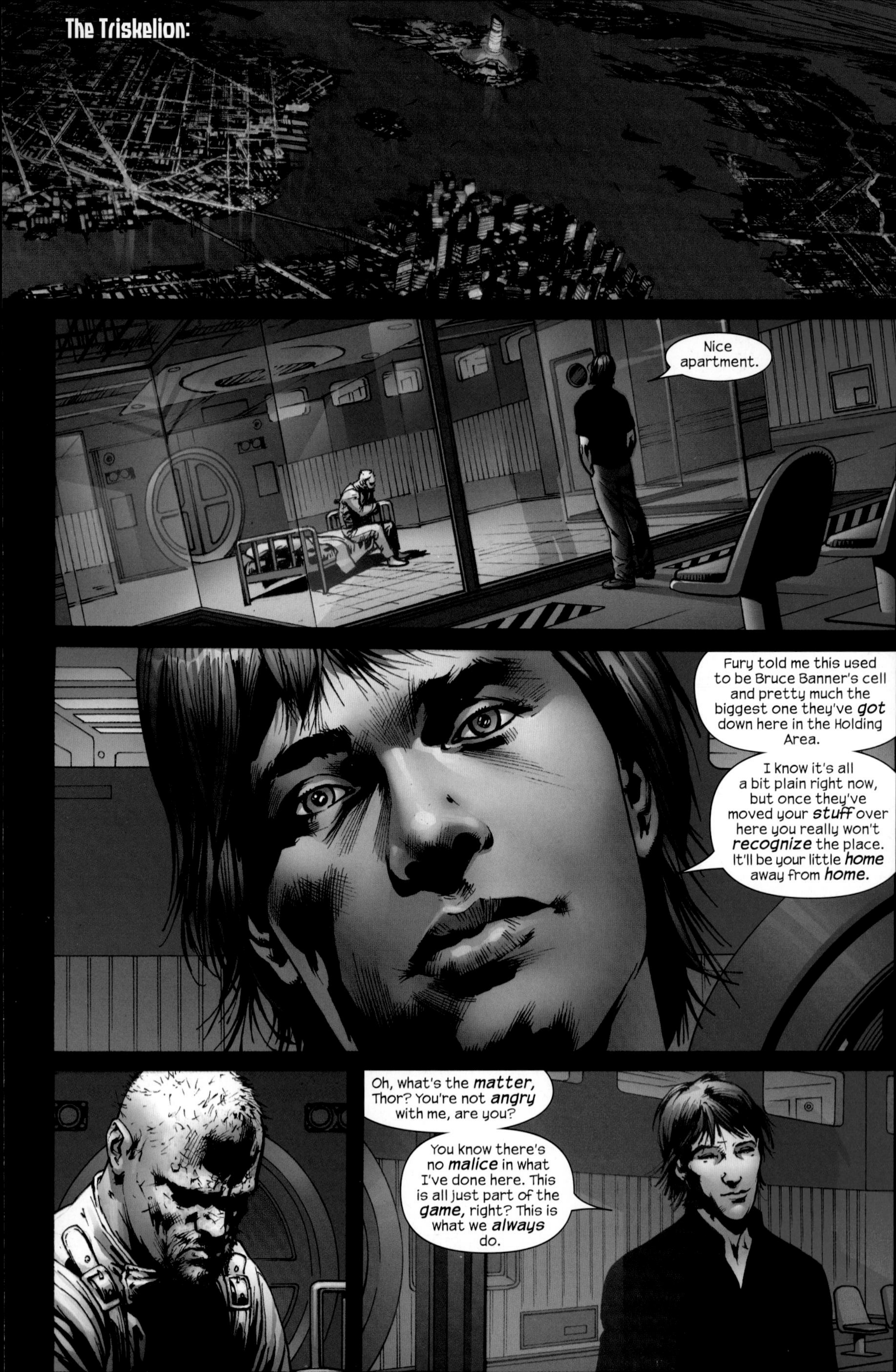
The Triskelion:
Nice apartment.
Fury told me this used to be Bruce Banner's cell and pretty much the biggest one they've got down here in the Holding Area.
I know it's all a bit plain right now, but once they've moved your stuff over here you really won't recognize the place. It'll be your little home away from home.
Oh, what's the matter, Thor? You're not angry with me, are you?
You know there's no malice in what I've done here. This is all just part of the game, right? This is what we always do.

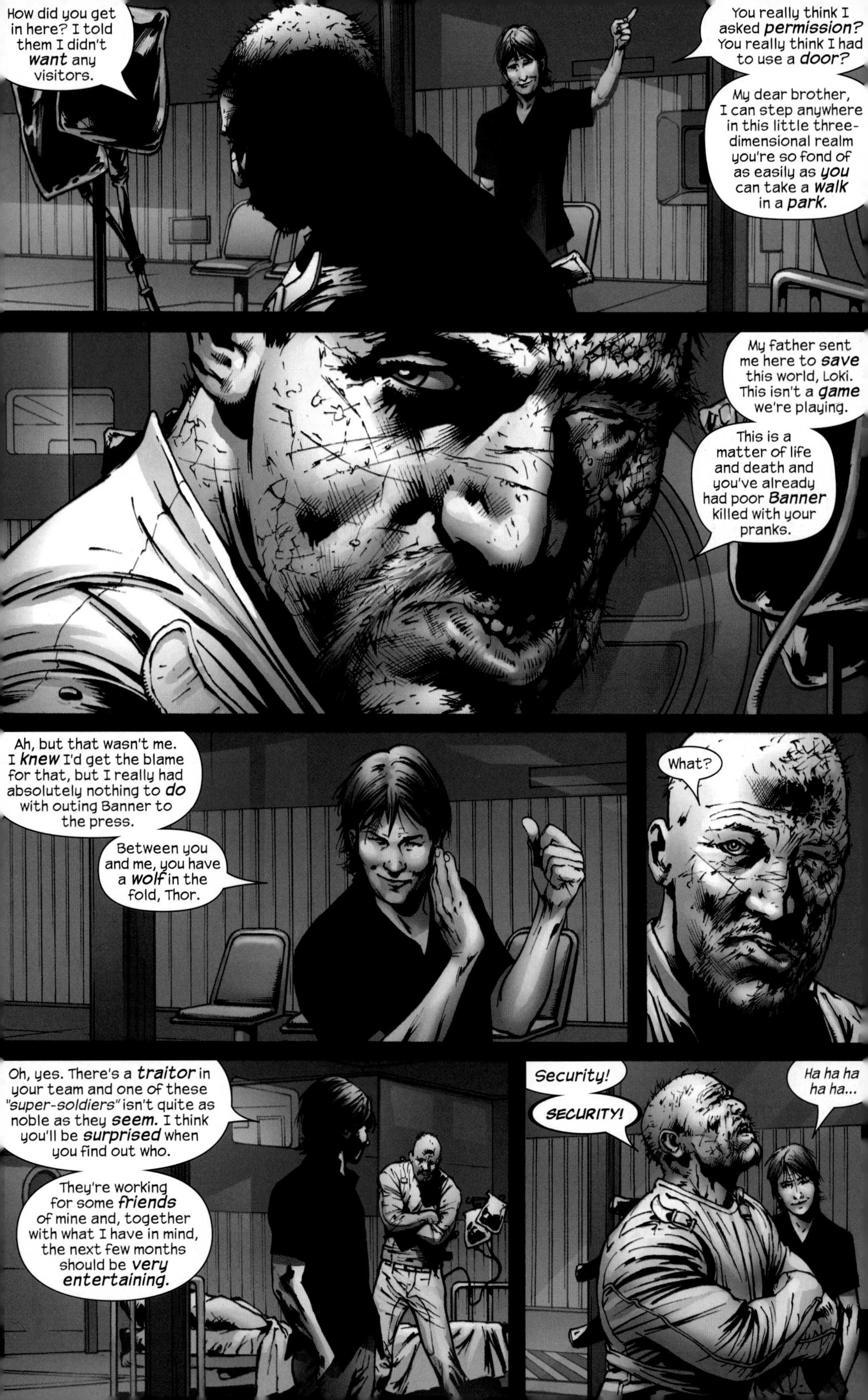
How did you get in here? I told them I didn't want any visitors.
You really think I asked permission? You really think I had to use a door?
My dear brother, I can step anywhere in this little three-dimensional realm you're so fond of as easily as you can take a walk in a park.
My father sent me here to save this world, Loki. This isn't a game we're playing.
This is a matter of life and death and you've already had poor Banner killed with your pranks.
Ah, but that wasn't me. I knew I'd get the blame for that, but I really had absolutely nothing to do with outing Banner to the press.
Between you and me, you have a wolf in the fold, Thor.
What?
Oh, yes. There's a traitor in your team and one of these "super-soldiers" isn't quite as noble as they seem. I think you'll be surprised when you find out who.
They're working for some friends of mine and, together with what I have in mind, the next few months should be very entertaining.
Security!
SECURITY!
Ha ha ha ha ha...

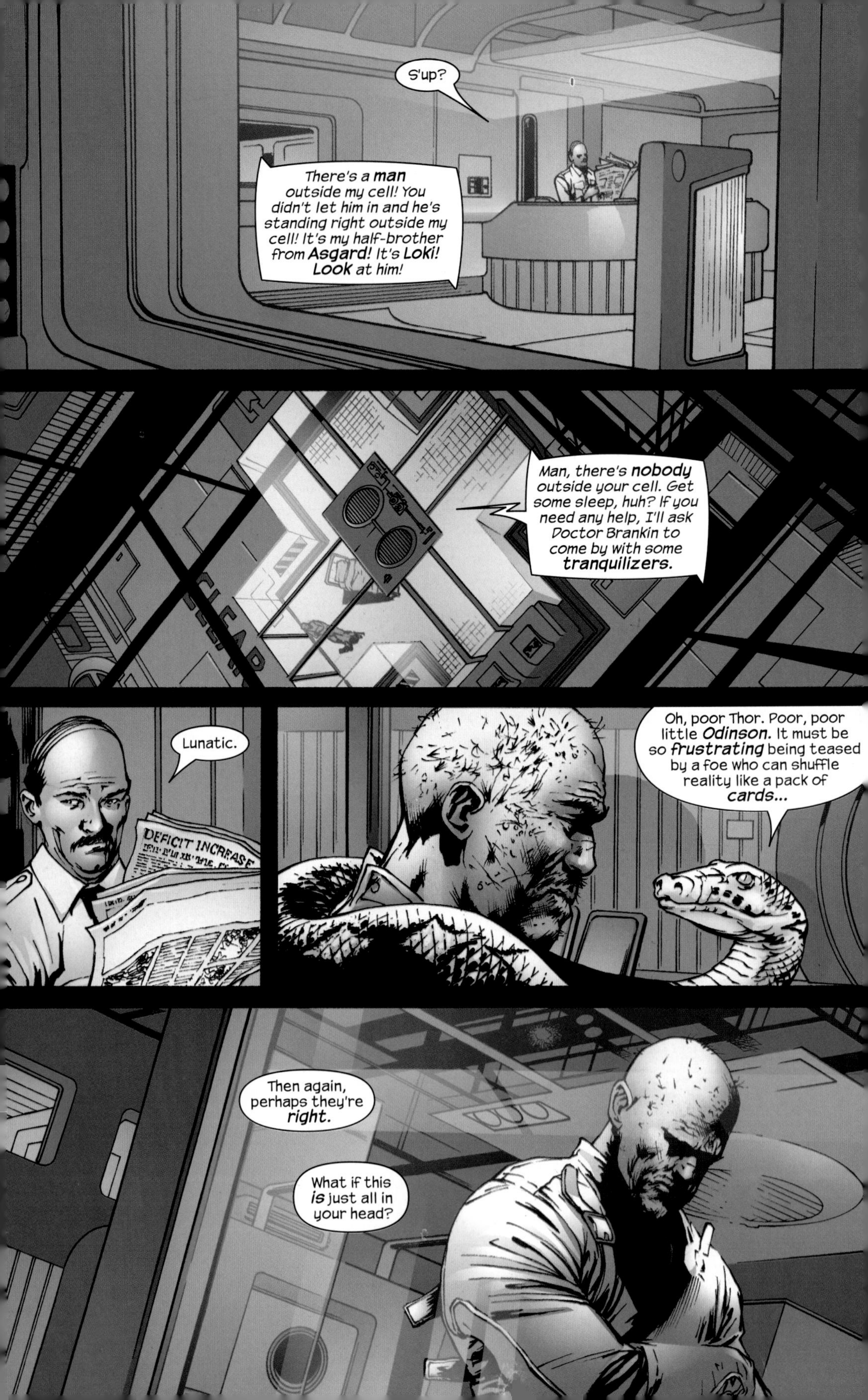
S'up?
There's a man outside my cell! You didn't let him in and he's standing right outside my cell! It's my half-brother from Asgard! It's Loki! Look at him!
Man, there's nobody outside your cell. Get some sleep, huh? If you need any help, I'll ask Doctor Brankin to come by with some tranquilizers.
Lunatic.
DEFICIT INCREASE
Oh, poor Thor. Poor, poor little Odinson. It must be so frustrating being teased by a foe who can shuffle reality like a pack of cards...
Then again, perhaps they're right.
What if this is just all in your head?

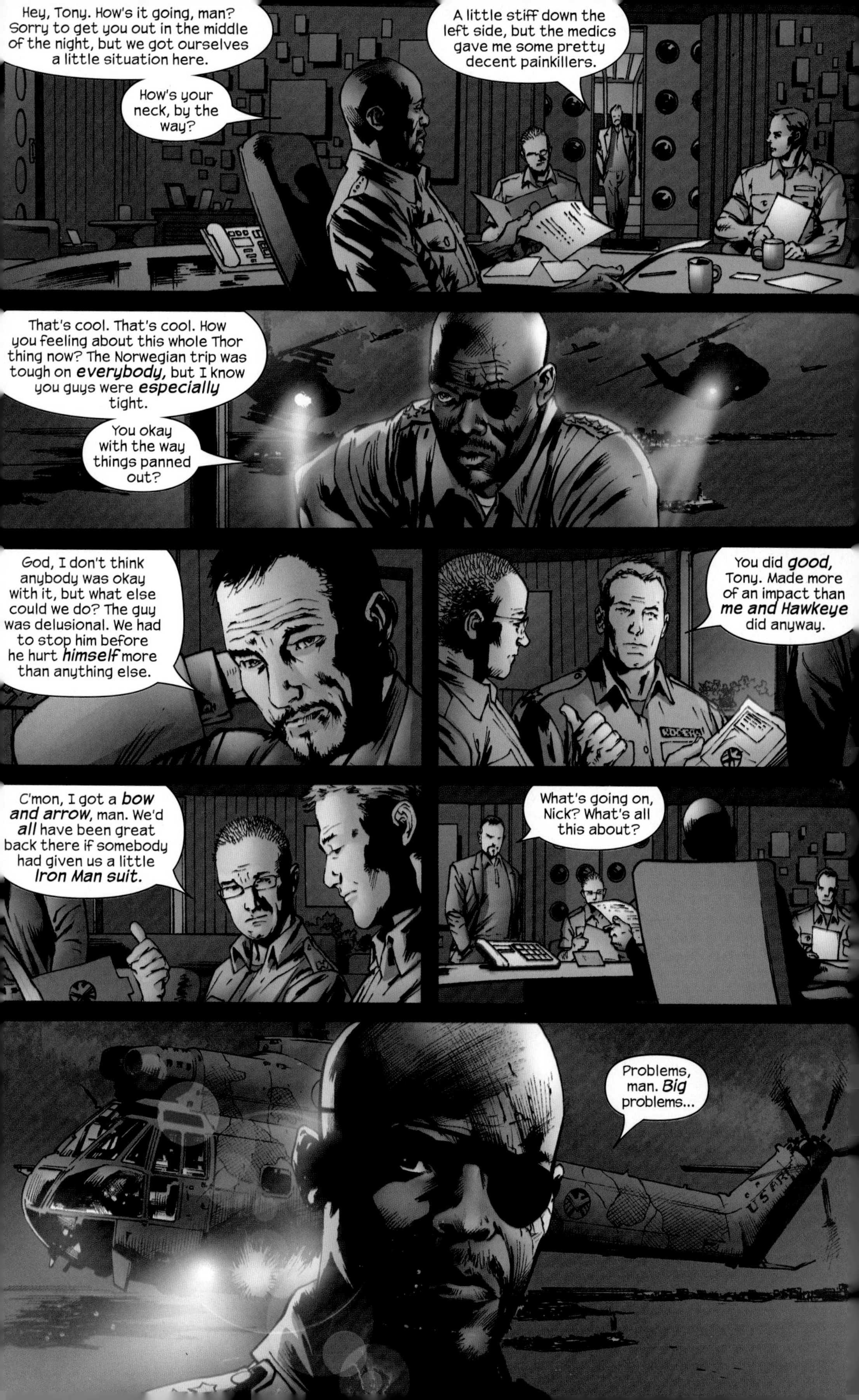
Hey, Tony. How's it going, man? Sorry to get you out in the middle of the night, but we got ourselves a little situation here.
How's your neck, by the way?
A little stiff down the left side, but the medics gave me some pretty decent painkillers.
That's cool. That's cool. How you feeling about this whole Thor thing now? The Norwegian trip was tough on *everybody,* but I know you guys were *especially* tight.
You okay with the way things panned out?
God, I don't think anybody was okay with it, but what else could we do? The guy was delusional. We had to stop him before he hurt *himself* more than anything else.
You did *good,* Tony. Made more of an impact than *me and Hawkeye* did anyway.
C'mon, I got a *bow and arrow,* man. We'd *all* have been great back there if somebody had given us a little *Iron Man suit.*
What's going on, Nick? What's all this about?
Problems, man. *Big* problems...

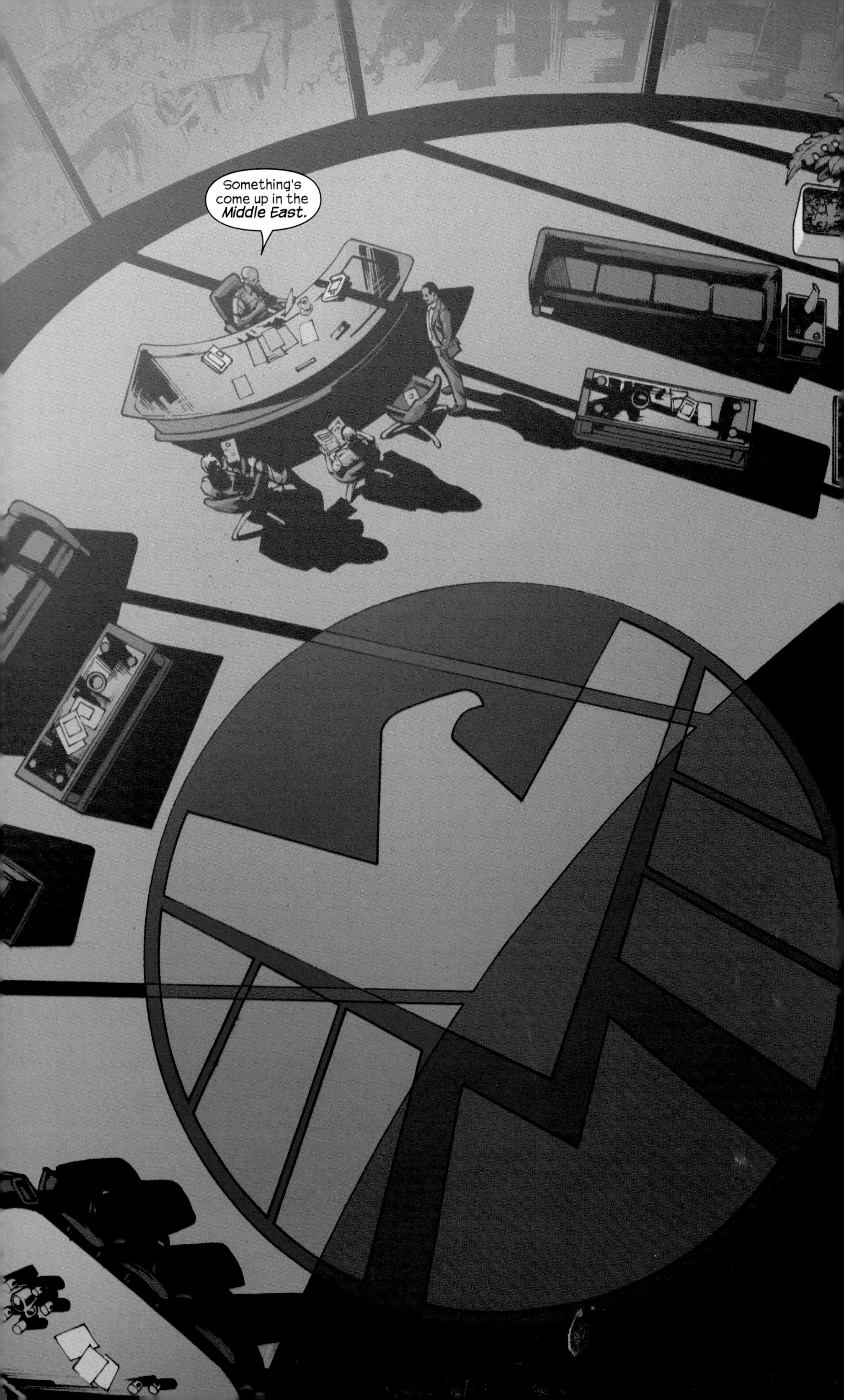
Something's come up in the *Middle East.*

THE DEFENDERS

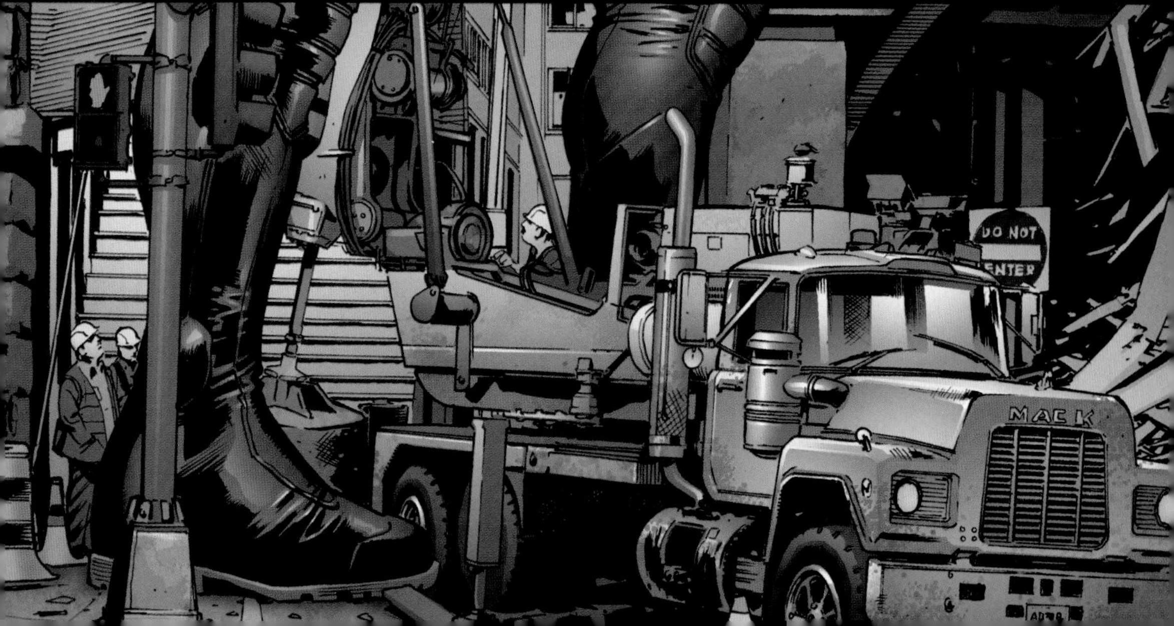
DO NOT
ENTER
MACK

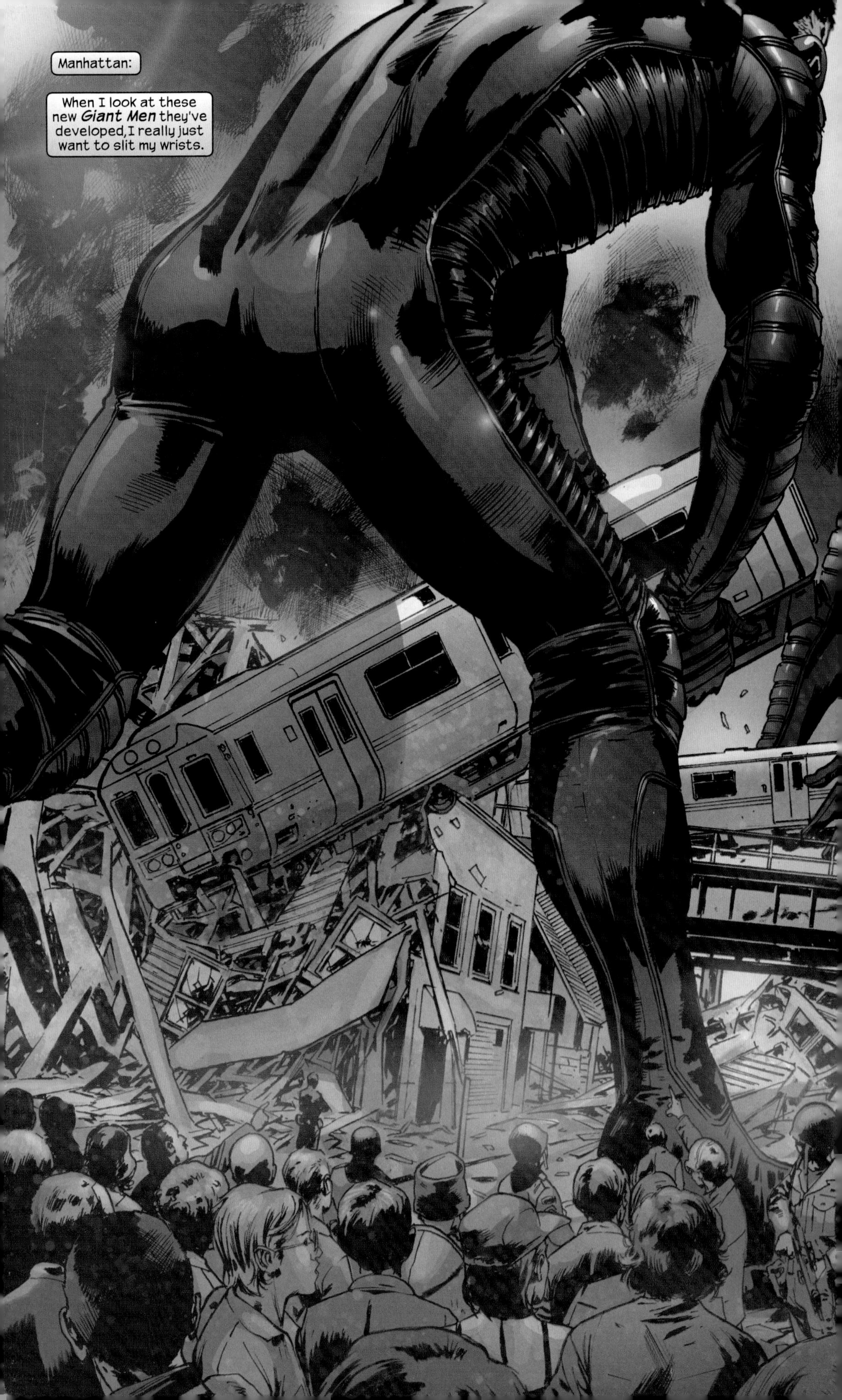
Manhattan:
When I look at these new *Giant Men* they've developed, I really just want to slit my wrists.

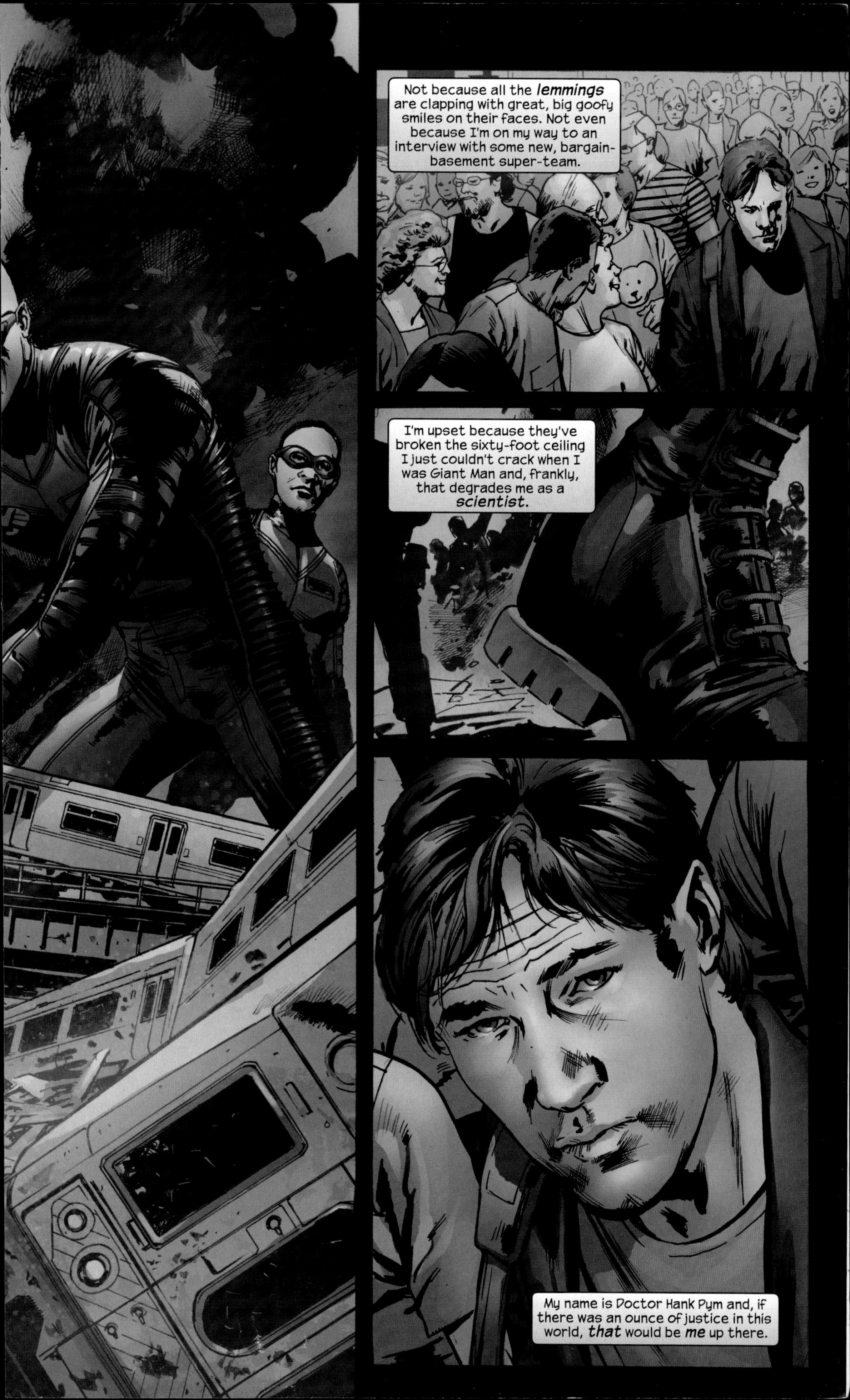

Not because all the *lemmings* are clapping with great, big goofy smiles on their faces. Not even because I'm on my way to an interview with some new, bargain-basement super-team.
I'm upset because they've broken the sixty-foot ceiling I just couldn't crack when I was Giant Man and, frankly, that degrades me as a *scientist*.
My name is Doctor Hank Pym and, if there was an ounce of justice in this world, *that* would be *me* up there.

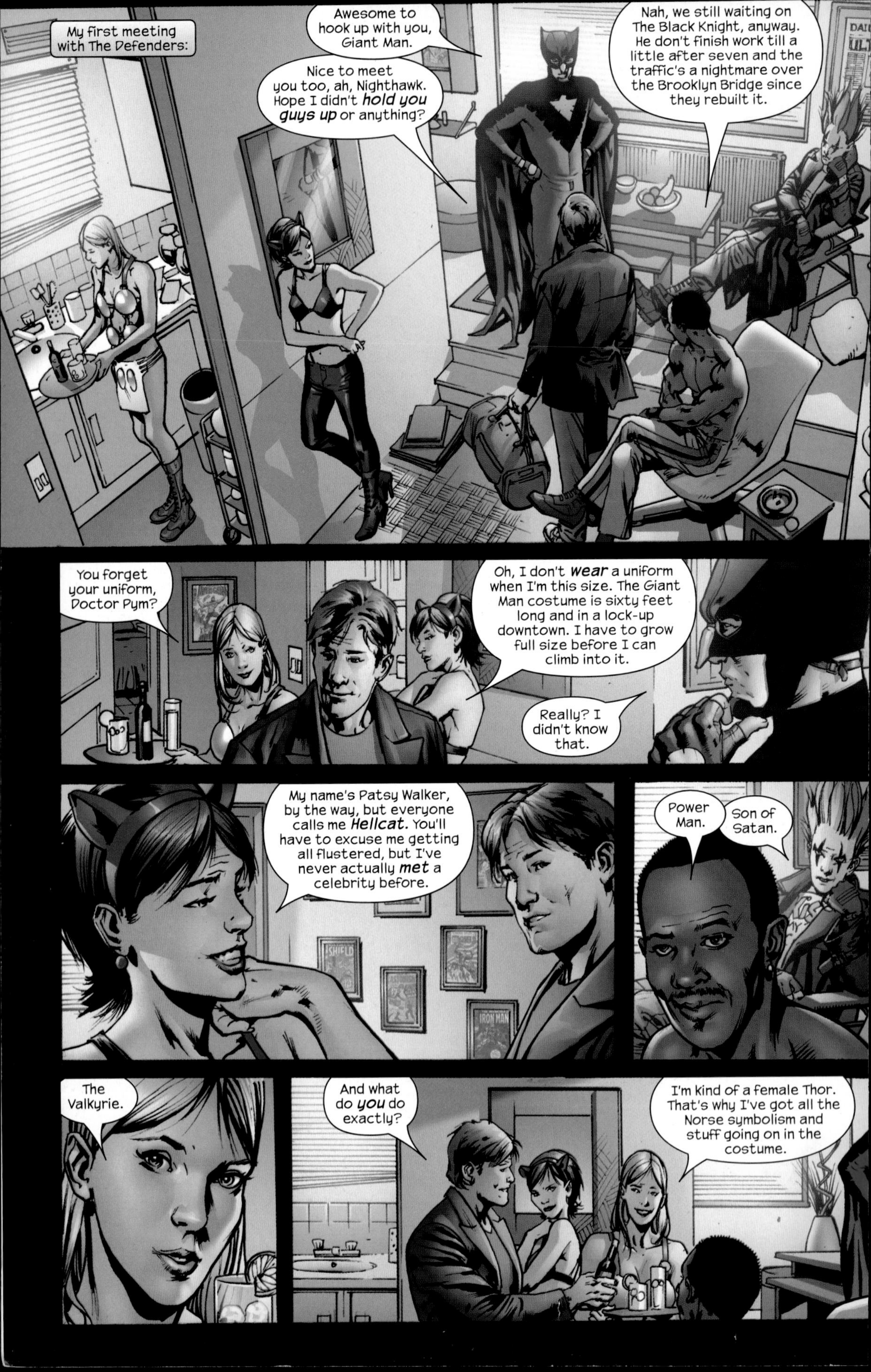
My first meeting with The Defenders:
Awesome to hook up with you, Giant Man.
Nice to meet you too, ah, Nighthawk. Hope I didn't *hold you guys up* or anything?
Nah, we still waiting on The Black Knight, anyway. He don't finish work till a little after seven and the traffic's a nightmare over the Brooklyn Bridge since they rebuilt it.
You forget your uniform, Doctor Pym?
Oh, I don't *wear* a uniform when I'm this size. The Giant Man costume is sixty feet long and in a lock-up downtown. I have to grow full size before I can climb into it.
Really? I didn't know that.
My name's Patsy Walker, by the way, but everyone calls me *Hellcat*. You'll have to excuse me getting all flustered, but I've never actually *met* a celebrity before.
Power Man.
Son of Satan.
The Valkyrie.
And what do *you* do exactly?
I'm kind of a female Thor. That's why I've got all the Norse symbolism and stuff going on in the costume.

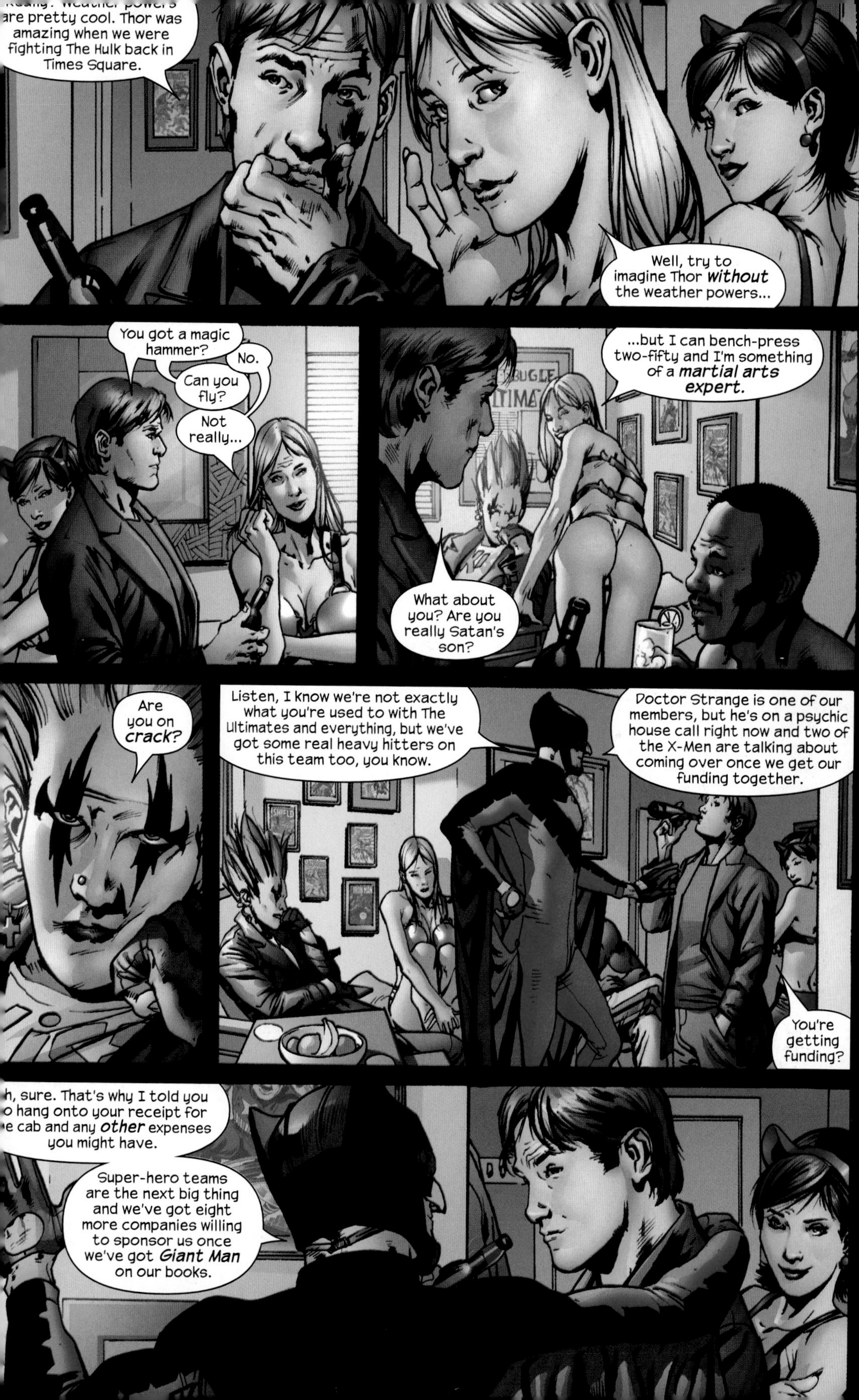
are pretty cool. Thor was amazing when we were fighting The Hulk back in Times Square.
Well, try to imagine Thor *without* the weather powers...
You got a magic hammer?
No.
Can you fly?
Not really...
...but I can bench-press two-fifty and I'm something of a *martial arts expert.*
What about you? Are you really Satan's son?
Are you on *crack?*
Listen, I know we're not exactly what you're used to with The Ultimates and everything, but we've got some real heavy hitters on this team too, you know.
Doctor Strange is one of our members, but he's on a psychic house call right now and two of the X-Men are talking about coming over once we get our funding together.
You're getting funding?
h, sure. That's why I told you o hang onto your receipt for e cab and any *other* expenses you might have.
Super-hero teams are the next big thing and we've got eight more companies willing to sponsor us once we've got *Giant Man* on our books.

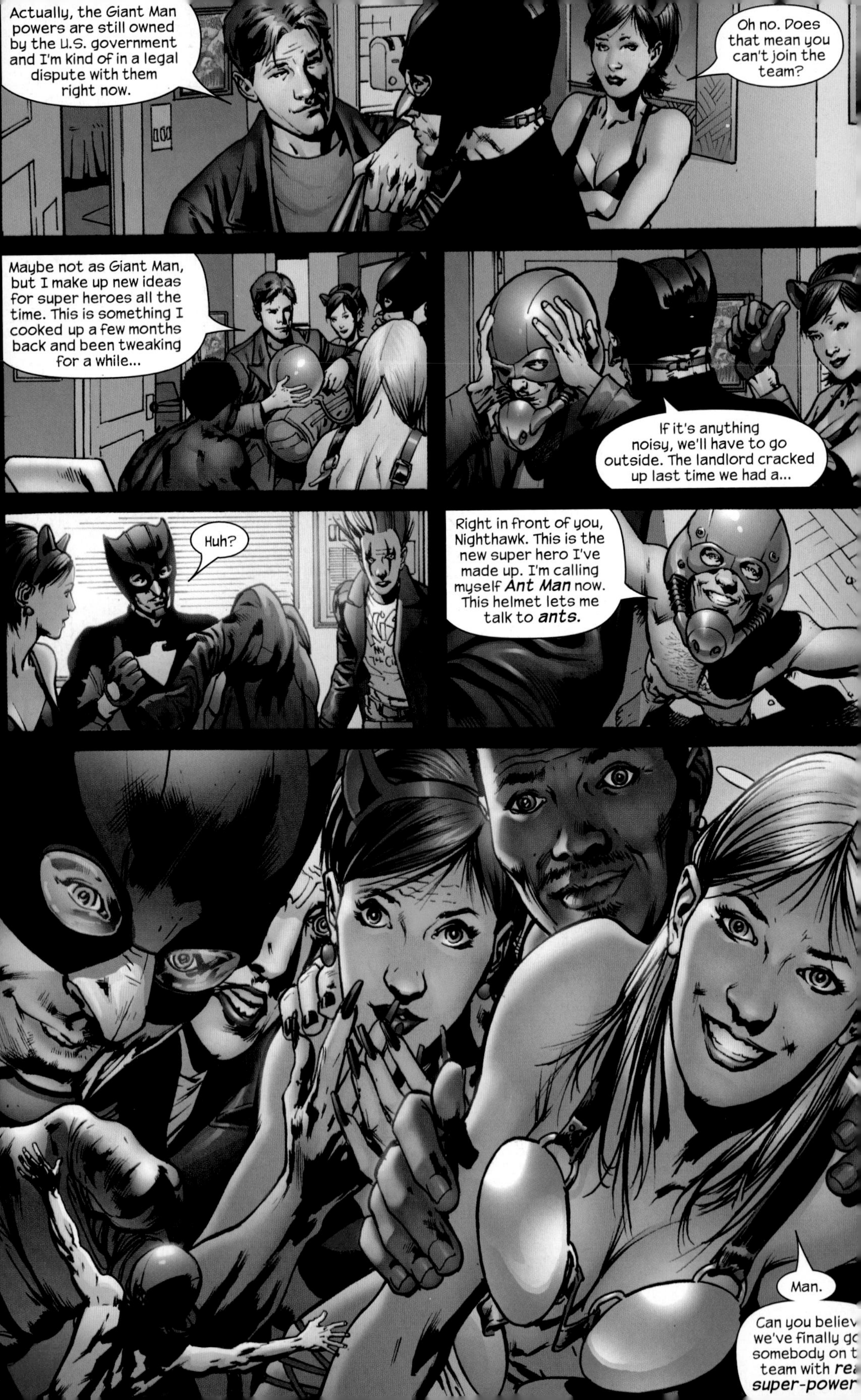
Actually, the Giant Man powers are still owned by the U.S. government and I'm kind of in a legal dispute with them right now.
Oh no. Does that mean you can't join the team?
Maybe not as Giant Man, but I make up new ideas for super heroes all the time. This is something I cooked up a few months back and been tweaking for a while...
If it's anything noisy, we'll have to go outside. The landlord cracked up last time we had a...
Huh?
Right in front of you, Nighthawk. This is the new super hero I've made up. I'm calling myself *Ant Man* now. This helmet lets me talk to ***ants.***
Man.

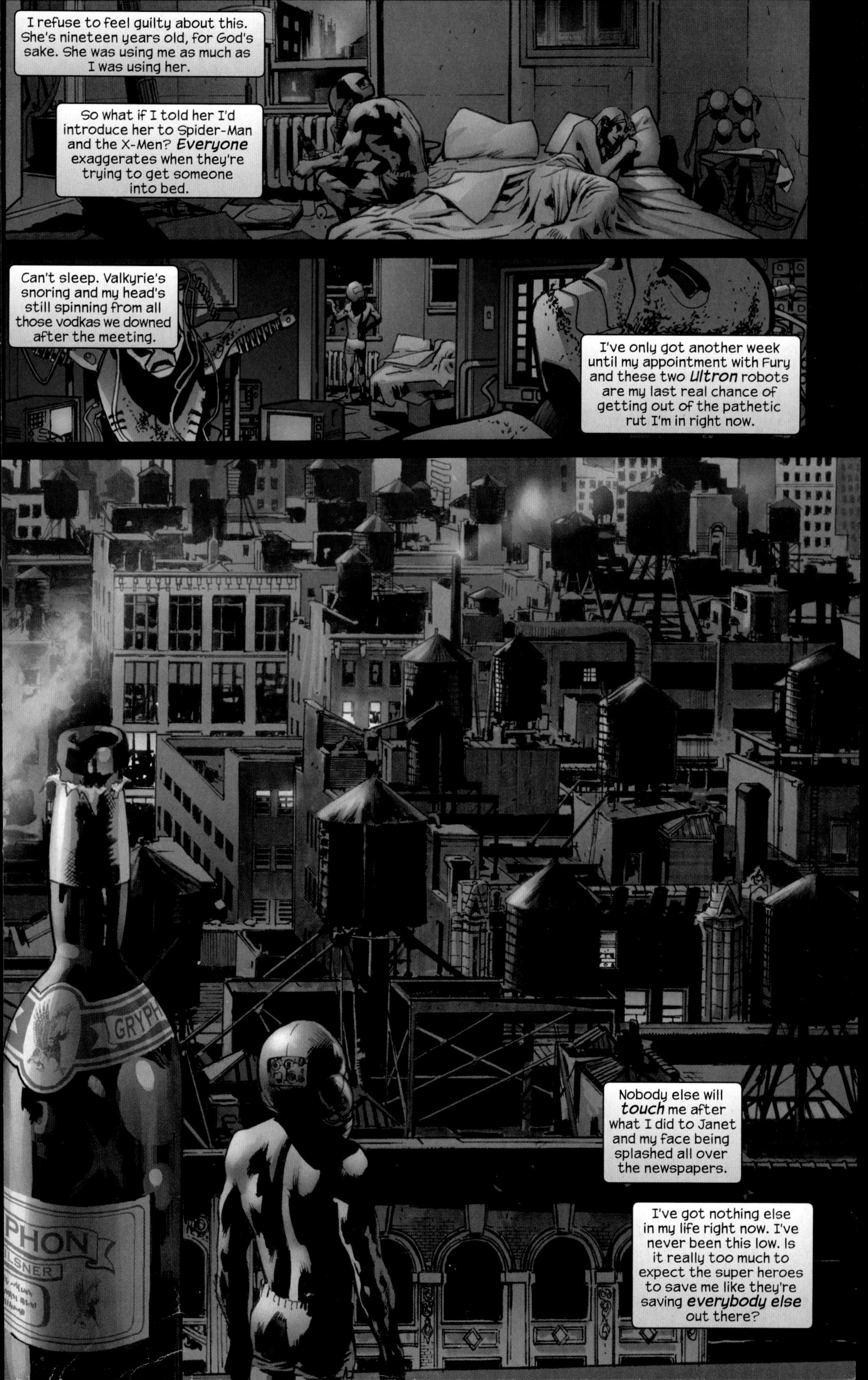

I refuse to feel guilty about this. She's nineteen years old, for God's sake. She was using me as much as I was using her.
So what if I told her I'd introduce her to Spider-Man and the X-Men? *Everyone* exaggerates when they're trying to get someone into bed.
Can't sleep. Valkyrie's snoring and my head's still spinning from all those vodkas we downed after the meeting.
I've only got another week until my appointment with Fury and these two *Ultron* robots are my last real chance of getting out of the pathetic rut I'm in right now.
GRYPH
PHON
Nobody else will *touch* me after what I did to Janet and my face being splashed all over the newspapers.
I've got nothing else in my life right now. I've never been this low. Is it really too much to expect the super heroes to save me like they're saving *everybody else* out there?

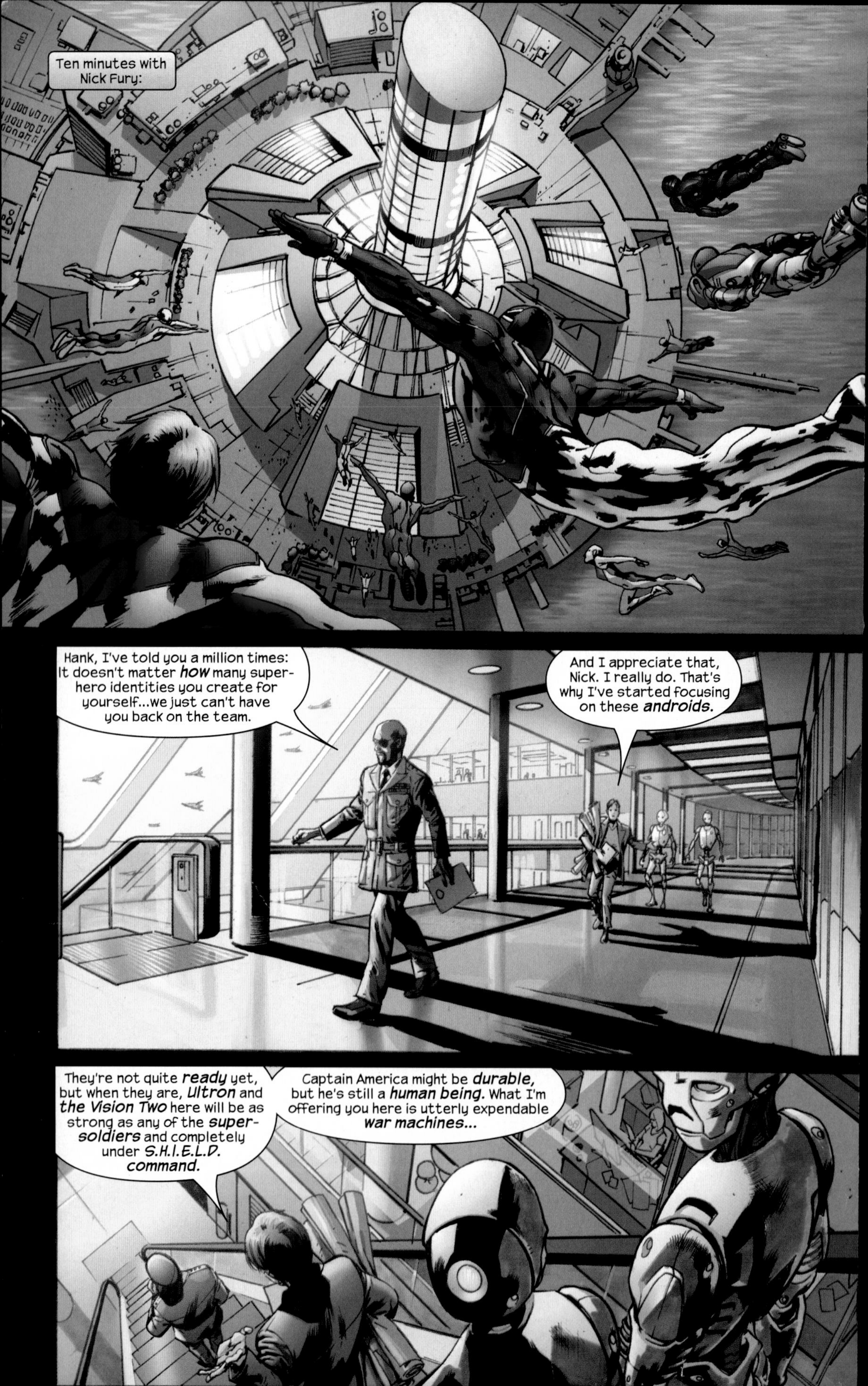
Ten minutes with Nick Fury:
Hank, I've told you a million times: It doesn't matter how many super-hero identities you create for yourself...we just can't have you back on the team.
And I appreciate that, Nick. I really do. That's why I've started focusing on these androids.
They're not quite ready yet, but when they are, Ultron and the Vision Two here will be as strong as any of the super-soldiers and completely under S.H.I.E.L.D. command.
Captain America might be durable, but he's still a human being. What I'm offering you here is utterly expendable war machines...

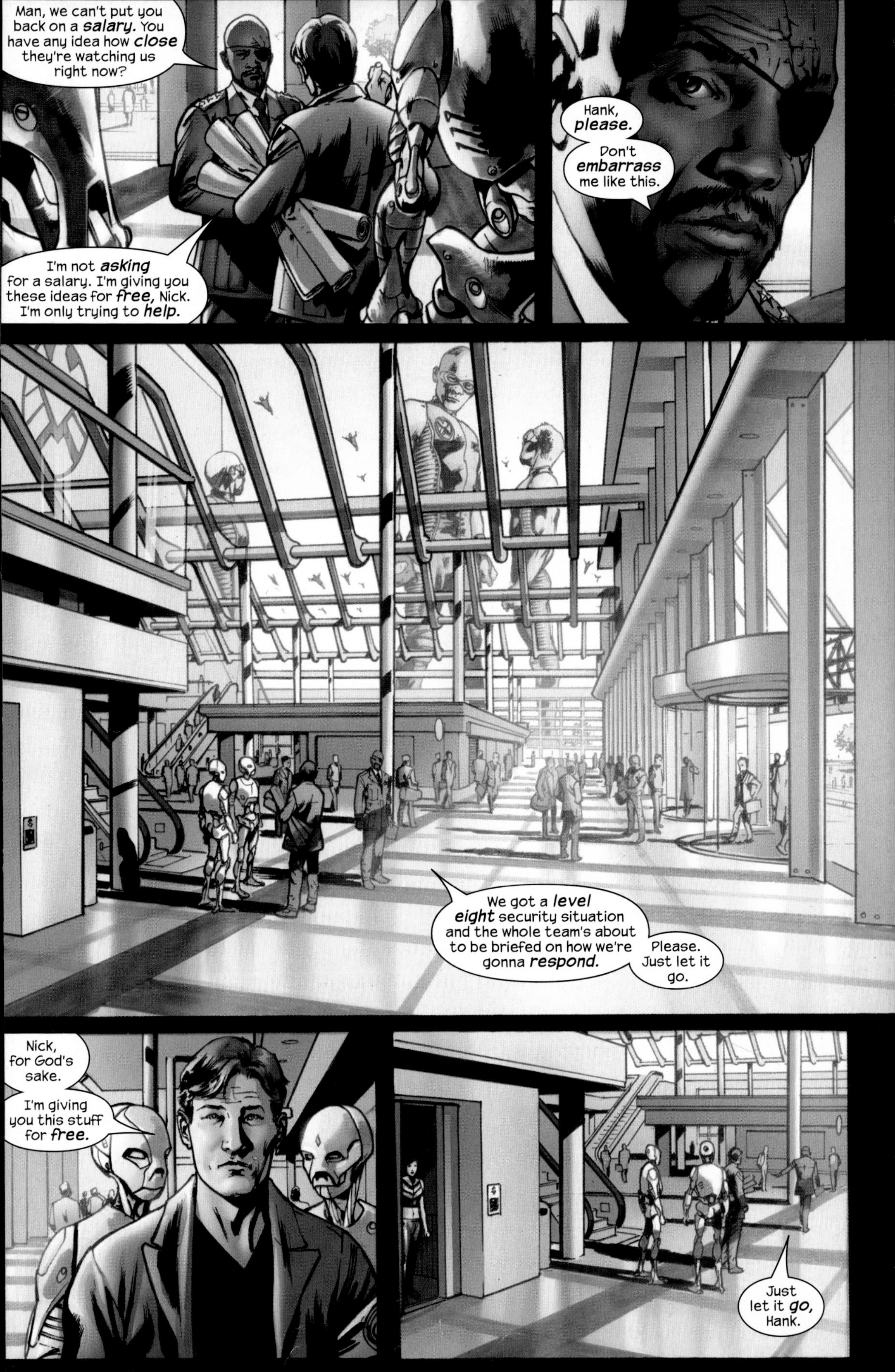
Man, we can't put you back on a salary. You have any idea how close they're watching us right now?
I'm not asking for a salary. I'm giving you these ideas for free, Nick. I'm only trying to help.
Hank, please.
Don't embarrass me like this.
We got a level eight security situation and the whole team's about to be briefed on how we're gonna respond.
Please. Just let it go.
Nick, for God's sake.
I'm giving you this stuff for free.
Just let it go, Hank.

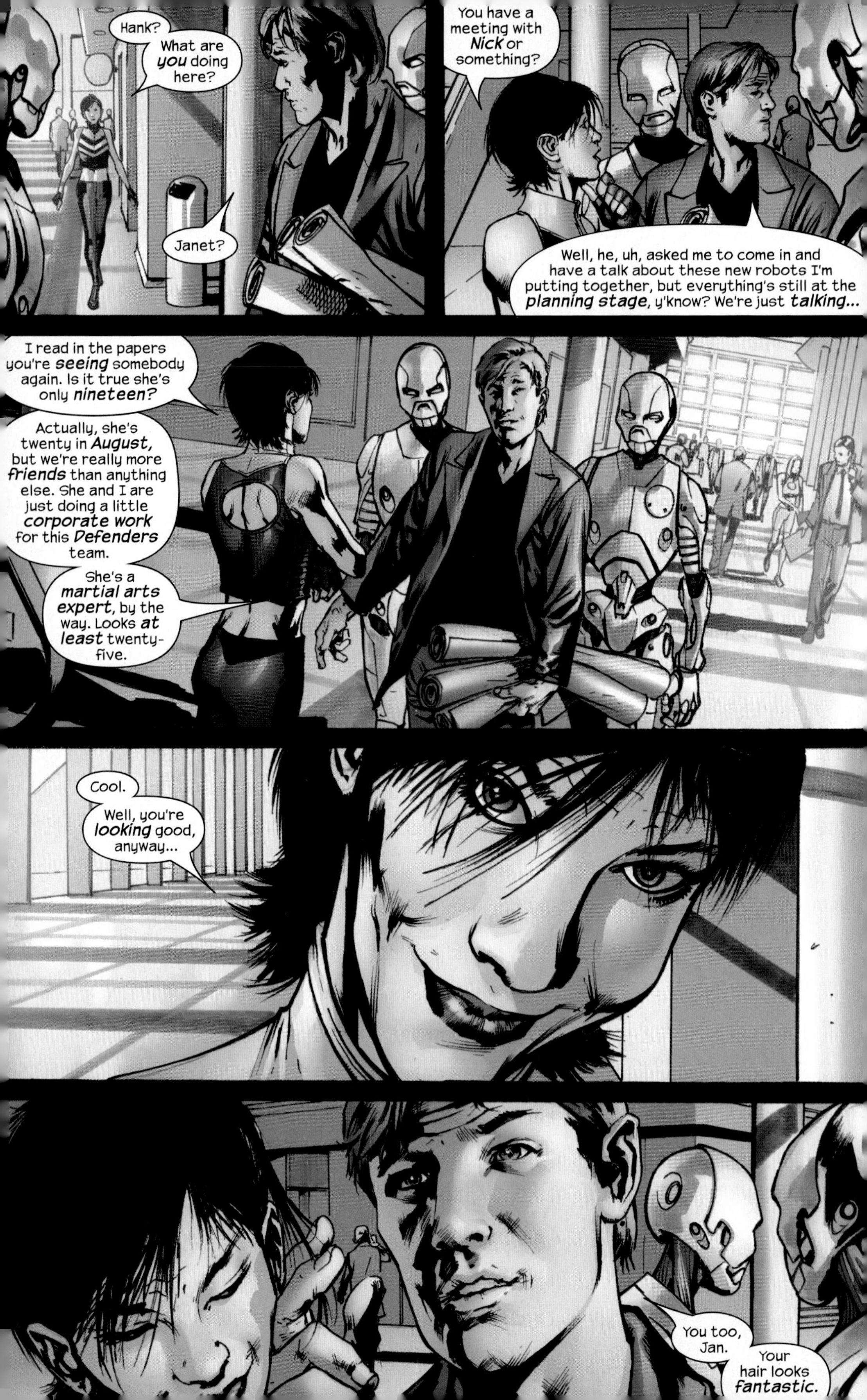
Hank? What are you doing here?
Janet?
You have a meeting with Nick or something?
Well, he, uh, asked me to come in and have a talk about these new robots I'm putting together, but everything's still at the planning stage, y'know? We're just talking...
I read in the papers you're seeing somebody again. Is it true she's only nineteen?
Actually, she's twenty in August, but we're really more friends than anything else. She and I are just doing a little corporate work for this Defenders team.
She's a martial arts expert, by the way. Looks at least twenty-five.
Cool.
Well, you're looking good, anyway...
You too, Jan.
Your hair looks fantastic.

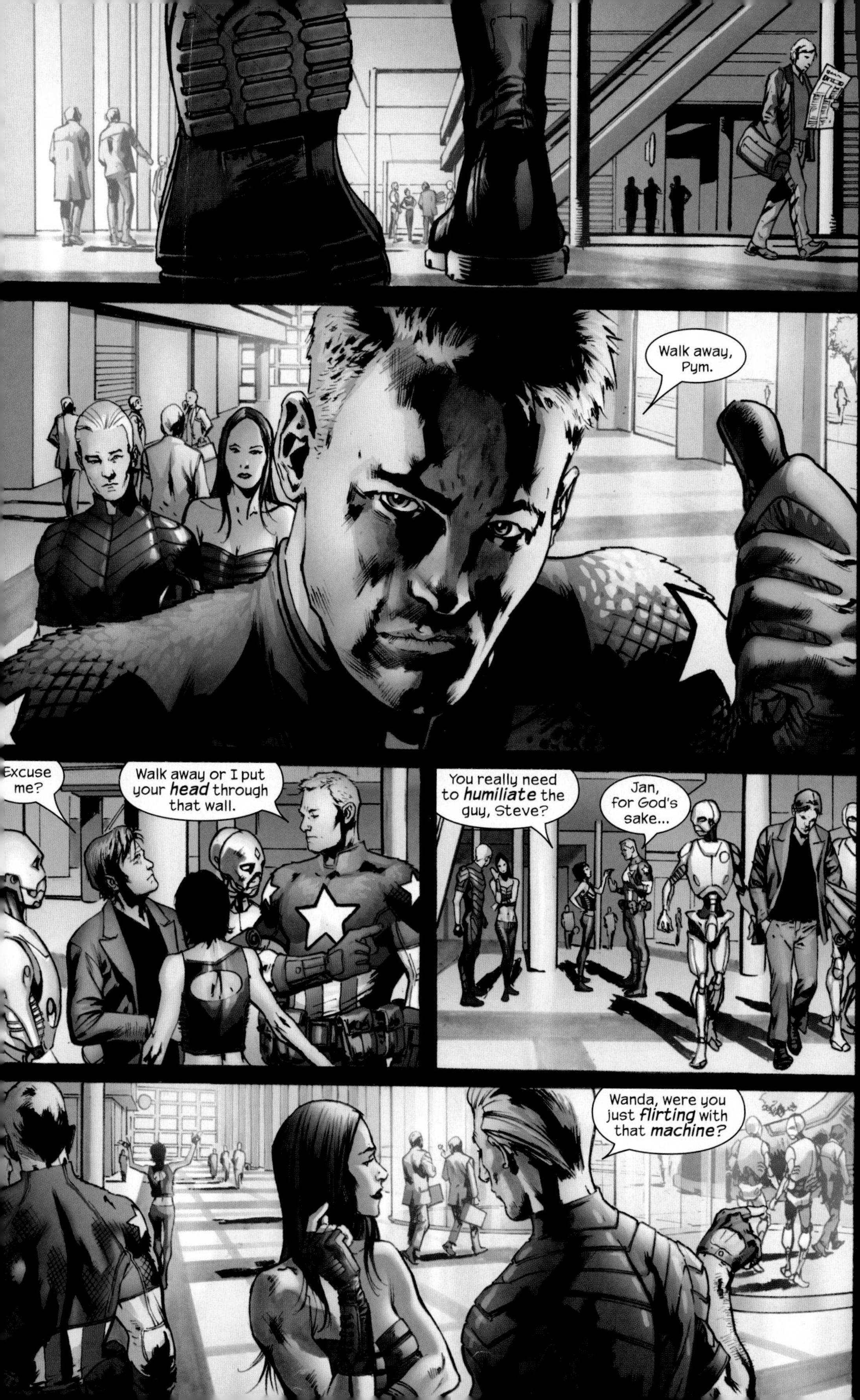

Walk away, Pym.
Excuse me?
Walk away or I put your *head* through that wall.
You really need to *humiliate* the guy, Steve?
Jan, for God's sake...
Wanda, were you just *flirting* with that *machine*?

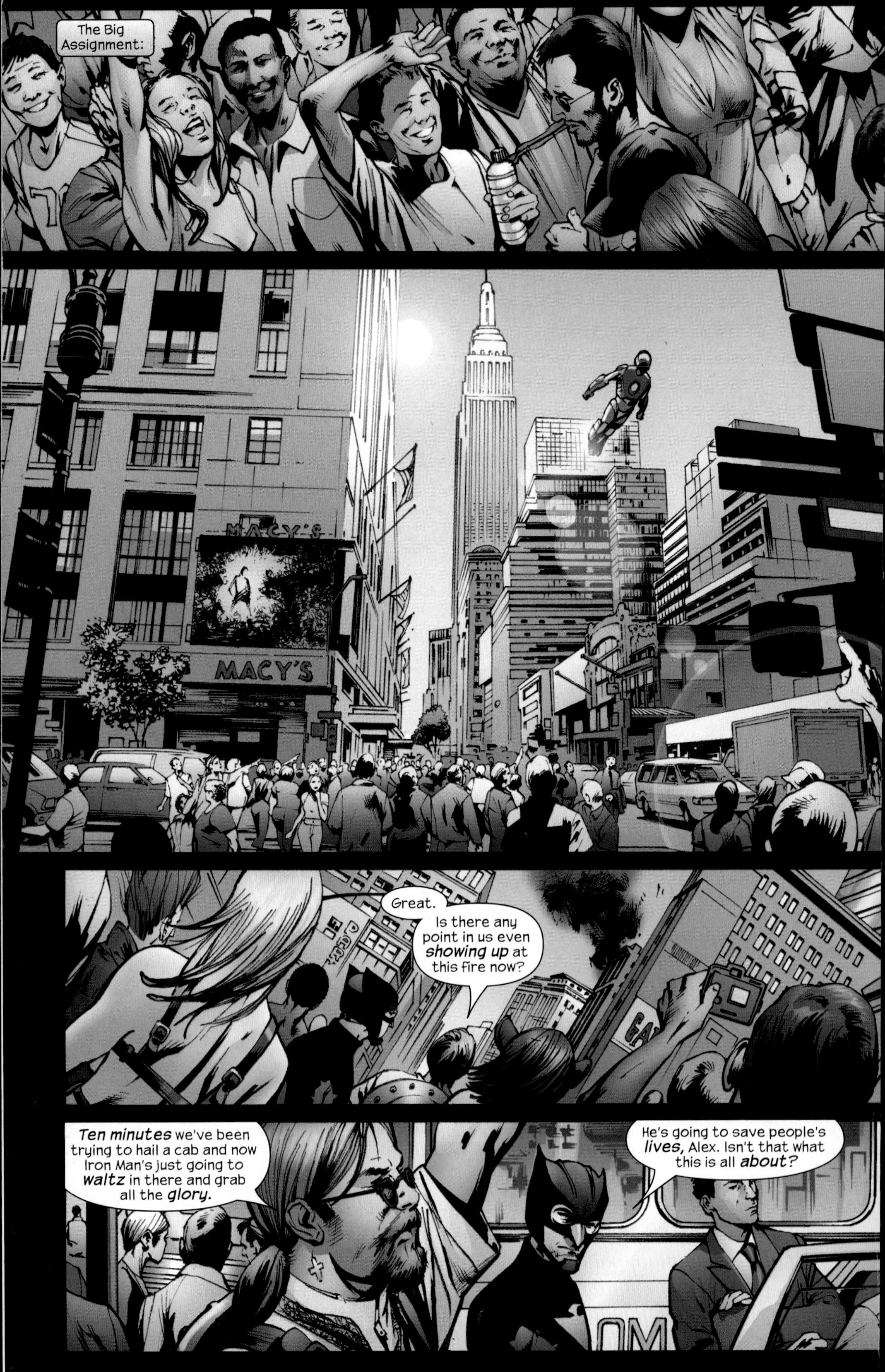

The Big Assignment:
MACY'S
MACY'S
Great.
Is there any point in us even *showing up* at this fire now?
Ten minutes we've been trying to hail a cab and now Iron Man's just going to *waltz* in there and grab all the *glory.*
He's going to save people's *lives,* Alex. Isn't that what this is all *about?*

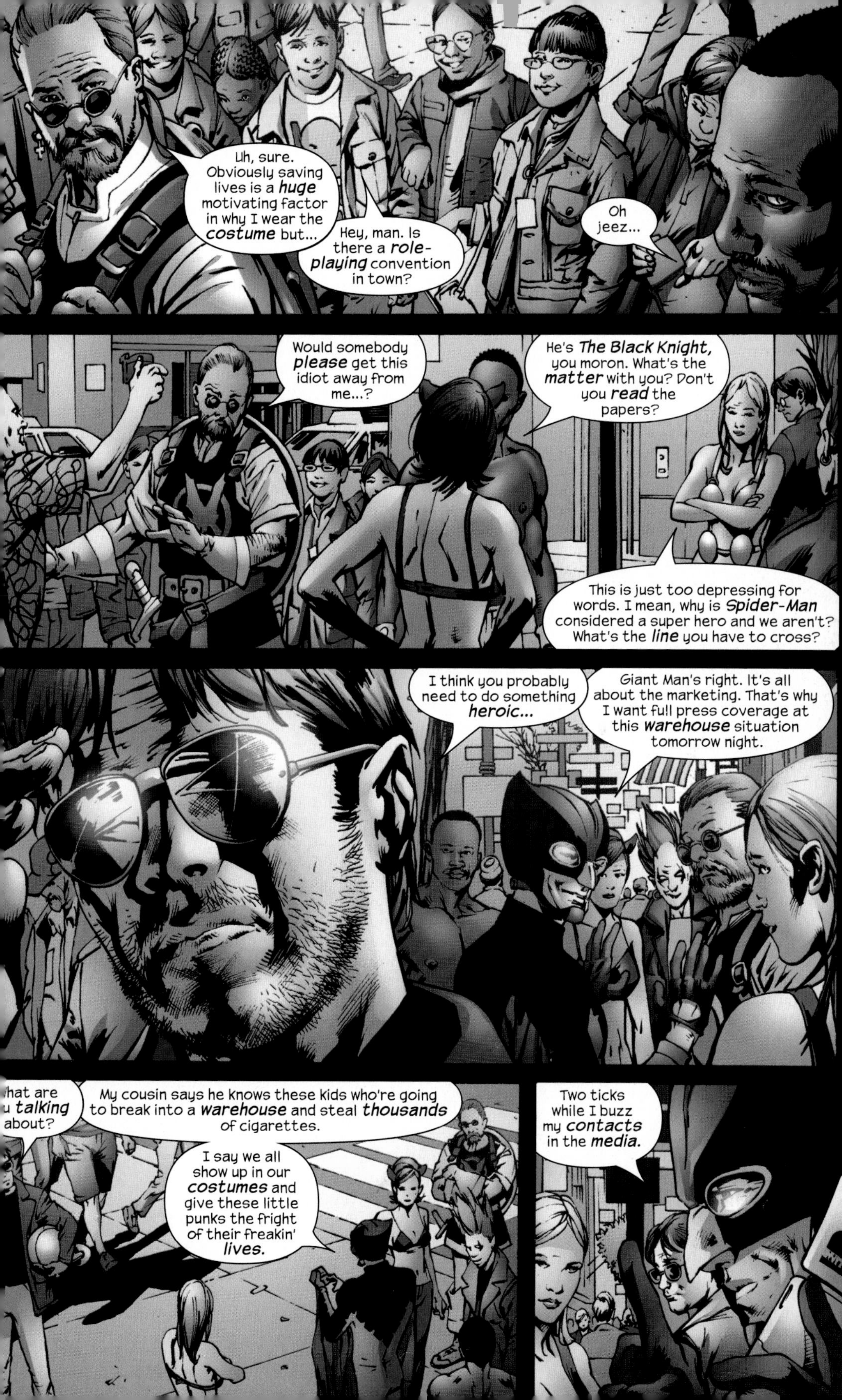

Uh, sure. Obviously saving lives is a *huge* motivating factor in why I wear the *costume* but...
Hey, man. Is there a *role-playing* convention in town?
Oh jeez...
Would somebody *please* get this idiot away from me...?
He's *The Black Knight,* you moron. What's the *matter* with you? Don't you *read* the papers?
This is just too depressing for words. I mean, why is *Spider-Man* considered a super hero and we aren't? What's the *line* you have to cross?
I think you probably need to do something *heroic...*
Giant Man's right. It's all about the marketing. That's why I want full press coverage at this *warehouse* situation tomorrow night.
hat are u *talking* about?
My cousin says he knows these kids who're going to break into a *warehouse* and steal *thousands* of cigarettes.
I say we all show up in our *costumes* and give these little punks the fright of their freakin' *lives.*
Two ticks while I buzz my *contacts* in the *media.*

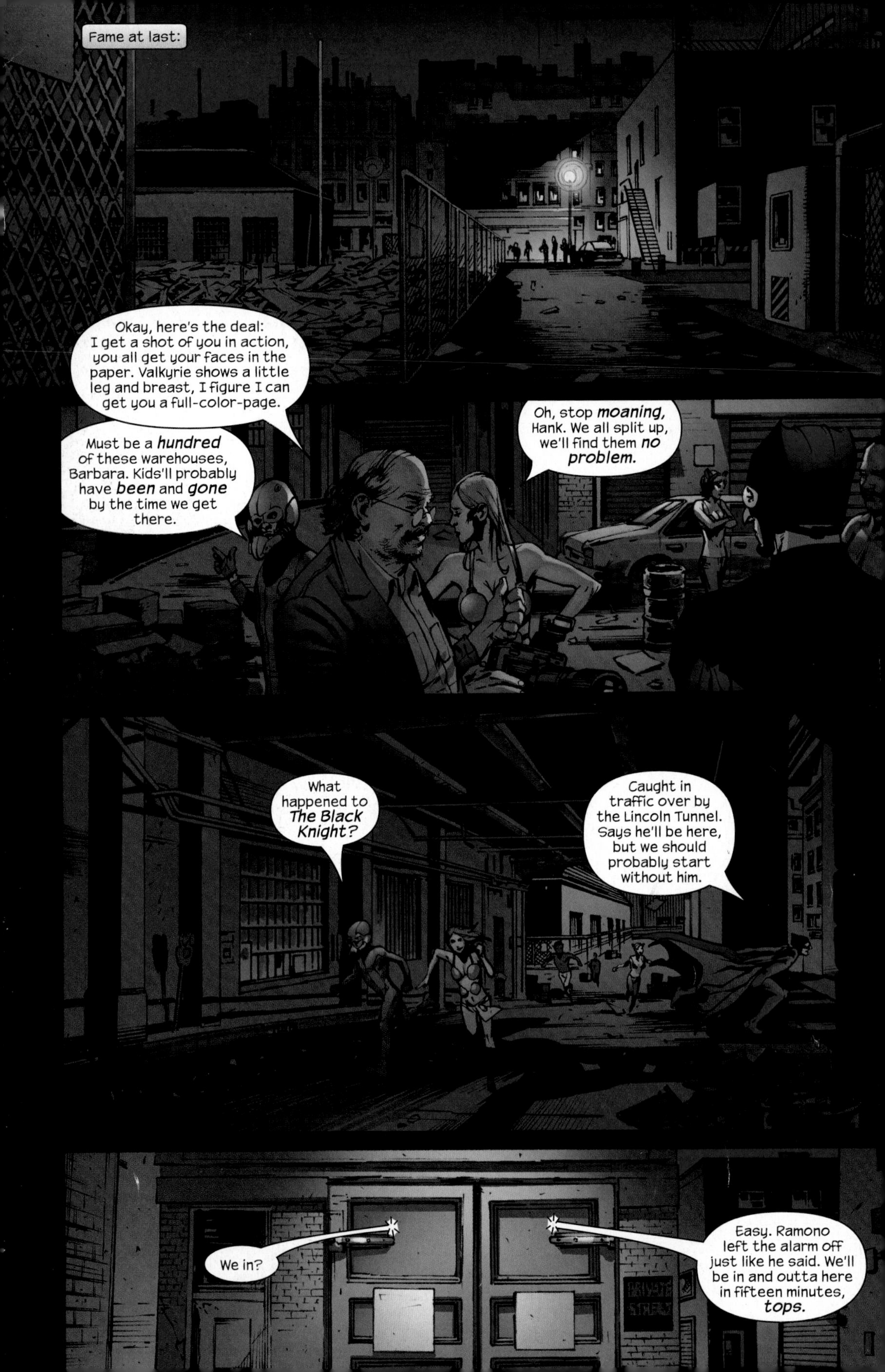

Fame at last:
Okay, here's the deal: I get a shot of you in action, you all get your faces in the paper. Valkyrie shows a little leg and breast, I figure I can get you a full-color-page.
Must be a *hundred* of these warehouses, Barbara. Kids'll probably have *been* and *gone* by the time we get there.
Oh, stop *moaning,* Hank. We all split up, we'll find them *no problem.*
What happened to *The Black Knight?*
Caught in traffic over by the Lincoln Tunnel. Says he'll be here, but we should probably start without him.
We in?
Easy. Ramono left the alarm off just like he said. We'll be in and outta here in fifteen minutes, *tops.*

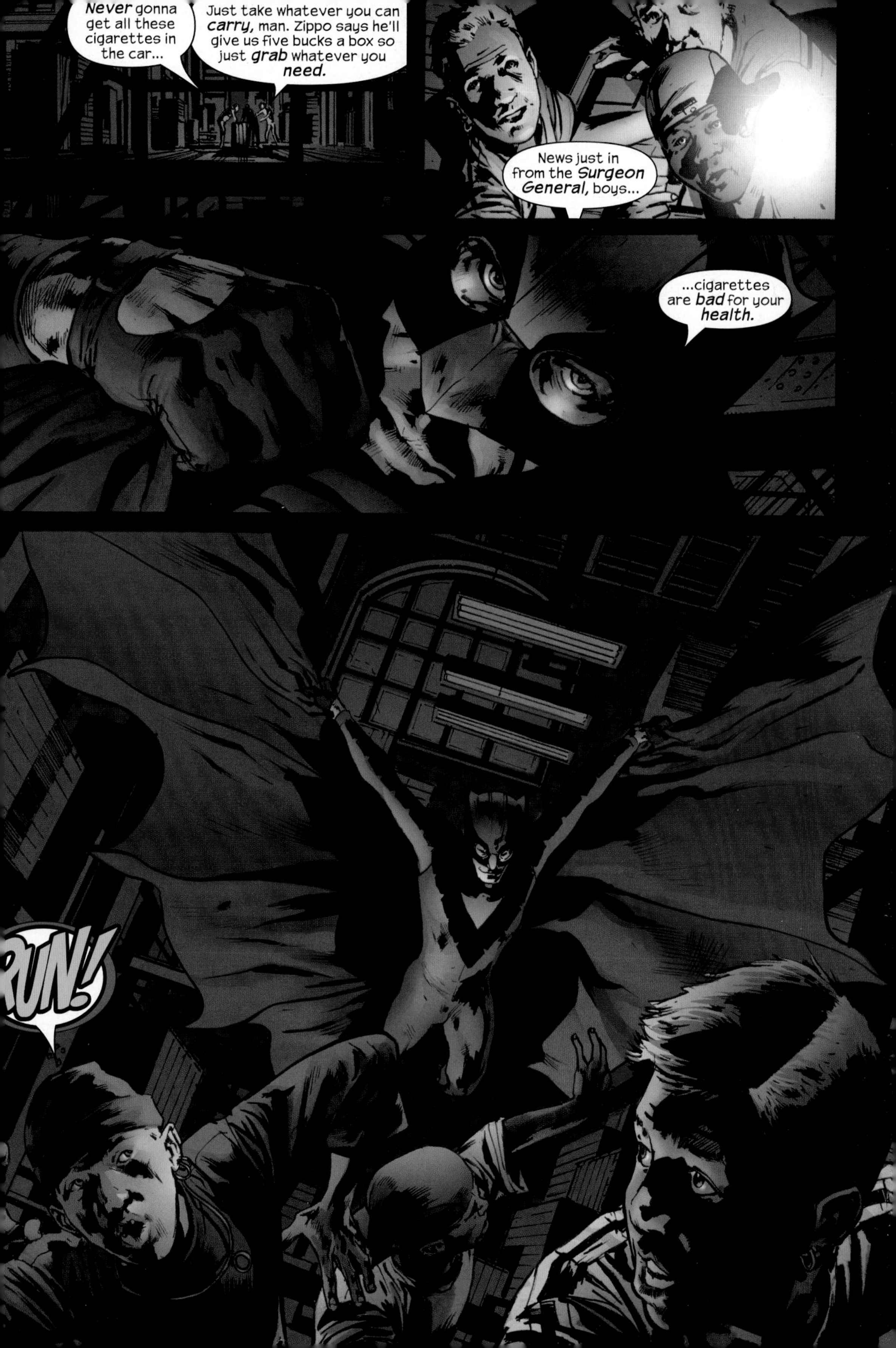

Never gonna get all these cigarettes in the car...
Just take whatever you can *carry,* man. Zippo says he'll give us five bucks a box so just *grab* whatever you *need.*
News just in from the *Surgeon General,* boys...
...cigarettes are *bad* for your *health.*
RUN!

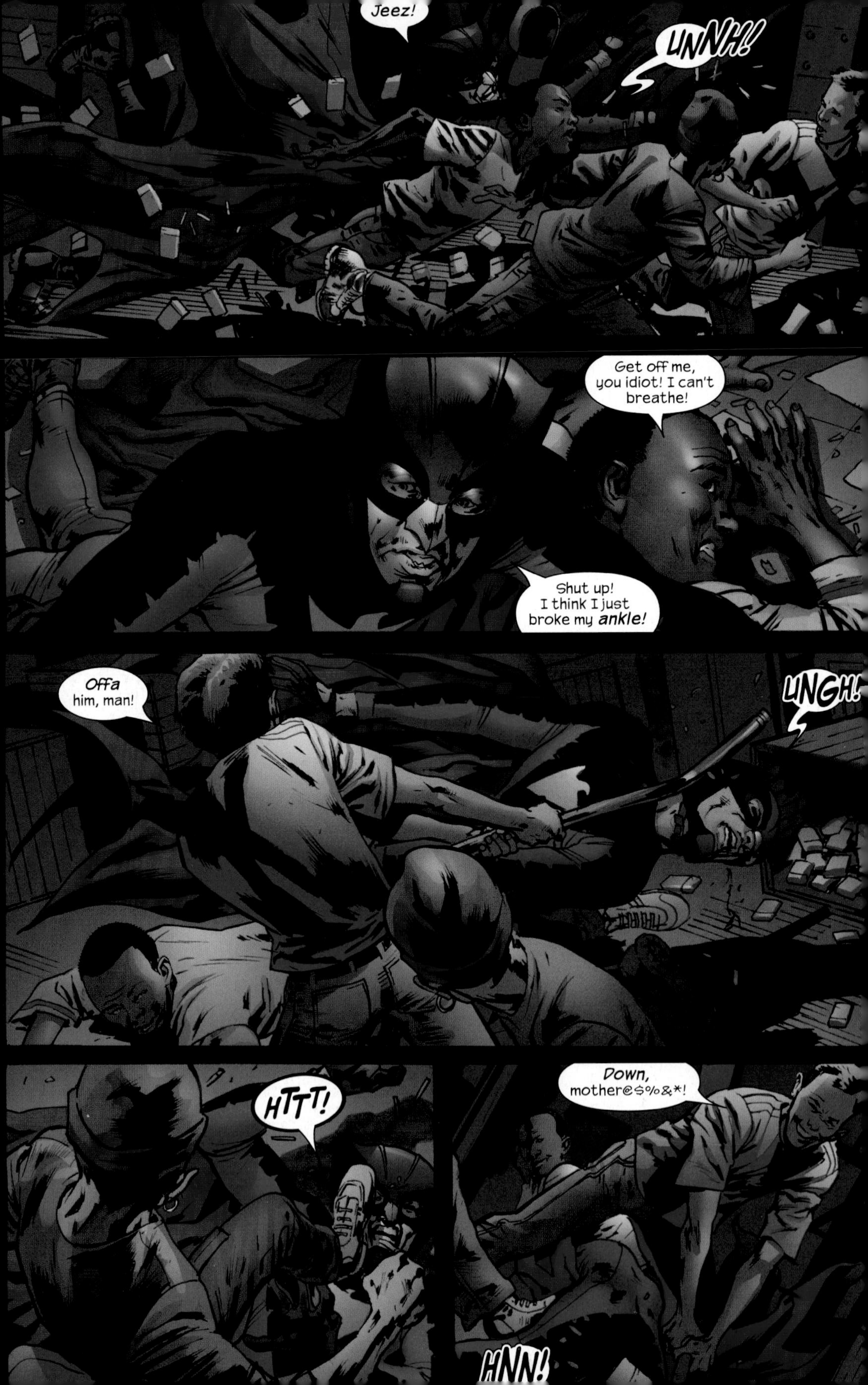
Jeez!
UNNH!
Get off me, you idiot! I can't breathe!
Shut up! I think I just broke my ankle!
Offa him, man!
UNGH!
HTTT!
Down, mother@$%&*!
HNN!

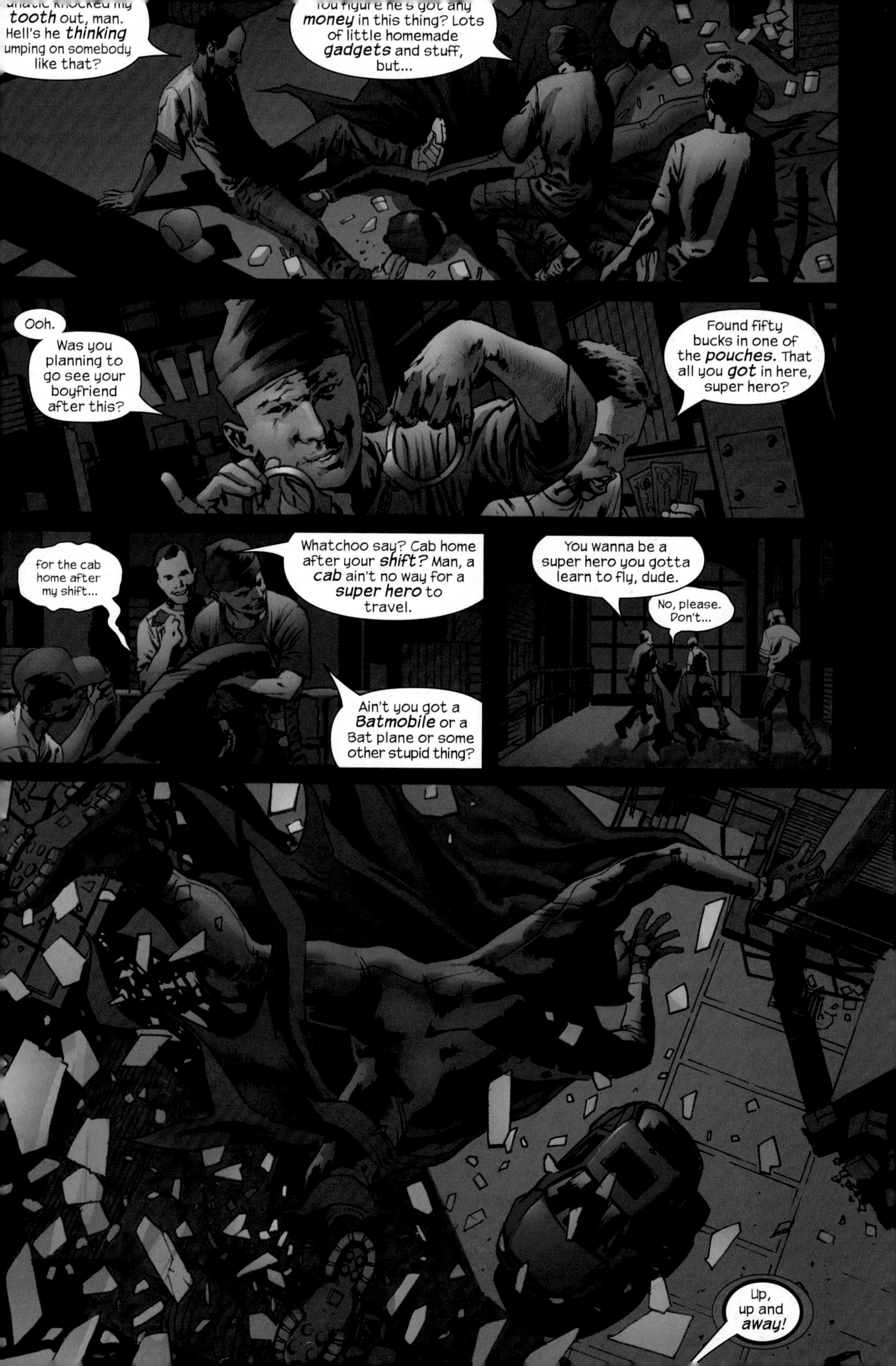

tooth out, man. Hell's he thinking umping on somebody like that?
You figure he's got any money in this thing? Lots of little homemade gadgets and stuff, but...
Ooh.
Was you planning to go see your boyfriend after this?
Found fifty bucks in one of the pouches. That all you got in here, super hero?
for the cab home after my shift...
Whatchoo say? Cab home after your shift? Man, a cab ain't no way for a super hero to travel.
Ain't you got a Batmobile or a Bat plane or some other stupid thing?
You wanna be a super hero you gotta learn to fly, dude.
No, please. Don't...
Up, up and away!

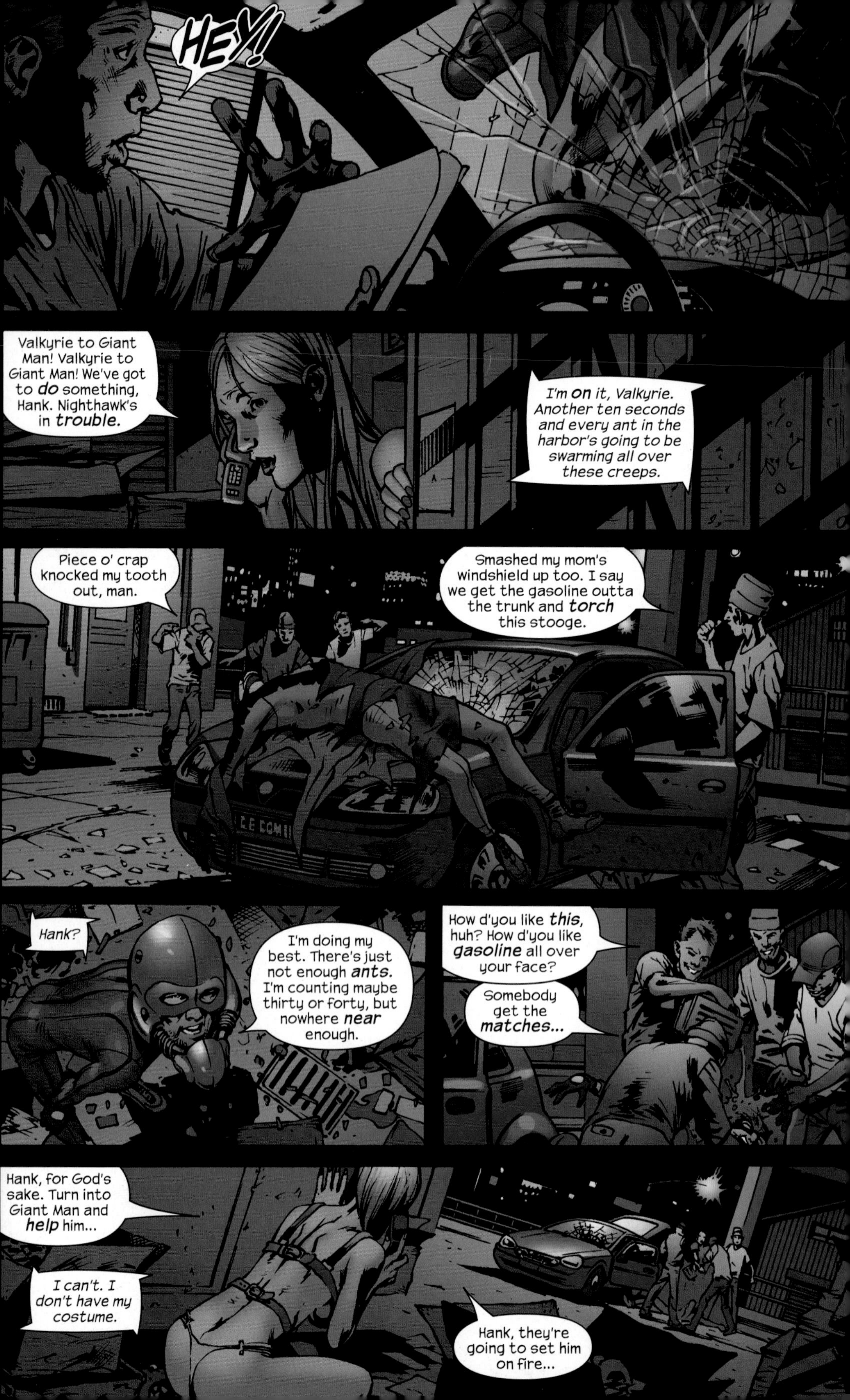
HEY!
Valkyrie to Giant Man! Valkyrie to Giant Man! We've got to do something, Hank. Nighthawk's in trouble.
I'm on it, Valkyrie. Another ten seconds and every ant in the harbor's going to be swarming all over these creeps.
Piece o' crap knocked my tooth out, man.
Smashed my mom's windshield up too. I say we get the gasoline outta the trunk and torch this stooge.
Hank?
I'm doing my best. There's just not enough ants. I'm counting maybe thirty or forty, but nowhere near enough.
How d'you like this, huh? How d'you like gasoline all over your face?
Somebody get the matches...
Hank, for God's sake. Turn into Giant Man and help him...
I can't. I don't have my costume.
Hank, they're going to set him on fire...

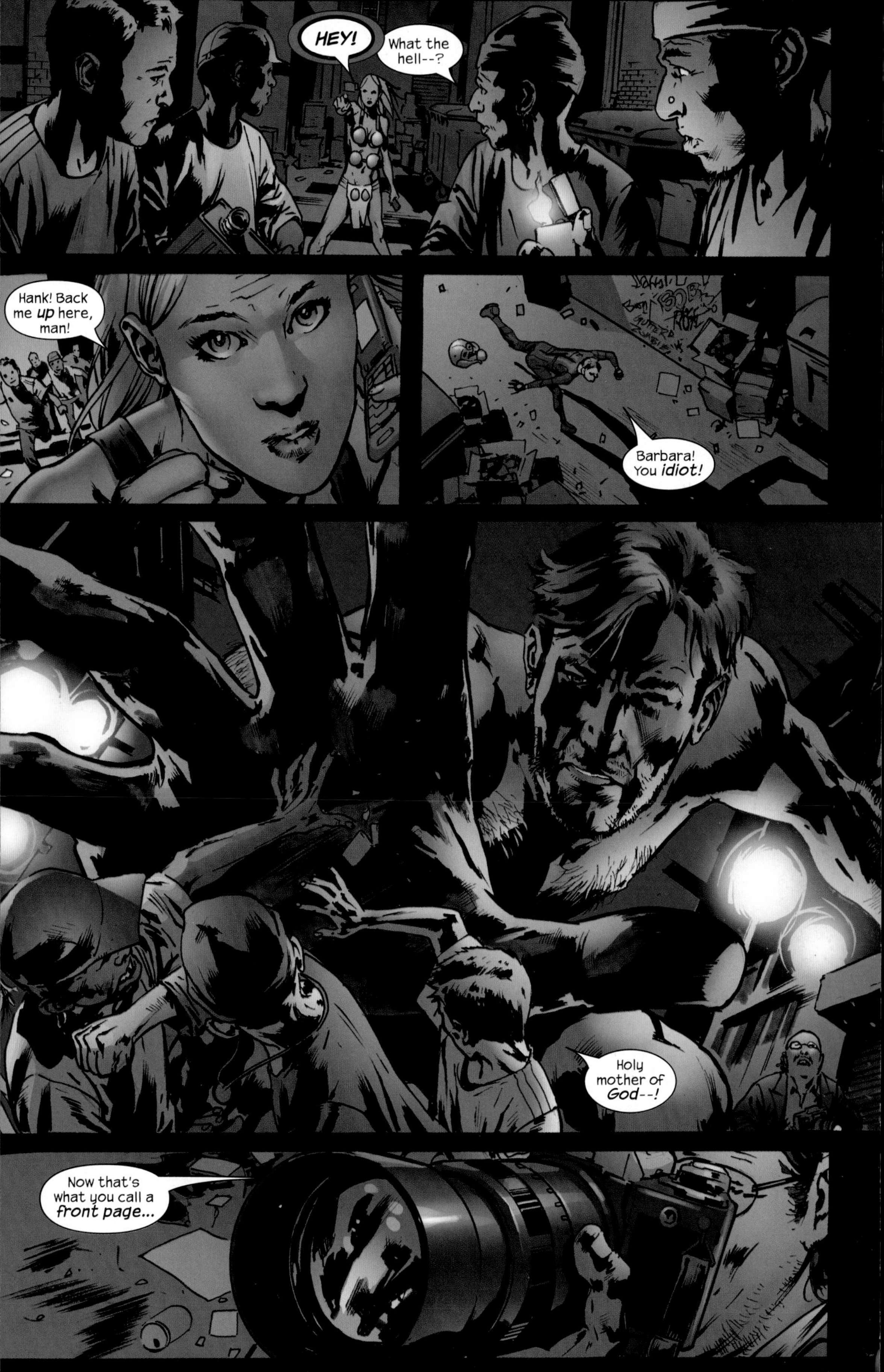
HEY!
What the hell--?
Hank! Back me up here, man!
Barbara! You idiot!
Holy mother of God--!
Now that's what you call a front page...

DAILY BUGLE

NEW YORK'S FINEST DAILY PAPER

BUTT-ER LUCK NEXT TIM

Super-Hero Debut Descends Into Far

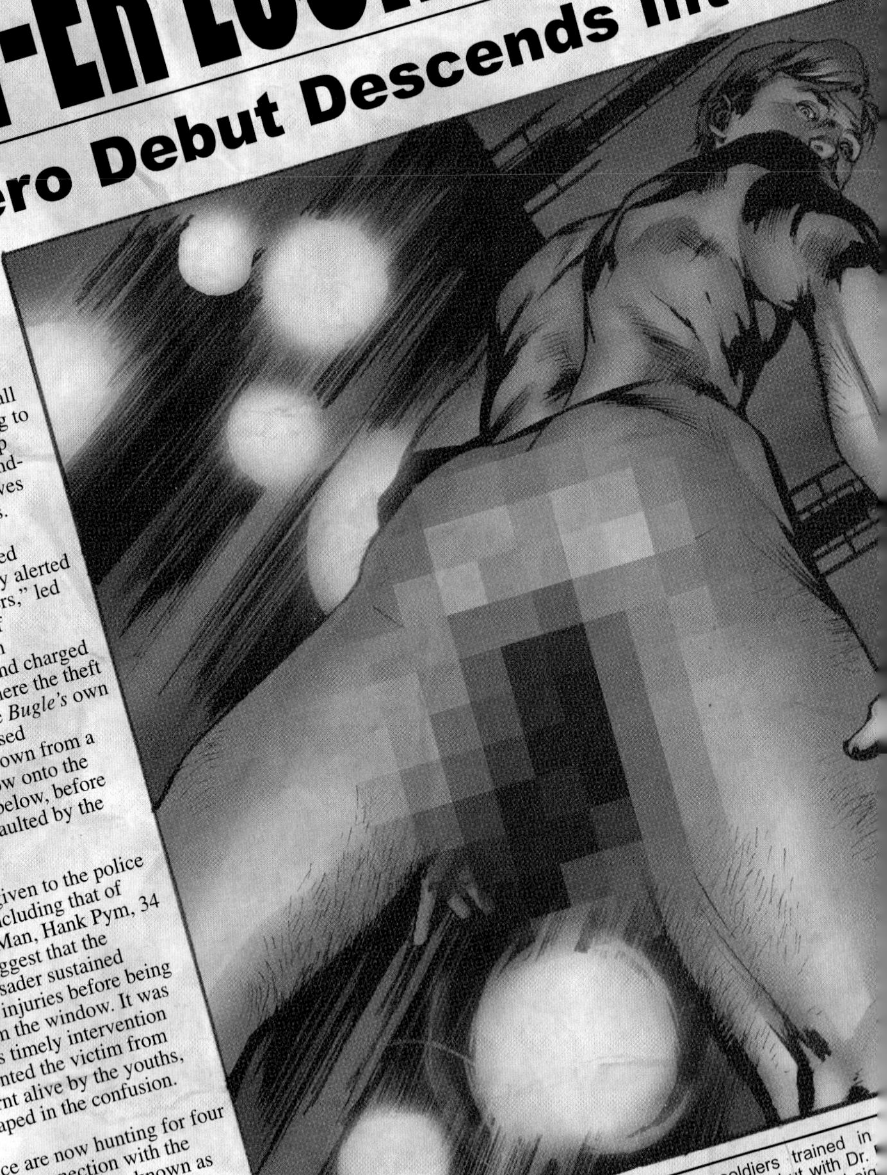

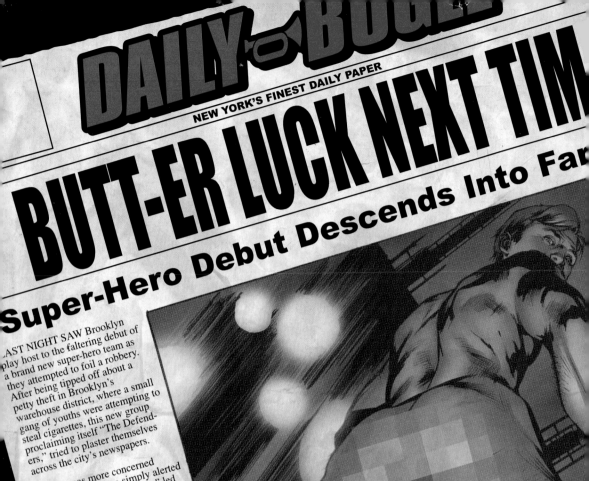

LAST NIGHT SAW Brooklyn play host to the faltering debut of a brand new super-hero team as they attempted to foil a robbery. After being tipped off about a petty theft in Brooklyn's warehouse district, where a small gang of youths were attempting to steal cigarettes, this new group proclaiming itself "The Defenders," tried to plaster themselves across the city's newspapers.

Whereas more concerned citizens might have simply alerted the police, "The Defenders," led by a man calling himself Darkhawk,dressed up in homemade costumes and charged into the warehouse where the theft was taking place. The *Bugle's* own photographer witnessed Darkhawk being thrown from a second-floor window onto the hood of a vehicle below, before being brutally assaulted by the youths.

Statements given to the police by witnesses including that of former Giant Man, Hank Pym, 34 (pictured), suggest that the wannabe crusader sustained severe head injuries before being thrown from the window. It was only Pym's timely intervention that prevented the victim from being burnt alive by the youths, who escaped in the confusion.

Police are now hunting for four youths in connection with the assault while the man known as Darkhawk remains in critical condition. Assistant district attorney Nick Setchfield is also looking into charging "The Defenders" with breaking anti-vigilante laws.

Once a member of the world's leading superhuman defense group, The Ultimates, Dr. Hank Pym's life is far from the glamor of Hollywood celebrity. Aside from his much-publicized divorce from fellow teammate Janet van Dyne (also known as The Wasp), he was fired from his position as head of the ultra-secret Super Soldier program at S.H.I.E.L.D. following allegations of physical abuse and a public brawl with Captain America in the backstreets of Chicago.

...the loss of Pym's position, medical breakthroughs saw a ... of Giant Men introduced to the Ultimates' line-... ws. "These new guys are amazing. Not only are they soldiers trained in situations, with experience in the Gulf, but with Dr. ... new treatments we have raised their ceiling heig... under two hundred feet--that's more than three time... height of Pym at his best. These Giant Men and the... have training in Tony Stark's specially commissio... exo-suits will make our Super Human Defense Initiative the greatest...

Triskelion insiders also suggest that Pym may be... illegal use of a controlled substance followin... tioned height multiplication in Brooklyn last night.

Dr. Pym was not available for comment.

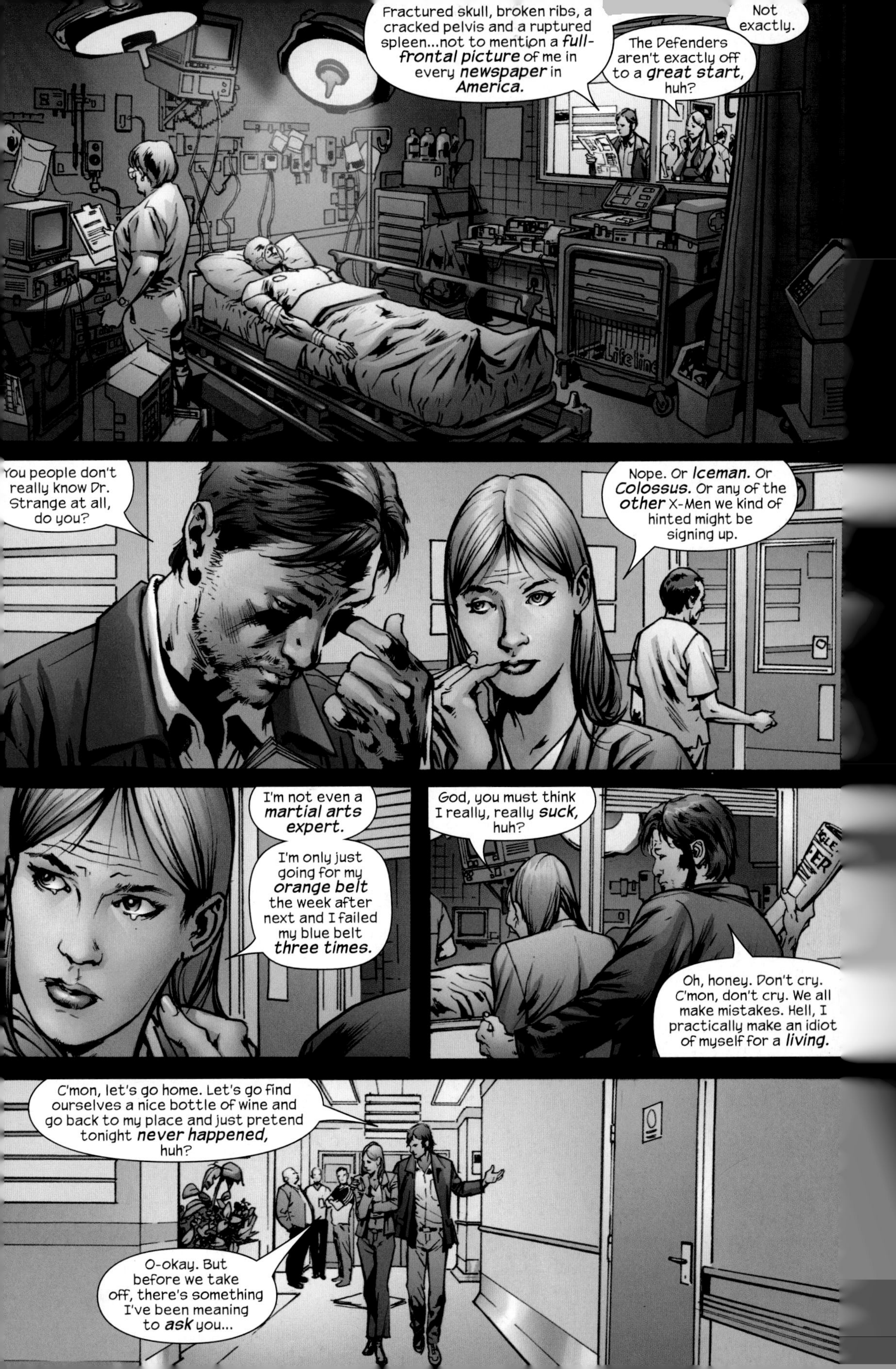
Fractured skull, broken ribs, a cracked pelvis and a ruptured spleen...not to mention a full-frontal picture of me in every newspaper in America.
The Defenders aren't exactly off to a great start, huh?
Not exactly.
You people don't really know Dr. Strange at all, do you?
Nope. Or Iceman. Or Colossus. Or any of the other X-Men we kind of hinted might be signing up.
I'm not even a martial arts expert.
I'm only just going for my orange belt the week after next and I failed my blue belt three times.
God, you must think I really, really suck, huh?
Oh, honey. Don't cry. C'mon, don't cry. We all make mistakes. Hell, I practically make an idiot of myself for a living.
C'mon, let's go home. Let's go find ourselves a nice bottle of wine and go back to my place and just pretend tonight never happened, huh?
O-okay. But before we take off, there's something I've been meaning to ask you...

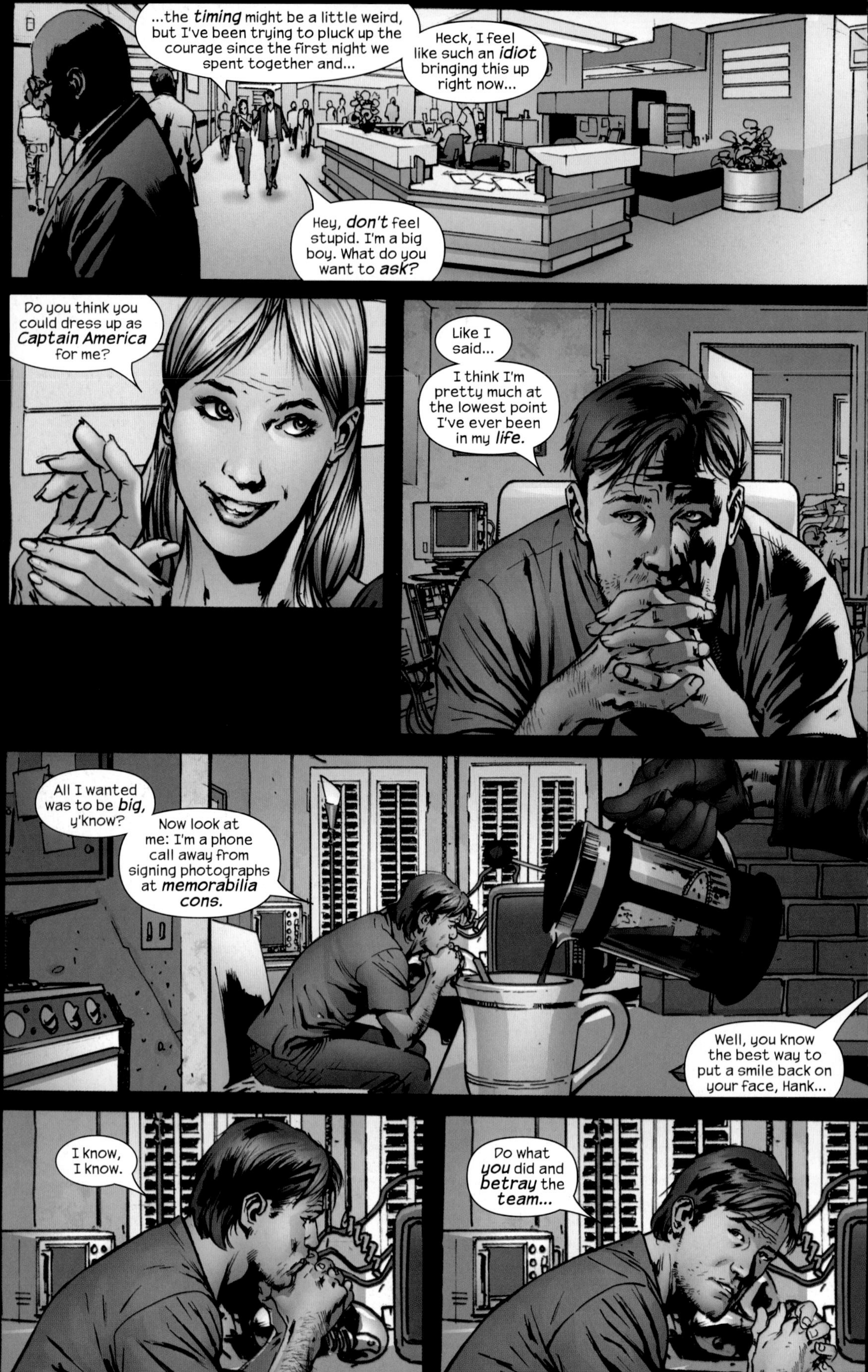
...the *timing* might be a little weird, but I've been trying to pluck up the courage since the first night we spent together and...
Heck, I feel like such an *idiot* bringing this up right now...
Hey, *don't* feel stupid. I'm a big boy. What do you want to *ask?*
Do you think you could dress up as *Captain America* for me?
Like I said...
I think I'm pretty much at the lowest point I've ever been in my *life.*
All I wanted was to be *big,* y'know?
Now look at me: I'm a phone call away from signing photographs at *memorabilia cons.*
Well, you know the best way to put a smile back on your face, Hank...
I know, I know.
Do what *you* did and *betray* the *team...*

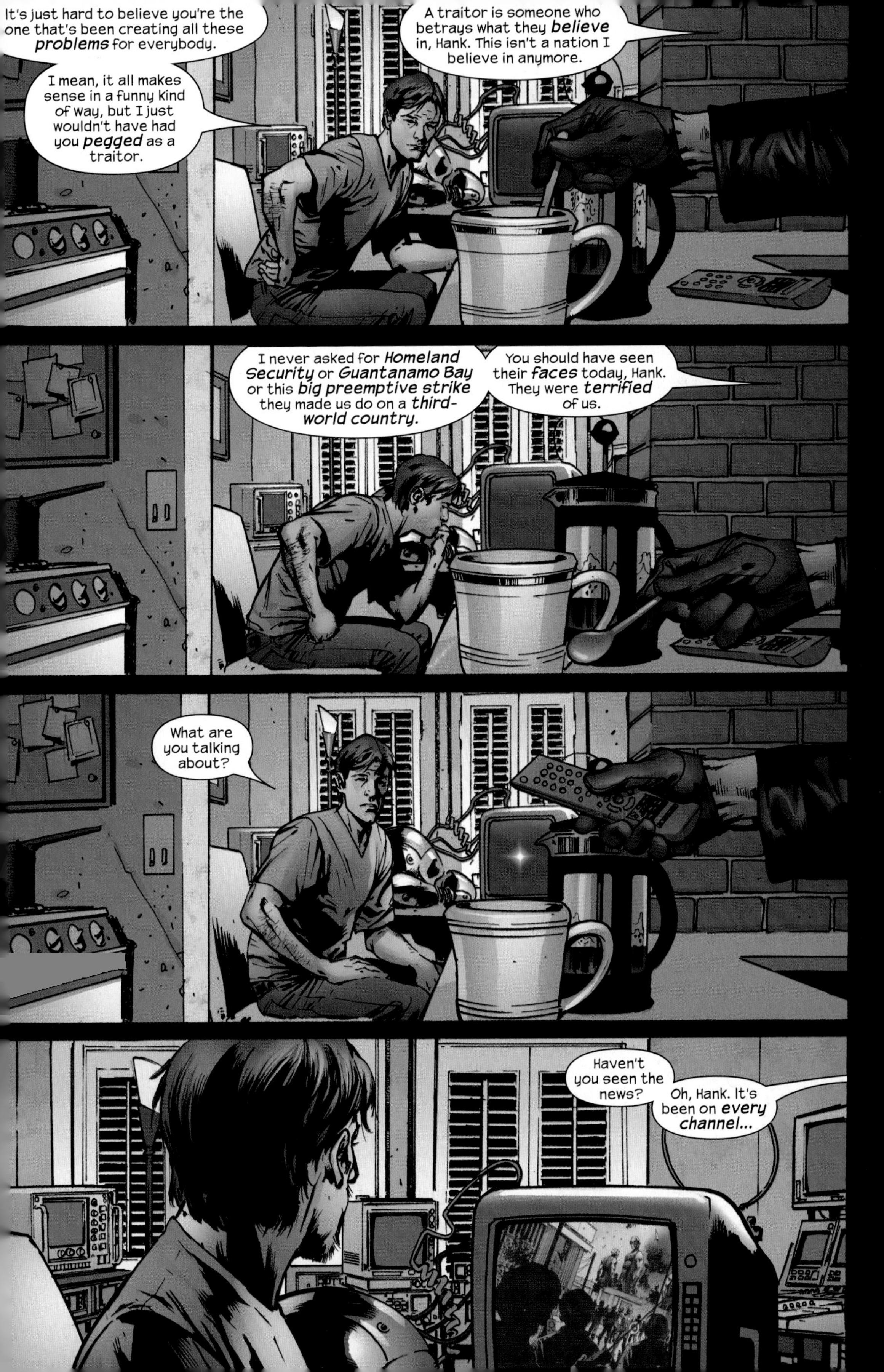

It's just hard to believe you're the one that's been creating all these *problems* for everybody.
I mean, it all makes sense in a funny kind of way, but I just wouldn't have had you *pegged* as a traitor.
A traitor is someone who betrays what they *believe* in, Hank. This isn't a nation I believe in anymore.
I never asked for *Homeland Security* or *Guantanamo Bay* or this *big preemptive strike* they made us do on a *third-world country.*
You should have seen their *faces* today, Hank. They were *terrified* of us.
What are you talking about?
Haven't you seen the news?
Oh, Hank. It's been on *every channel...*

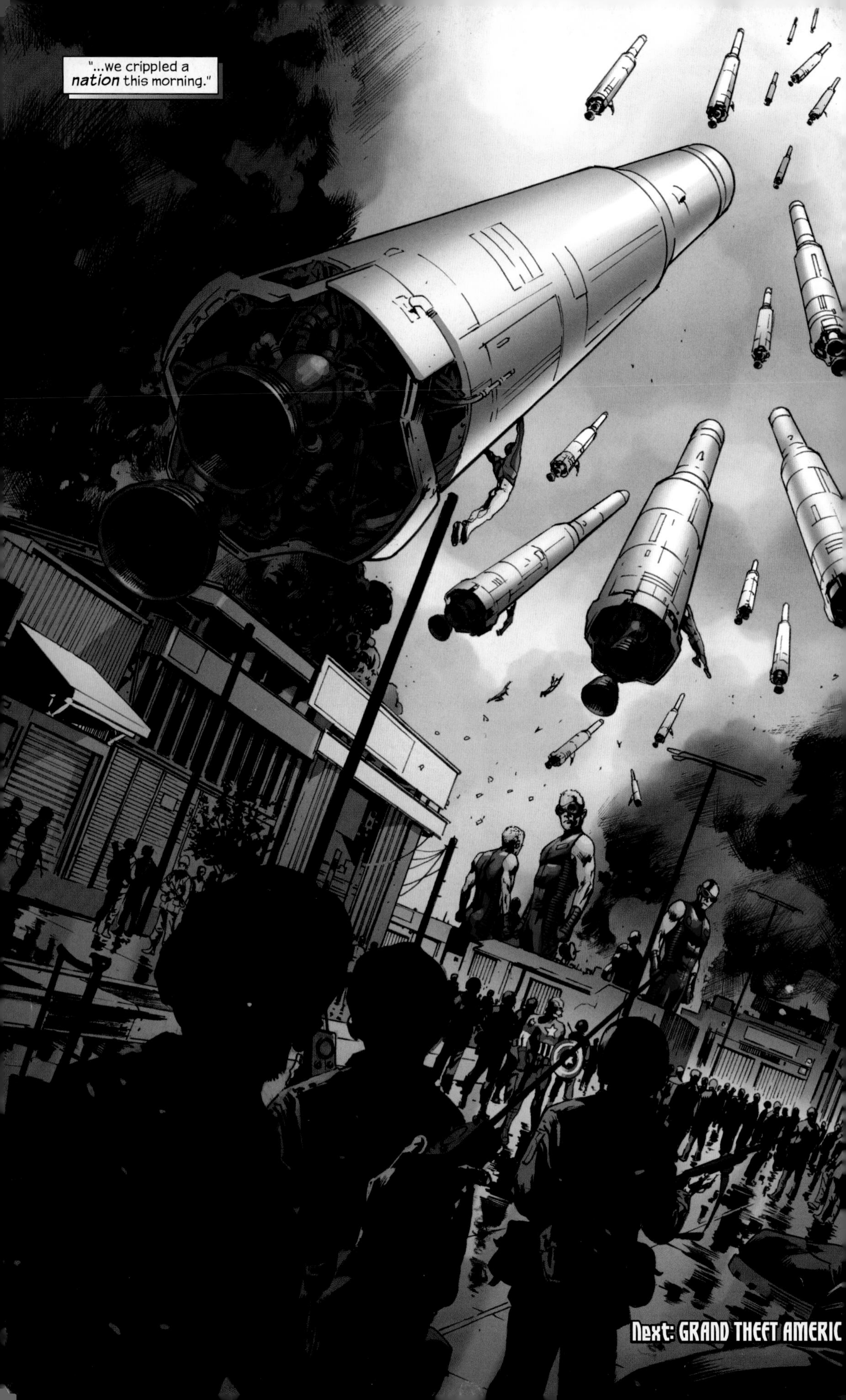
"...we crippled a *nation* this morning."
Next: GRAND THEFT AMERIC

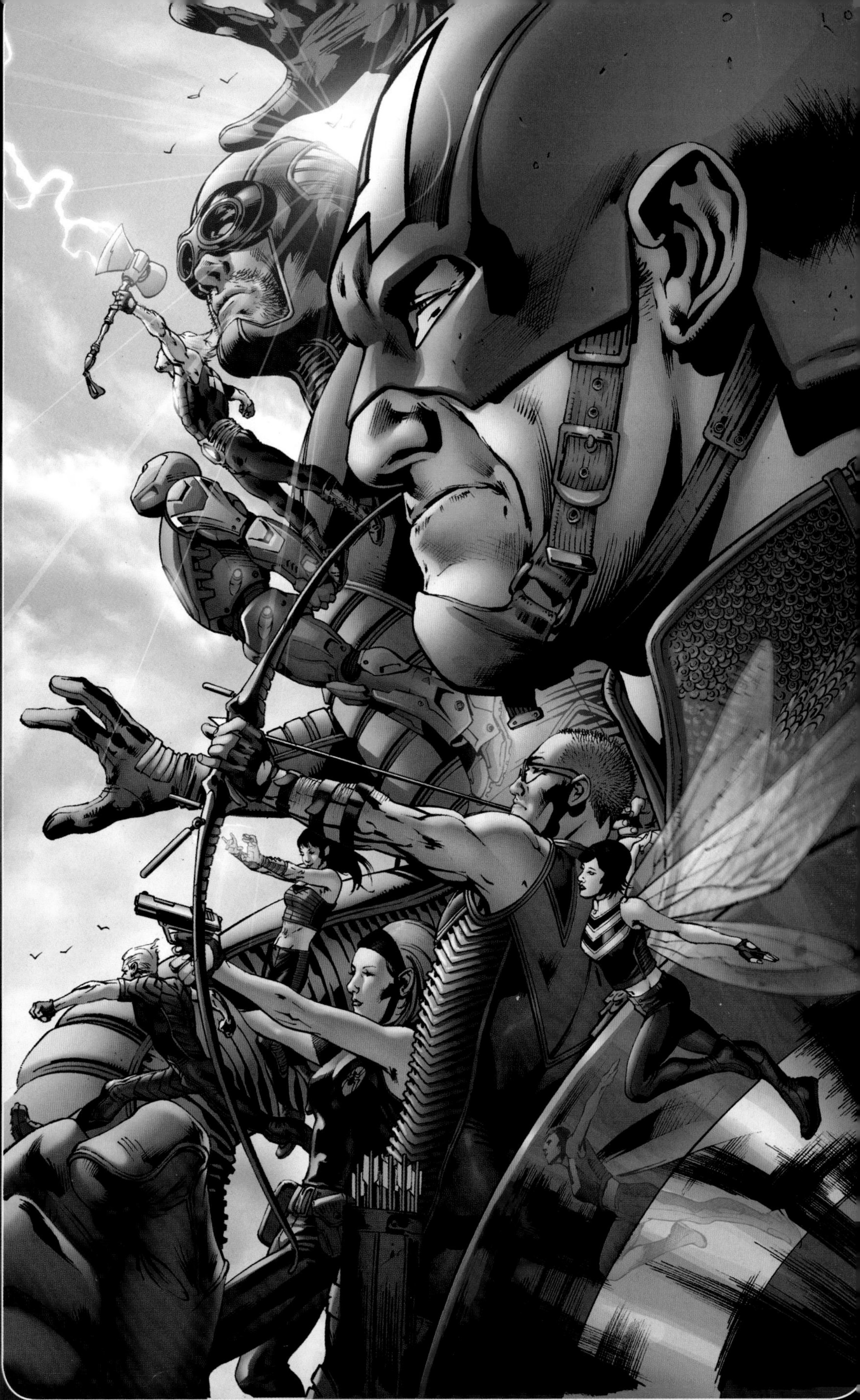

ONE

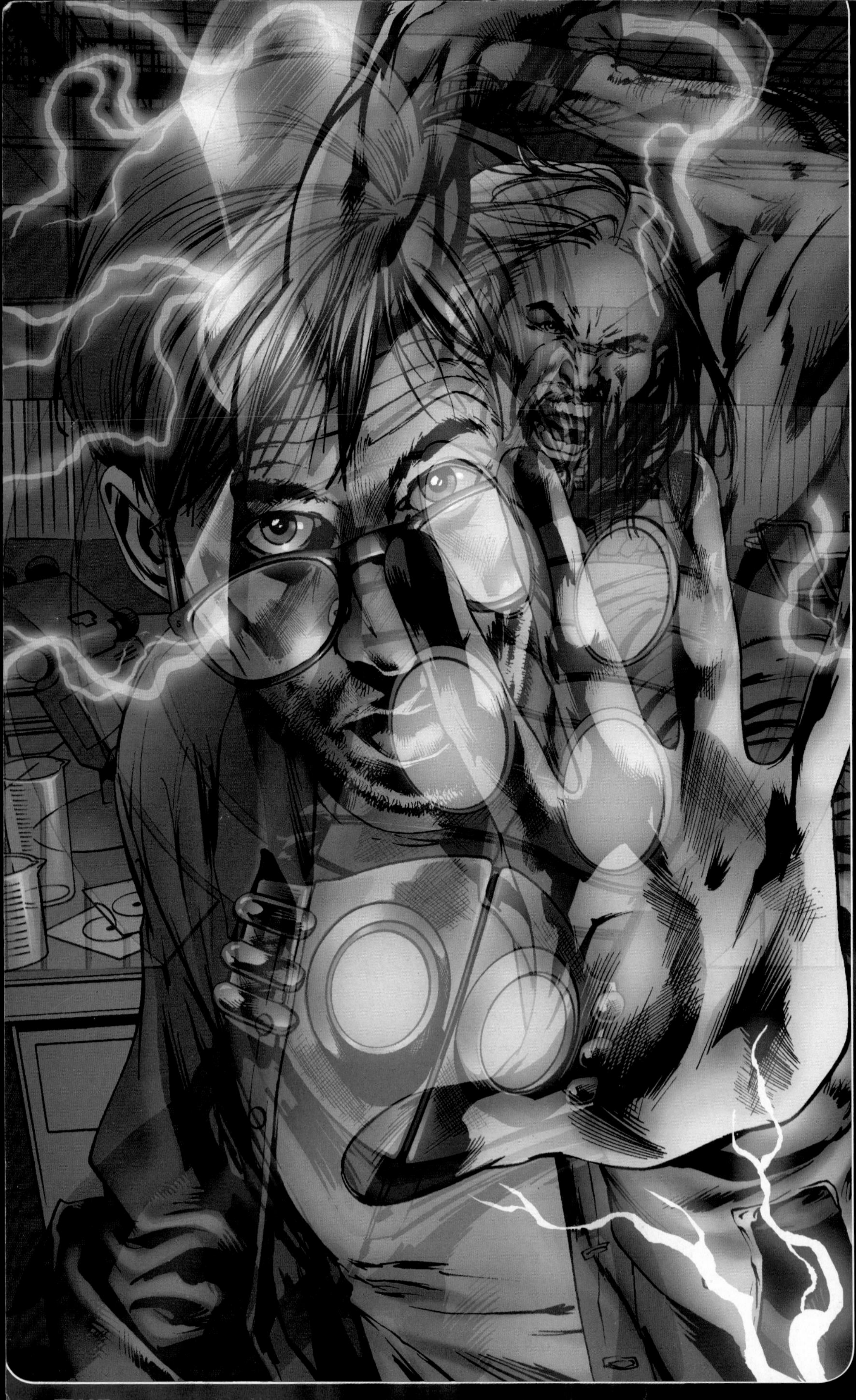

TWO

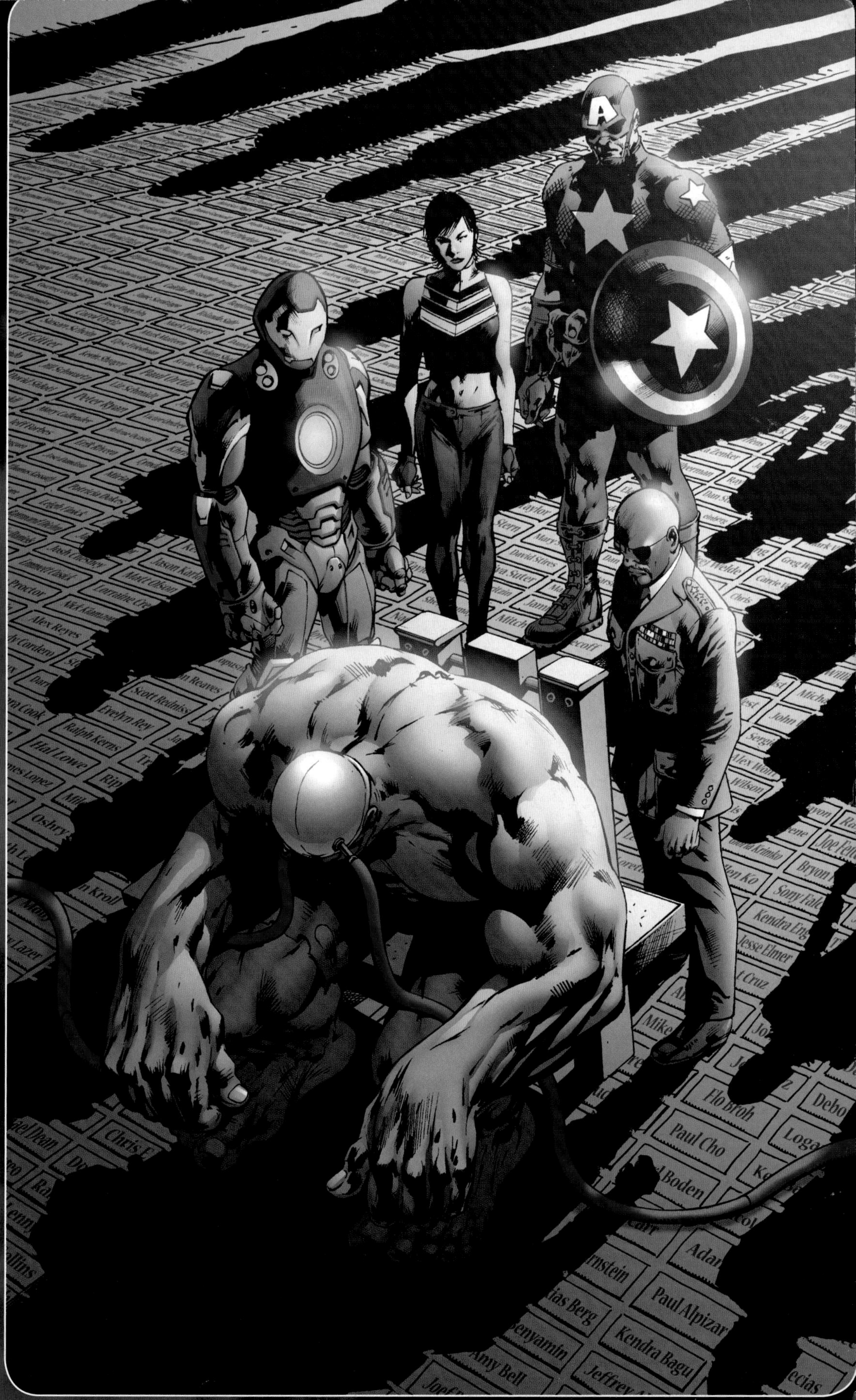
Paul Cho
Paul Alpizar
Amy Bell
Jesse Elmer
Alex Reyes
Ralph Kerns
Hal Lowe
Evelyn Rey
David Stires
Matt Olsen

THREE

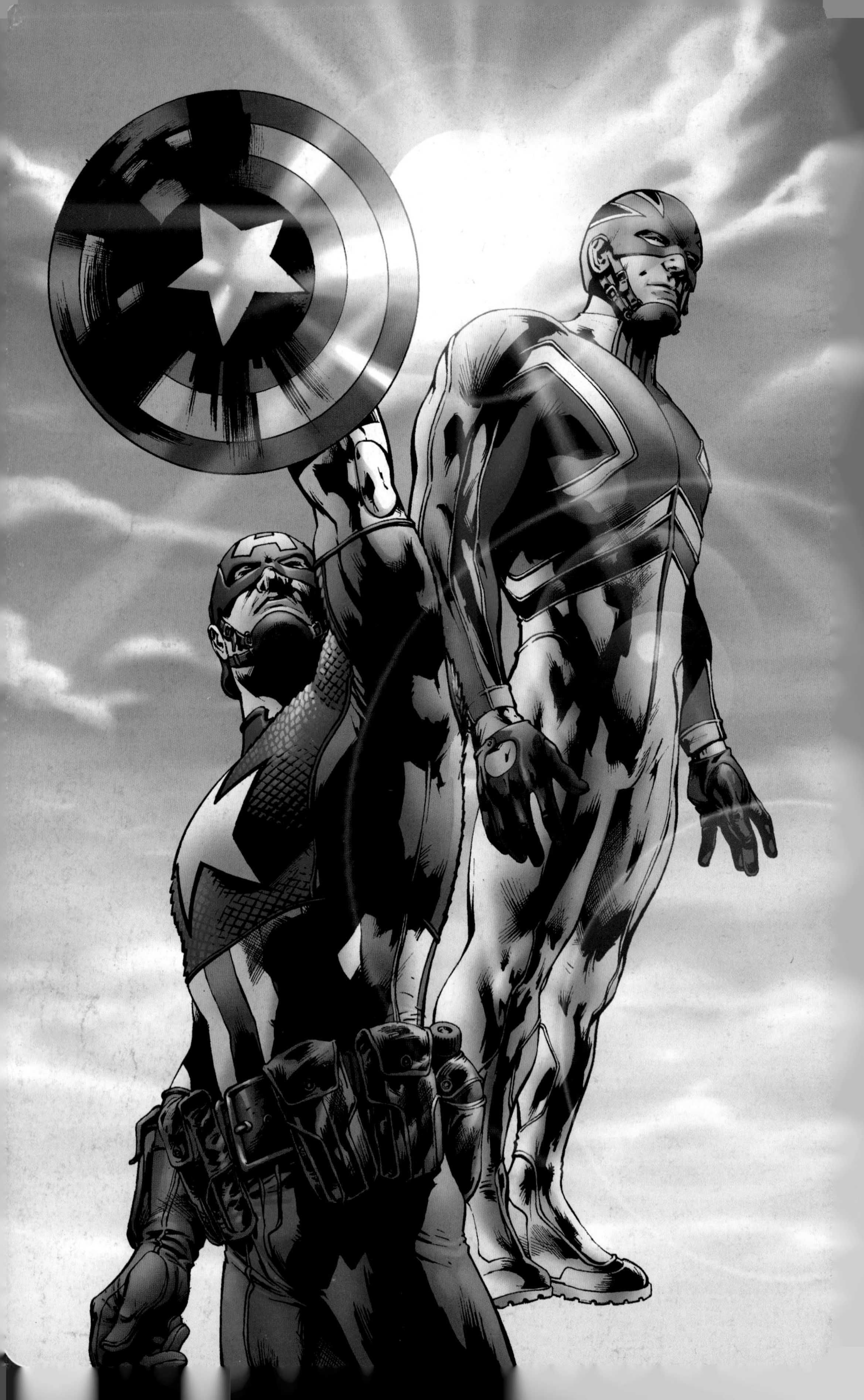

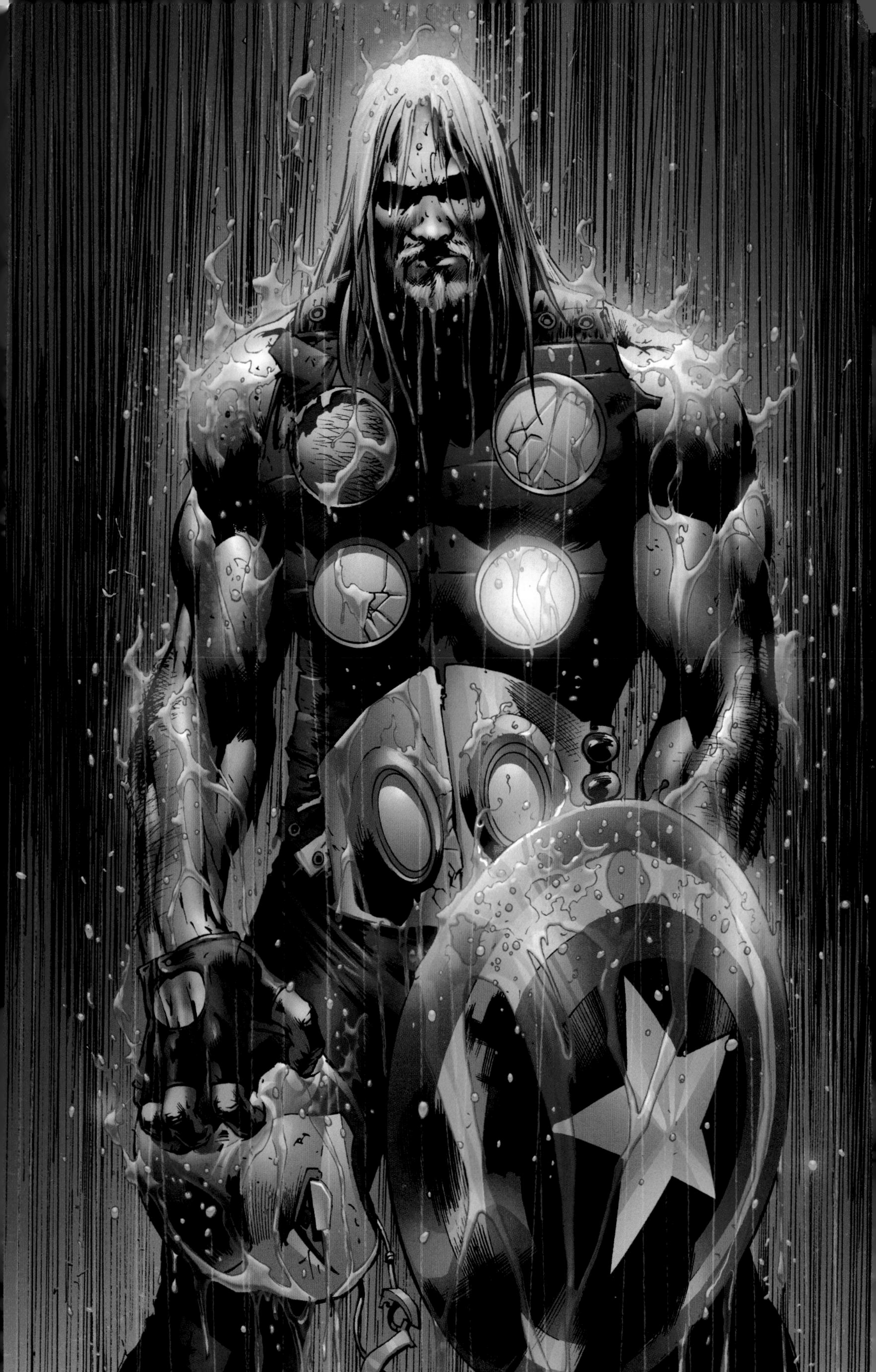

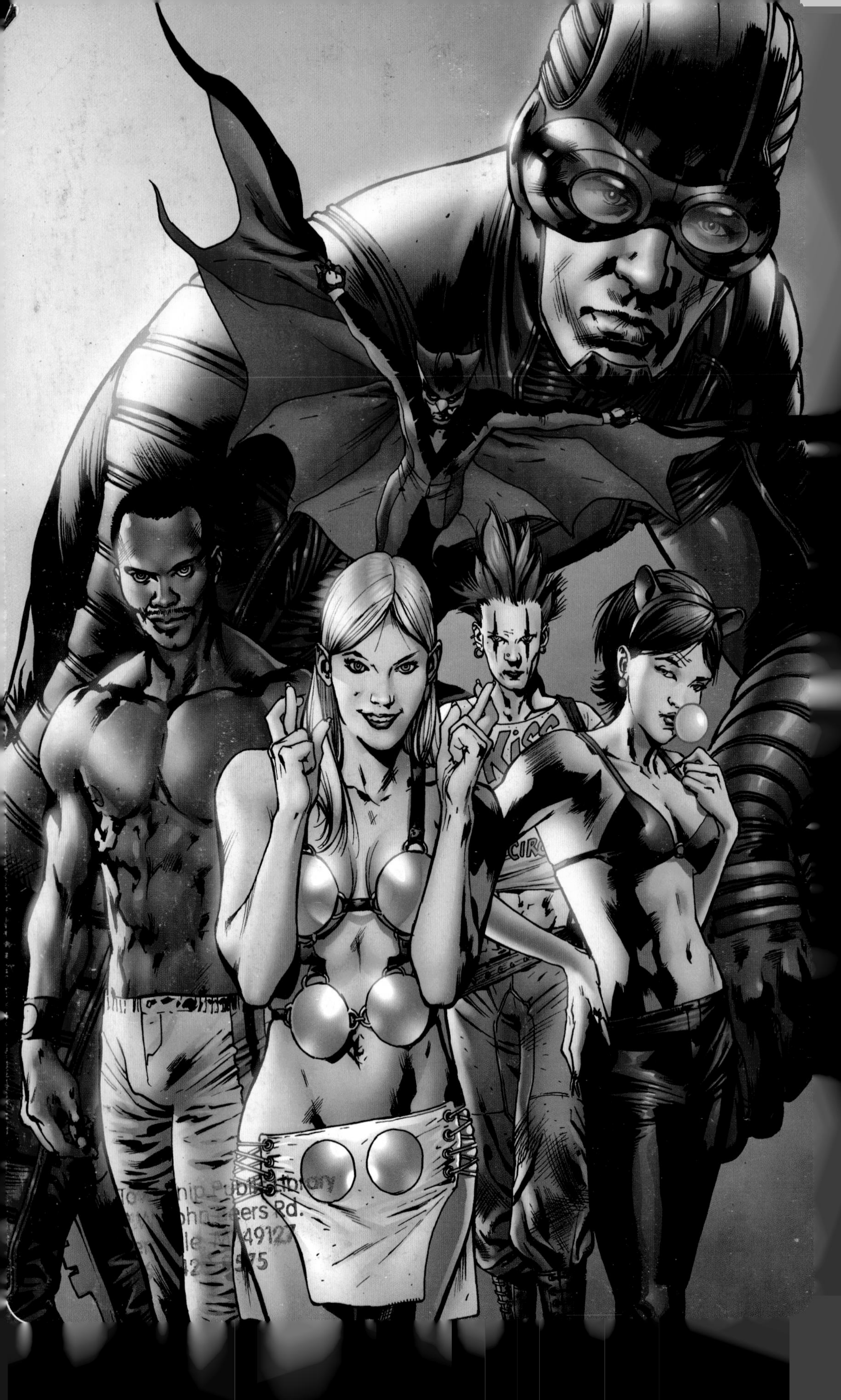